AF147218

Raps of
Resistance

Raps of Resistance

How Kendrick Lamar and J. Cole Reignited a Hip-Hop Tradition

Jeremy C. McCool and Earl Hopkins

BLOOMSBURY ACADEMIC
NEW YORK · LONDON · OXFORD · NEW DELHI · SYDNEY

BLOOMSBURY ACADEMIC
Bloomsbury Publishing Inc, 1359 Broadway, New York, NY 10018, USA
Bloomsbury Publishing Plc, 50 Bedford Square, London, WC1B 3DP, UK
Bloomsbury Publishing Ireland, 29 Earlsfort Terrace, Dublin 2, D02 AY28, Ireland

BLOOMSBURY, BLOOMSBURY ACADEMIC and the Diana logo are trademarks of
Bloomsbury Publishing Plc

First published in the United States of America 2026

Copyright © Bloomsbury Academic, 2026

For legal purposes the Acknowledgments on pp. 181–182 constitute an extension of this
copyright page.

Cover design: Sally Rinehart
Photos of J. Cole and Kendrick Lamar (c) Scott Hemenway/Alamy
Additional images (c) iStock.com/FG Trade; iStock.com/urbazon

All rights reserved. No part of this publication may be: i) reproduced or transmitted in
any form, electronic or mechanical, including photocopying, recording or by means of
any information storage or retrieval system without prior permission in writing from the
publishers; or ii) used or reproduced in any way for the training, development or operation
of artificial intelligence (AI) technologies, including generative AI technologies. The rights
holders expressly reserve this publication from the text and data mining exception as per
Article 4(3) of the Digital Single Market Directive (EU) 2019/790.

Bloomsbury Publishing Inc does not have any control over, or responsibility for, any third-
party websites referred to or in this book. All internet addresses given in this book were
correct at the time of going to press. The author and publisher regret any inconvenience
caused if addresses have changed or sites have ceased to exist, but can accept no
responsibility for any such changes.

Library of Congress Cataloging-in-Publication Data Available

ISBN: HB: 979-8-8818-0125-0
ePDF: 979-8-2163-7889-1
eBook: 979-8-8818-0126-7

Typeset by Newgen KnowledgeWorks Pvt. Ltd., Chennai, India
Printed and bound in the United States of America

For product safety related questions contact productsafety@bloomsbury.com.

To find out more about our authors and books visit www.bloomsbury.com
and sign up for our newsletters.

Contents

Preface

The concept of *Raps of Resistance* came at one of the lowest points in recent hip-hop history. In July 2023, two lifelong fans of the genre met for the first time at a swanky cigar lounge in Downtown Philly. They bonded over their favorite emcees and top cultural moments. Outside of being massive fans, both of them dedicated much of their lives' work to preserving the legacy of the genre and culture. As a professor, Dr. Jeremy C. McCool did so in the classroom, creating curriculum and teaching college courses on socially conscious hip-hop. As a journalist, Earl Hopkins did so by contributing essays and music history guides to big-name publications, interviewing iconic hip-hop artists about their musical journeys, and reviewing the artwork they released to the world.

During this meeting, they addressed their glaring gripes about the current state of hip-hop. It wasn't glamorous. For the longest stretch in thirty years, rap was without a No. 1 album atop the Billboard 200. The second-longest streak dates back to 1993. The record that ended the commercial drought was Lil Uzi Vert's 2023 album, *The Pink Tape*, which did little to move the needle amid one of the genre's grandest milestones.

To commemorate fifty years of hip-hop, there were televised tributes, legacy award show performances, and year-long editorial campaigns to celebrate hip-hop icons, both past and present. After reflecting on rap's recent failures, with the decline of conscious rap among the biggest missteps, those same hip-hop fans decided there needed to be a cultural reset. Someone had to point to hip-hop's decline, and both Dr. Jeremy C. McCool and Earl Hopkins decided they were the messengers willing to relay the thoughts of fellow hip-hop purists far and wide.

Simply, there were too few artists with lyrical substance who addressed social issues like poverty, mass incarceration, and political corruption, who were championed the same way as other mainstream acts. That's what hip-hop represents, but over time, these traditions were lost on new-age emcees. There was an oversaturation of untalented emcees and online personalities-turned-musicians, who refused to rap about the social, cultural, or political issues affecting *real people*, especially those in the very communities or enclaves they came from. Instead, they decided to glamorize violence, drug abuse, and materialism, without injecting teachable moments or showcasing the power of redemption.

Conscious rap didn't go anywhere in the 2020s. Even with the popularity of certain sounds, subgenres, or trends that led to hip-hop's descent, there were still figures like Joey Bada$$, Denzel Curry, Lupe Fiasco, Noname, Saba, LaRussel, JID, and others who addressed topics traditionally associated with rap's greatest poets and lyrical freedom fighters. However, there were two emcees who struck similar chords as conscious artists, while still reaching the pinnacle of mainstream success, even when it felt the two couldn't coexist. Those two artists are Kendrick Lamar and J. Cole.

Weeks after McCool and Hopkins's cigar session, their thoughts were in full alignment. The cultural reset would be in the form of a book. Not only would it address the history of conscious rap and its evolution over the decades, it would demonstrate how icons like Kendrick and Cole have been torchbearers of conscious rap and hip-hop's most heralded traditions. They are the lone superstars of a sound and movement that's grown out of favor with mainstream audiences. Despite its decline on contemporary radio and its diminishing presence on Spotify playlists and other music streaming services, Cole and Kendrick have stood their ground as artists and cultural titans.

The two names are forever synonymous with one another. Cole and Kendrick have certainly ventured down separate paths as artists, businessmen, and influencers, but their presence in rap has always spiraled within the same funnel. While they have their differing viewpoints, messaging, and musical approaches, consciousness has always been the foundation of their artistry. They have garnered platinum plaques, critical praise, and hardware on Grammy night, while advocating for and directly supporting community initiatives and youth programs everywhere. And unlike other artists of the same vein, it shows up in ways outside the studio booth. They *live* it.

Cole and Kendrick always have and continue to use their voices for the betterment of listeners. K.Dot echoed the struggles and misfortunes of those from Compton to Senegal, and reinvigorated their minds and hearts with empowering songs about Black pride. Cole has focused on the mistreatment of Black women and the wrongful imprisonment of Black men, who are both ridiculed for existing in a country (and world) that routinely disregards them.

Raps of Resistance is here to further prove their impact. This isn't to vilify any subgenre or artist who doesn't follow the traditional mold of consciousness. Even certain tales of violence, gang warfare, and drug use or distribution can be conscious, depending on what listeners can draw from the record or project. If there's transparency on the pros and cons associated with a particular lifestyle or decision, that's conscious. If it demystifies a new or lesser-known movement that's either healing or hurting the Black community, that's conscious. Or if it draws on a heartfelt moment that changed an artist's life for the better, or for the worse, that can also be conscious.

Raps of Resistance isn't to undermine the work of current or past contributors. It's a way to remind people of hip-hop's beauty and show how its foundation shaped pop culture and the world for the better. Embarking on this project meant delving into all ends of rap history, so showing its grandeur and coarser elements was necessary context. Without revealing both sides would be a disservice to readers and lovers of hip-hop culture.

Raps of Resistance is an embodiment of it all—the good, bad, and the ugly. The book also unveils a path of correction for artists, record executives, and the consumers of today's musical product. One of the many remedies is to encourage all parties to endorse music with a message. Cole and Kendrick are figures who prove it inspires societal change and advancement.

That's how figures like Grandmaster Flash, Common, Public Enemy, OutKast, A Tribe Called Quest, Scarface, Goodie Mob, and others pierced through the musical and cultural stratosphere. Cole and Kendrick have taken notes from each of their careers to craft their own gumbo of conscious records and chart-topping hits for a well-balanced serving of hip-hop.

Through a series of interviews with fellow hip-hop artists, record executives, music journalists, hip-hop studies scholars, and elected officials, *Raps of Resistance* chronicles the rise of Cole and Kendrick, the obstacles they faced on their way to stardom, and the paths they ventured on to become musical and cultural icons.

1
The Birth of Conscious Rap

There are few hip-hop debates without the names Kendrick Lamar and J. Cole at the top of the ballot. Whether it's a list of the most lyrical emcees or the best all-around talents, Cole and Kendrick are among the first names drawn. Even past generations have embraced the two musical heavyweights, who have solidified themselves as some of the greatest artists the genre has ever seen. Their skillset alone has drawn comparisons to rap legends like Jay-Z, Nas, Rakim, 2Pac, and The Notorious B.I.G., but it's their ability to reach commercial milestones while remaining true to hip-hop tradition that's been the root of their admiration. While their mainstream hits have turned them into global music stars, it's their dedication as conscious artists that's made them such integral figures in hip-hop.

To understand the notion of "consciousness," one must understand the parallel between Black music and the lived Black experience. Black expression is the heartbeat and pulse of American music. People across the world congregate to mourn, celebrate, or dance to stories of triumph, love, joy, pain, sadness, and dysfunction. These same audiences love to watch the story of an underdog play out in real-time, and there has been no group in history with a plight congruent to that of Black Americans.

This plight has been told through various forms of artistic expression, namely musical genres such as jazz, blues, soul, funk, and rock n' roll. These genres have all reigned over the music industry at one time or another and have gone on to cement the legacies of early visionaries like Nat King Cole, B.B. King,

Louis Armstrong, Nina Simone, Miles Davis, and other musicians across time. However, the emergence of hip-hop forever changed the landscape of music and media worldwide. Its impact and artistic layers can be traced back to the conditions surrounding its creation in the Bronx borough of New York City.

At the height of financial strife, industrial decline, and the sociopolitical dismay that stemmed from the War on Drugs, New York City in the 1970s was a shell of its former self. The unemployment rate soared with the slicing of city jobs, and upwards of 820,000 middle-class families escaped to the suburbs in what's known as White flight. Those unable to flee the nearly bankrupt city were forced to shrug off the growing decay, depopulation, and violence.[1] Amid the socioeconomic plague, a new art form called hip-hop bloomed from the abandoned ghettos and trash-laden streets during a late summer party in the West Bronx on August 11, 1973. The host was an eighteen-year-old DJ and emcee named Clive "DJ Kool Herc" Campbell, who helped his younger sister Cindy organize a party inside their apartment rec room to raise money for back-to-school clothes.[2]

Back then, the growing presence of New York gangs turned Bronx nightclubs into war zones, and people started gravitating to smaller and more intimate parties. Herc's parties were tailored for a ready-made crowd. The Jamaican-born immigrant, whose family moved from the politically torn Caribbean country to the United States in the late 1960s, made his name in Bronx's graffiti circles. But with his father's influence and upbringing in Kingston, his love of funk, reggae, dance music, and massive sound systems helped usher in a new artform. In a *2023 interview with Spin Magazine*, Herc stated:

> I would say my start came from Jamaica, and my father was a mechanic at Kingston Wharf. I'll never forget "White Christmas." I played that. All that stuff. His favorite person was Ella Fitzgerald. So, I know my records. But in Jamaica, there were other groups called Byron Lee and the Dragonaires. Then come the Skatalites, and then the Paragons and U-Roy and Big Youth. I learned from that.

Herc, equipped with a sound system of two turntables, paired records from James Brown and the Bongo Band to a growing crowd at 1520 Sedgwick Avenue. The same back-to-school jam is where he put his now-famed

"Merry-Go-Round" DJing style to use. The technique separates and replays the drum breaks on dance and funk records for a continuous loop of party tracks, and that very moment is credited as the point of hip-hop's inception. It birthed a sound and a cultural movement that changed the fabric of music and ignited the spirit of Black America.

While most historians point to Herc's party as hip-hop's launch point, others like Questlove say hip-hop was oven-baked with the ingredients of older, more seasoned genres that came before. "I don't totally accept the Kool Herc party as a hard-and-fast origin story," Questlove wrote in his 2023 chronology, *Hip-Hop Is History*. "There were artists before him that did some of the same things that rappers would later do, whether it was raging against the establishment or prioritizing rhythmic vocals over melodic ones."[3] The legendary drummer of The Roots believes hip-hop was a product of boogie, soul, and disco music, but there's no denying hip-hop is a gumbo of sound and influence. No single person is responsible for its creation. It was forged by an amalgamation of musical and cultural luminaries.

What's referred to as "emceeing" or "rapping" occurred in Black American music long before hip-hop's arrival. One of the earliest examples is the 1946 song "Noah" by Florida gospel group, The Jubalaires. You can also hear the rhythmic style and wordplay from early spoken word acts such as Gil Scott-Heron and the Last Poets. The influence of past genres, combined with the burgeoning music scene in New York City during the 1970s, spawned the new movement. The first DJs plugged their speakers into streetlights, and hip-hop's earliest emcees drew crowds in local parks and playgrounds.

Hip-hop made a commercial splash with the release of The Sugarhill Gang 1979 hit "Rappers Delight," which became rap's first song to reach the Top 40. Far more records were in circulation at the time, but the lively and disco-inspired record elevated the newly established genre to national audiences. What was deemed a short-lived fad became one of the most influential artforms the world has ever seen. Communities across continental lines have been drawn to all five elements, which include emceeing, DJing, breaking, graffiti, knowledge, and others depending on the scholar.

The genre has spun into an abundance of subgenres since its inception. But the one that's gone on to define and shape hip-hop the most is socially conscious rap, or "conscious rap" for short. Conscious rap consists of artists using their voice, music, or platform to speak on social, political, and cultural issues that exist in the world. These topics range between poverty, mass incarceration, racism, political corruption, mental health, and other societal concerns. Since hip-hop was formed by Black artists, conscious music has largely shed light on how these affairs affect Black Americans and other disenfranchised communities.

It's All in "The Message"

In the eyes of most hip-hop scholars, Grandmaster Flash and The Furious Five's "The Message" is considered the most transformative conscious rap song ever recorded. It veered from the party jams and braggadocious raps of the period and administered a fresh dose of reality rap at a pivotal point in the country. "The Message" was released at the start of the crack epidemic in New York City and former US President Ronald Reagan's administration, which was criticized for cutting social programs and reducing taxes for high-income earners. The result of Reagan's economic policy, often referred to as "Reaganomics," widened income inequality and increased poverty rates.

Author, journalist, and NYU professor Kathy Iandoli said "The Message" broke new ground in mainstream hip-hop by echoing the thoughts of many living in impoverished conditions, and often in ways news organizations failed to do at the time. "I think of 'The Message' because of the way hip-hop was used as a vessel and a vehicle for being the true watchdogs of journalism in a way that wasn't in the newspapers and wasn't covered in magazines," she said. The record reflects life in the ghetto—the violence, drug abuse, and sex trafficking that permeated street corners—and the inescapable feeling that arose during these hardened times. "Broken glass everywhere. People pissing on the stairs, you know they just don't care. I can't take the smell, can't take the noise. Got no money to move out, I guess I got no choice," the legendary emcee Melle Mel rapped on the song.

"The Message," released under the pioneering Sugar Hill Records imprint, inspired future generations of artists to weave social commentary in their music. It also displayed both the power and responsibility of the emcee. While earlier records like 1979's "King Tim III (Personality Jock)" are credited for first placing the emcee at the heart of a hip-hop song, "The Message" showcased the extent of an emcee's lyrical abilities. Back then, the grand mixers and DJs were at the center of most records, but the resounding voice and descriptive lyrics of Melle Mel and Ed "Duke Bootee" Fletcher pushed artists and listeners to focus on the messages rappers conveyed in each stanza.

The song has been rightly crowned one of the best in hip-hop history. Music publications like *Rolling Stone* have even ranked it among the best in music history. The song fell at No. 51 on *Rolling Stone*'s list of the 500 Greatest Songs of All Time in 2004, making it the highest-ranked hip-hop record on the list.[4] In a 2021 interview with media personality DJ Vlad, Melle Mel said he was surprised "The Message" has had such lasting power. "I didn't think the record was going to do anything," Melle Mel said. "It didn't resonate nothing that was going on [in the] basic hip-hop world. It wasn't a hip-hop song. It didn't have any beats in it. You couldn't break dance to it. But it resonated [with] the general public."[5]

While "The Message" is the first conscious rap song to be widely consumed, Brother D and his crew Collective Effort first posed questions about the state of Black America over a beat from Cheryl Lynn's disco smash "Got to Be Real." In the groovy track, "How We Gonna Make the Black Nation Rise?," he talked about the rise in unemployment, gaps in education, mass incarceration, and other issues affecting low-income Americans. The song, and others like Run-DMC's 1983 breakout "It's Like That," influenced socially conscious creatives to wet their musical paintbrushes and put them to sonic canvases. Without the contributions of iconic acts like Gil Scott-Heron, the Last Poets, Watts Prophets, Nina Simone, and George Clinton & Parliament-Funkadelic, the bounds for conscious rap would never have been set.

With an infusion of spoken word poetry, jazz, and a proto-rap delivery, Scott-Heron set the template for future conscious rappers to follow. Records like "The Message" can be traced back to the bold proclamations blared by Scott-Heron on tracks like "Home Is Where the Hatred Is" and "Message to the Messengers." Scott-Heron's "The Bottle" addressed the harmful effects of alcoholism, and "Gun" illustrated the nation's growing violence and tension with the circulation of firearms. His most well-known record, "The Revolution

Will Not Be Televised," confronted the dangers of commercialization. It turned the gifted revolutionary into a touchstone of hip-hop history. His emphatic manifestos and artistic musings, which earned him the designation as the "Godfather of Rap," have since been interpolated and sampled by the likes of Common, 2Pac, Kanye West, now known as "Ye," Kendrick Lamar, and countless others. In a 2010 interview with *The New Yorker*, Chuck D stated:

> They are the roots of rap—taking a word and juxtaposing it into some sort of music. Gil Scott-Heron is the manifestation of the modern word … In combining music with the word, from the voice on down, you follow the template he laid out.[6]

In the same vein as Scott-Heron, the work of the Last Poets and the Watts Prophets was at the root of Black consciousness in the 1970s. Their sharp flows, commanding tone, and grounded tellings of the Black experience elevated street poetry to new heights and inspired future acts to place their impassioned monologues on wax, similar to Isaac Hayes's "Ike's Rap" in 1970. By the late 1980s, acts like Jungle Brothers, A Tribe Called Quest, and Schoolly D used new-age sampling technology to further illuminate the musical lineage between street poetry and the hip-hop audiences are familiar with today.[7] In honoring the Last Poets' contributions, artists like Kanye West and Common featured the iconic group on 2005's "The Corner," a song reflecting the hardships and struggles endured by people occupying the street corners of Chicago.

Along with the influence of street poetry, George Clinton's Parliament-Funkadelic was the personification of Black identity, self-liberation, and anti-establishment. The word "funk" symbolized a form of enlightenment and a force of liberation, which was reflected in the group's music. On songs like 1977's "Bop Gun (Endangered Species)," the funk and psychedelic-soul collective devised a motivational jam about the defense and advancement of Black Americans. Records like "One Nation Under a Groove" and "Free Your Mind and Your Ass Will Follow" became songs of unification, while others like "Paint the White House Black" blended funk and hip-hop for a critique of the nation's political structure. Clinton's legacy and conscious messages were amplified through collaborations with Ice Cube, Kendrick Lamar, and other emcees, and indirectly through the sampling of his work.

Next to James Brown and the "Funky Drummer" Clyde Stubblefield, Clinton and P-Funk remain one of the most sampled artists in hip-hop history, and many conscious acts like Public Enemy put their artistic mastery to good use for 1990's "911 Is a Joke." The mashing of poetry, soul, funk, and disco is at the heart of hip-hop, but it's the messages these genres and artists carried that ultimately shaped conscious rap. But Timothy Welbeck, college professor and the inaugural director of Temple University's Center for Anti-Racism, argues the root of conscious rap—and the genres that preceded its development—ultimately stemmed from the Motherland. The hip-hop scholar said cultural traditions once rooted in West Africa have evolved into some of the world's most transformative artforms, and hip-hop is one of its greatest descendants. Welbeck stated:

Black music at its core is political because Black life is political. And if you look at the beginnings of Black music in America, you're looking at people who were enslaved from West Africa and were brought across the Atlantic. It means to be property, subjugated, and robbed of their cultural lineage. But they held on to various forms and vestiges of their culture as a means to further their humanity and connect with each other. They took the various elements of traditional West African music-making, and they blended that with the psalms, hymns, and spiritual songs in America, we call spirituals. And from spirituals, we get ragtime, jazz, blues, gospel, soul, funk, and reggae, all of which are ancestors of hip-hop. By the time hip-hop comes on the scene, it becomes something recognizable. There is a sense of social consciousness and awareness among rappers. We don't get that at the infancy of emceeing, but by the time emceeing formed into something that we recognize today, we began to see some of the roots of it.

The Heart of Conscious Rap

There would be no socially conscious rap without the civil rights era, and the later formation of the Black Power Movement in the late 1960s and 1970s. Many artists, driven by the messages and ideologies expressed by civil rights figures, were encouraged to speak boldly about social issues in their music.

As the son of a member of the Black Panther Party, a revolutionary organization that spearheaded the Black Power movement, Tupac "2Pac" Shakur was driven to weave social and political messages into his early solo projects. On his 1991 debut, *2Pacalypse Now*, a twenty-year-old 2Pac rapped about the mental and physical dangers of imprisonment on "Trapped," the community-wide effects of teen pregnancy on "Brenda's Got a Baby," and the nation's hypocrisy as a "free country" on "Words of Wisdom." The album, and the series of projects that followed, delivered timely messages when police brutality, drug addiction, and a widening wealth gap were among the biggest issues in America.

Years before 2Pac's emergence, KRS-One and Boogie Down Productions' "Stop the Violence" addressed the wealth gap in America and the government's mistreatment of military veterans, and foreshadowed the potential end of hip-hop if violence surrounding the genre continued to ensue. The record was released the same year KRS-One, who was nicknamed "The Teacher" for his educational messaging, formed the Stop the Violence Movement alongside hip-hop journalist Nelson George. The movement launched after a series of violent incidents erupted at rap concerts in the Tri-State area, most notably at the Nassau Veterans Memorial Coliseum. On August 12, 1988, several concertgoers were stabbed at a Run-DMC concert.[8] A month later, another violent attack broke out at the Uniondale, New York venue, but this time it was fatal.[9] At the "Jam '88" concert, featuring artists like Eric B. and Rakim, Kool Moe Dee, and Doug E. Fresh, nineteen-year-old Julio Fuentes was fatally stabbed. More than a dozen other concertgoers were injured in the attack.[10]

Following the string of incidents, mainstream media outlets began blaming rap music for the violent attacks, despite artists' constant attempts to deescalate the situations. The Nassau Coliseum and other venues across the country began banning rap shows, which left the genre at a critical crossroads. As anti-rap campaigns began to populate, George tapped KRS-One and Jive/RCA executive Ann Carli, credited as Tokyo Rose, to lead a social charge. They decided to release a one-off, posse cut to respond to the acts of violence and address the unfair criticism aimed in hip-hop's direction.

When news outlets began dismissing the progress hip-hop carved out in Black America, KRS-One was one of many luminary artists who stepped up in the genre's defense. The song "Self Destruction," produced and mixed by BDP's D-Nice, featured Public Enemy, Doug E. Fresh, Ms. Melodie, Kool Moe Dee, MC Lyte, Heavy D, and others as part of the all-star lineup of emcees. The record was released under the Stop the Movement banner on what would have been the sixtieth birthday of Martin Luther King Jr. (January 15, 1989). A portion of the profits went to the National Urban League to fund educational programs focused on combating crime. Despite initial resistance from urban radio stations, "Self Destruction" became the top-selling 12-inch single in the history of RCA distribution at the time, generating more than $100,000 for the National Urban League.

The contributions of the KRS-One-led troupe and 2Pac were a testament to the power of conscious rap music at a vulnerable time in hip-hop and were in congruence with the birth of one of the nation's most prestigious civil rights leaders in Dr. King Jr, and the thoughts of other revolutionaries throughout history. Other conscious records drew even more attention to social issues impacting communities in and outside of hip-hop circles. Many even became the soundtrack to protests and rallies worldwide.

Shades of Consciousness

Throughout hip-hop history, conscious rap has illuminated the effects of racial inequality, and social and political disenfranchisement, in some ways, becoming an extended form of protest. Rather than hitting the pavement with large signs and verbal chants, artists took to the airwaves to acknowledge their pain and grievances. And through trials of fire, progress was eventually made.

At its core, conscious rap is a subgenre of meaning. It tends to reject drug abuse and the perils of materialism. There is a clear distinction in messaging from conscious artists. When speaking about negative acts they have committed in the past or are engaged in currently, it's typically to raise awareness of the issue. They tend to speak to the negative outcomes caused by the behaviors or circumstances, instead of glorifying the behavior themselves. Whether it's tackling political injustices, street violence, or the racial divide in America, there's a semblance of perspective unfelt in other subgenres. It's not a weaponization of truth, it's a platform of change with artists serving as its very agent. Their voices and their listeners' ears move mountains and have done so through years of formation.

Conscious rap isn't a monolith. The artists and their messages vary in tone and delivery. Some rappers choose a *testimonial* method, which addresses how certain personal occurrences impacted their own lived experiences. Some rappers speak about the obstacles that they've faced themselves or in depth about the harsh realities that they have observed of their peers, friends, family, and community. One example is 2Pac's 1995 hit "Dear Mama." Within this heartfelt track, Pac expresses the dysfunction that his family faced as he was growing up between the East and West Coast. While he details his own imperfections as well as his mother's, he also shines a light on her strength and perseverance during her times battling drug addiction. He paints a vivid picture of how there is beauty in overcoming obstacles, praising his mother for doing so for his family's betterment.

In other cases, these rap artists use exaggerated or fictionalized storytelling to drive points home. This process allows artists' lyrical creativity to shine through. The message delivered within these stories is oftentimes more important than the characters. One example is Slick Rick's "Children's Story." The 1988 hit details the story of a seventeen-year-old boy who chooses the path of becoming a stick-up kid and robbing people to make cash. The song ends with him being killed by an undercover police officer. While it's unclear whether this story is real or not, the idea of a life of crime leading to disastrous consequences was an effective and potent tale.

Other artists choose a more direct approach called a *vocalized protest*. Instead of a personal narrative, artists use their music as a call to action or a vehicle to vent their anger and frustration. Songs like N.W.A.'s "Fuck Tha Police" and Public Enemy's "Fight the Power" were sonic gut punches, addressing the corruptive powers of law enforcement, elected officials, and the proprietors of White supremacy. In a 1988 interview with BBC Late Show reporter Mary Harorn, Ice Cube stated:

I'm sick of getting hassled I was tired of seeing my friends come home with scars and stuff, police beating them up for anything and everything, so I was like, "Yo, it's time to retaliate, you know, it's time to retaliate in song."[11]

The fiery N.W.A. record—and the landmark album *Straight Outta Compton*—firmly established Los Angeles' foothold in rap, and the legacy of future legends Ice Cube, Eazy-E, and Dr. Dre. The group, an acronym for Niggaz Wit Attitudes, also shone a light on the corruption of the LAPD, which former chief Daryll Gates admitted in an interview with PBS was an overly aggressive squadron at the time of the song's release.[12] The same legislative force nearly bludgeoned to death a 27-year-old LA motorist named Rodney King in 1991.

Four LAPD officers were caught on camera beating King, and their acquittal in the infamous court case incited days of looting, arson, and assault in Southern California. "Fuck Tha Police" perfectly encapsulated the emotions and frustrations of those rioters then and continues to echo those shared by activists and freedom fighters sparring with today's oppressors. "Fuck the police comin' straight from the underground. A young nigga got it bad 'cause I'm brown," Ice Cube's thundering voice rapped.

Along with "Fuck Tha Police," Public Enemy's 1989 smash "Fight the Power" became one of the more heralded rap songs in genre history. The record was featured in Spike Lee's 1989 classic film *Do the Right Thing*, and ignited an internal flame in the hearts of Black Americans and hip-hop fans worldwide. It's the anthem of international protest and social unrest, with the words of Chuck D echoing in the minds of those prepared to set the world ablaze. "Got to give us what we want. Gotta give us what we need. Our freedom of speech is freedom or death." The song reached the top of Billboard's Hot Rap Singles charts and would later be listed as one of the best hip-hop records of all time. It also inspired Kendrick's "Alright" and Cole's "Be Free," which became civil rights anthems in their own right.

Over the years, conscious rap began to expand. After melding Jamaican dancehall and hip-hop in classics like "Remix for P is Free" under the trio Boogie Down Productions, KRS-One embraced a more brash and politically leaning approach with 1993's "Sound of da Police." The defiant track unmasked the tumultuous relationship between Black Americans and badged figures, with the Bronx legend comparing New York City cops to plantation overseers during the slave trade.

New York duo Dead Prez took a more militant approach with "Police State." The song dismantles the idea of the nation's watchdogs—from police to military forces—and sheds light on America's economic struggles. And Yasiin Bey, formerly known as Mos Def, broke these topics down in statistical form on "Mathematics." Acts like Queen Latifah, De La Soul, Monie Love, A Tribe Called Quest, and the Jungle Brothers brought Pan-Africanism to conscious rap as the mega group Native Tongues. People from around the country wore dashikis, Black Power T-shirts, and donned beads radiating with colors of African country flags thanks to songs like "Ladies First," "Straight Out the Jungle," and "U.N.I.T.Y."

Outside the East and West Coast, southern acts like OutKast, Goodie Mob, and the Geto Boys delivered stimulating records with the same conscious-like appeal. OutKast's "Git Up, Git Out" was a motivational tune for those struggling with past trauma and low self-esteem, and the Geto Boys' "Mind Playing Tricks on Me" was one of rap's first songs to directly address the coarse effects of mental health issues. Rap fans admired the subgenre's expansion and felt it encapsulated the best hip-hop had to offer to the world, as an art form and culture. And the success of these artists was indicative of their fervor and fans' attachment.

The music was more fulfilling in concept and scope, but it required added effort to digest, unlike the party records and mindless jams that blared from car and club speakers. In some ways, conscious rap was a stance against materialism, showmanship, drug-dealing and gun-toting declarations, and the mafioso themes that became increasingly popular in the mid-1990s. It was about soulful connections and the inherent desire to see hip-hop fans and Black America evolve in ways previously unseen. But over time, it lost much of its luster.

Rejecting the Subgenre

In the past, conscious rappers were endlessly met with praise. However, sometime between the early 2000s and 2010s, they have been widely underappreciated and marginalized by the masses. Casual hip-hop fans have deemed the work of artists like Immortal Technique, Common, and Talib Kweli as "backpack rap." The term has been associated with boorish music with little to no commercial appeal.

It doesn't help that big-name artists have subscribed to the same ideology. On Jay-Z's "Moment of Clarity," the Brooklyn-bred emcee acknowledged the exchange of high-octane lyrics and musical concepts for simplistic hits and multiplatinum records. "If skills sold, truth be told, I'd probably be lyrically Talib Kweli. Truthfully, I wanna rhyme like Common Sense. But I did 5 mill. I ain't been rhyming like Common since." And Malice, one-half of the duo Clipse, expressed his disdain for the subgenre on 2009's "Footsteps," "I hate conscious rap," he said.

It's easy to interpret their stance on conscious rap as one of contempt. However, what Jay-Z, Clipse, and a plethora of other artists, rap fans, and pundits are pointing to are the extremes of conscious rap, the kind of artists or listeners who feel anything outside of conscious rap is unconscious, and that their existence could slowly cripple Black America. That's always been the divide, and it's one that's ultimately led to the widening of the gap between conscious rap and everything else.

There's value in the dark, reality rhymes of Mobb Deep and Wu-Tang Clan, the hustler and drug-dealing confessions of Jay-Z, and the romantic exploits of artists like TLC and Salt-N-Pepa. Those artists offer threads of human connection and balance to a culture built on a medley of talent and an amalgamation of influences. Besides, they have a variation of conscious rap songs, too.

J. Cole and Kendrick Lamar are two of the few artists capable of balancing the varying worlds, all while experimenting with new creative pathways, themes, and social topics they deem worth addressing. Cole broke down the essence of his upbringing in North Carolina and detailed how he came to grips with certain traumas, past mistakes, and other hitches faced in his adolescence on albums such as *Born Sinner* and *2014 Forest Hills Drive*. Kendrick detangled the lessons he's learned in fatherhood, the woes of infidelity, and his battle with alcoholism on projects like *good kid, m.A.A.d. city*, and later *Mr. Morale & The Big Steppers*. Other contemporary artists have also followed suit.

Artists like YG and the late Nipsey Hussle made "Fuck Donald Trump" following the shockwave of the 2016 US presidential election. Jay-Z unpacked the value of generational wealth on *4:44*, and Compton's Westside Boogie proclaims the need for *More Black Superheroes*. Southern rap titans like

Rapsody, Big K.R.I.T., Killer Mike, and others continue to push the boundaries of rap, demanding that added substance is administered in the culture. But given Cole and Kendrick's commercial success, they stand as the two greatest examples of conscious rap and its importance in empowering Black Americans today.

Modern Rap: Medicine in the Candy

The influence of Grandmaster Flash and the Furious Five's "The Message" and the global awakening of Public Enemy's "Fight the Power" later inspired other artists to take on similar cultural and societal topics. Among the biggest stars of the early 1990s were 2Pac and Nasir "Nas" Jones, who both inspired a young Kendrick Lamar Duckworth and Jermaine Lamarr Cole.

In Kendrick's eyes, 2Pac embodied the essence of West Coast rap and showed him how passion-filled artists can move the world with words and action. In many respects, Lamar has inherited the spirit and fearlessness of a young Pac. He's never shied away from cultural or sociopolitical issues, and he's openly addressed his personal battles with alcoholism, infidelity, and generational trauma. Despite outside noise, he's embraced his role as a "conscious nigga." Kendrick made the claim on Future's "Mask Off Remix," rapping, "How y'all let a conscious nigga go commercial. While only makin' conscious albums?" The same can be said for Cole.

Cole's reverence for Nas was evident on "Let Nas Down," a song that highlighted the perceived disappointment in his debut album's release. Cole unveiled a conversation between himself and the Queensbridge legend, who was deemed a prophetic child of East Coast rap following his debut album, *Illmatic*. Nas's poetic lyrics and enriching tales of street life inspired a generation of superstar emcees, including J. Cole. When recalling his idolization of Nas as a kid at the 2014 VIBE Impact Awards, J. Cole stated:

> As a rapper, there are very few greats that I study and I still continue to study, and Nas is obviously one of them. I really had his lyrics printed on my wall ... I would print these joints out and I would hang them up on my wall and if you'd walk in my room [you'd be like], "What is wrong with this kid?" I'd just be there standing and reading the lyrics. I really wanted to know

what it was like to be that good. I was rapping at the time and it was my goal to be that good. I somehow wanted to master the style.[13]

Cole's song, and Nas's response "Made Nas Proud," opened fans' eyes to their kinship and the parts of Nas that existed in Cole, especially when it came to conceptual and provocative records. Cole's "Love Yourz" is a declaration of self-love and appreciation, while songs like "Change" conjure a sense of faith and "Crooked Smile" emboldens women to embrace their beauty, flaws and all. "We ain't picture perfect but we worth the picture still."

Like their predecessors, Cole and Lamar continue to inscribe tales of street life, bouts with mental health, and the past challenges of their adolescence. Decades after the emergence of conscious rap, Cole and Lamar are the last two superstars of the musical fashion. Grammy-nominated sound engineer Ben Thomas said their stance is a credit to their ability to mask such messaging underneath Billboard hits, summer jams, and club records. Other artists shed conscious messaging to garner mainstream success, but neither Cole nor Kendrick has been forced to conform. Thomas said their level of production is how Cole and Kendrick weave in conscious messages so seamlessly:

I think sonically it's all about production and beat selection. If you have an instrumental that has a mainstream feel, then you're able to sneak messages into it that you may not be able to do on other songs. I don't want to say we're past the age where rappers can do that because anything can happen, but the boom-bap rap songs and beats aren't going to play well on the radio. They don't have the sort of energy that people are looking for in music. But when it comes to Kendrick, I think the beat choices allow for him to make a "Humble" or "DNA" with that same sound and bounce.

They haven't singularly carried the torch. Other artists have captured the spirit of their musical forefathers, but none have quite reached the level of the two rap stars. They have been the faces of the subgenre since their first collaboration on 2011's "HiiiPoWeR," and it's no mistake that they have been considered two of the best rappers in hip-hop today. Their presence is even more significant given the decline of conscious rap in mainstream music.

It dwindled with rap becoming a larger international export, and with the oversaturation of artists in the genre.

With the formation of YouTube, SoundCloud, and other music-sharing apps, there are more rappers and musical artists than ever before. In today's musical landscape, people can record, upload, and share music through mobile apps and build fan bases via social media. The days when newcomers were forced to scrape together money for studio time or purchase expensive at-home equipment have long disappeared.

The barrier for creating and sharing music is lower than it's ever been. This access has opened doors for newer conscious rappers to emerge in the 2010s, namely Chance the Rapper, Mick Jenkins, NoName, Denzel Curry, and others who arose amid the SoundCloud era. While music-making apps and platforms like SoundCloud have opened pathways for talented emcees, who would have been potentially overlooked in past decades, it's weakened the barrier of entry for lackluster artists as well. The talent pool has grown wider, but the concentration of rap's musical talent has also gotten weaker. And their desire and ability to invoke conscious messaging in their music has also tapered off over time.

Rather than contribute quality music embedded with conscious messaging, a growing number of artists are choosing to make easily consumable records that have viral appeal. In the 2010s, artists like Lil Pump, Ugly God, SmokePurrp, and others of that tier generated buzz from records with little craftsmanship or shelf-life. They had virality, which sparked momentary interest and a significant boost to their profiles, but once their momentum faded months or years later, they had little else to show for it. For artists with music that draw from or directly tackle social issues, their success proves that quality lyrics and musical substance rise to the top. But the overabundance of talentless rap stars, and the state of mainstream rap today, is proof not all hip-hop fans feel the same sentiment.

The Shift from Consciousness

The idea of success is relative to an individual's own expectations. Lebanese-American poet Kahlil Gibran once said, "To understand the heart and mind of a person, look not at what he has already achieved, but what he aspires to." Many judge it based on the status of their peers or colleagues, but a person's success is completely subjective. This sentiment is also true for music artists and the decisions they make. One element that has impacted rappers in hip-hop is the desire to reach the masses and become "mainstream."

While hip-hop has always been a Black art form and culture, the music reaches far beyond this demographic. Some rappers want to stay true to their authentic sound and cater to the audience that brought them to prominence. Others feel pressure to appeal to new audiences and garner newfound superstardom. Sometimes this pressure comes from record labels with the hopes of increasing an artist's revenue and longevity, while other times artists fight the internal battle of staying true to their sound or becoming more "successful." Many artists within the industry make amends by altering their sound or messaging to expand and garner hit records. Sometimes it works and they create new fans while keeping their original audience, and other times it appears forced and their initial fanbase feels abandoned.

One example is Nas, who's celebrated for his introspective lyrics, deep storytelling, and vivid depictions of street life in New York. His debut album, *Illmatic*, is regarded as one of the greatest hip-hop albums of all time by hip-hop critics and fans. Since that moment, Nas has been acknowledged as a lyrical genius who discusses the world profoundly.

In 1999, Nas released a song that deviated from his usual sound called "Owe Me." The song, produced by Timbaland and featuring popular R&B singer Ginuwine, was a clear attempt at a mainstream hit. The record lacked the usual depth that fans expected from Nas, and contained messaging that many fans felt was beneath him as an artist. A song with a hook about women owing him for all the jewelry and money he spends on them seemed childish and ignorant to fans who fell in love with the thought-provoking nature of his music. While the song was a minor hit on the Billboard Hot 100, fans view it as a career misstep. Nas has since returned to his lyrical aptitude, releasing more critically acclaimed and impactful projects in the years since the 1999 single.

Nas is surely not the only artist to veer out of their typical lane to make more mainstream appealing tunes. People had similar criticisms when Fugees star Wyclef Jean branched out of the group's dark, hard-hitting, and introspective hip-hop sound to make an upbeat single called "We Trying to Stay Alive" in 1997. The song sampled the disco classic "Staying Alive" by the Bee Gees, and featured a 1970s-themed music video to match.

Just five years later, one of the most revered emcees, Common, was also heavily criticized for his album *Electric Circus*. Influenced by the rock stylings of legendary acts like Pink Floyd and Jimi Hendrix, the project was the opposite of the more soulful album *Like Water for Chocolate* that preceded it. His fans disliked the album so much that they blamed soul and R&B singer Erykah Badu, his significant other at the time, for this deviation from the sound they loved.

It's common for artists to alter their brand or musical style to attract mainstream success. As a younger or more inexperienced creator, there's even more pressure to score a hit record. And while the recipe for a "hit" has changed over time, the benefits of landing a Billboard-topping track have always been desired. It can turn a little-known artist into a superstar or reinvigorate the careers of well-established musicians who hit a musical plateau. As the industry shifted in the late 1990s, emcees were less inclined to release conscious records as potential radio smashes, or craft records with lyrical substance at all.

There's no singular point of its decline, but many consider the growth and exploitation of gangsta rap and other subgenres in the late 1990s and early 2000s as the catalyst for its eventual downswing. Aside from acts like OutKast, Eminem, Lauryn Hill, Black Star, and later Kanye West, emerging artists and rap fans were gravitating toward these other genres. Gangsta rap was first launched by pioneers like Schoolly D, Ice-T, and Just-Ice in the mid-1980s, and the momentum forged by stars like Dr. Dre, Snoop Dogg, Wu-Tang Clan, 2Pac, and others carried it over into the late 1990s and 2000s. The meteoric rise of artists like 50 Cent was indicative of its mass appeal, and offshoots like trap and drill music would shift the genre even further in the 2010s.

The period also gave birth to crunk, trap, and snap music. The subgenres brought trunk-rattling beats, catchy hooks, and high-intensity chants to rap, but it also placed lyricism on the back burner. Younger audiences were more interested in learning synchronized dances than they were in artists' lyrics. The same goes for the content of gangsta music in the 2000s. Often the image of the artist was more profound than the music they created, which made it harder for conscious rap artists to break through into the mainstream. The proof is in the decline of radio play and album sales.

Conscious rappers didn't go anywhere, but for a time record labels placed their marketing dollars and strategies toward other subgenres. Unless an artist was aligned with a growing underground sound or was boosted by a big industry cosign, conscious artists were beginning to struggle for visibility and widespread success. Record executives were prioritizing profit over musical messaging. For every Kanye West or Lupe Fiasco, there were ten artists whose music differed from their brand of hip-hop. It wasn't until the rise of artists like Kendrick Lamar and J. Cole that conscious rap regained its footing in mainstream music.

2
The Millennial Shift

Hip-hop dominated throughout the 1990s and into the new millennium, becoming the epicenter of pop culture, style, defiance, and artistry. Its massive popularity was backed by growing album and concert sales. While Whodini's 1984 album *Escape* is considered the first hip-hop record to go platinum, there would be a total of thirty releases to receive an RIAA certification in 1998.[1] That year alone accounted for nearly one-fifth of all platinum-selling albums in hip-hop up to that point, a figure that would grow exponentially in the years that followed.

Growing album sales led to larger opportunities for commercialization. High-profile artists were invited to perform on late-night TV shows. They had their own cartoons and clothing labels, and even big-budget movie roles. Hip-hop became a pop cultural commodity, with an endless flow of potential gain. Everyone in the entertainment industry wanted to get their hands on it. But for hardcore rap fans, they felt the music was beginning to lose much of its essence.

The lyrics weren't as potent, the songs weren't as meaningful, and fewer mainstream artists were willing to challenge the powers of oppression. Those elements represented the foundation of hip-hop, but purists were often left reminiscing on music of the past, with few hopes for the future of the genre. However, a new crop of rap stars emerged in the late 2000s with the ability to deliver chart-topping hits that evoked conscious messages that stuck to the bones. Kendrick Lamar and J. Cole were ahead of the class.

Backed by legends like Dr. Dre and Jay-Z, Cole and Kendrick carved out distinctive lanes with high-level storytelling, intricate concept albums, and commentary on social issues that transcended continental lines. Their groundbreaking emergence filled a noticeable gap in hip-hop, which widened as the genre transitioned from the "Golden Era" of rap to the bad and downright embarrassing period of the 2010s.

The Essence of Real Rap

The late 1980s and early 1990s are widely heralded as the "Golden Era" of hip-hop and one of the more transformative moments in music history. By then, hip-hop was a firmly established genre with a troop of new artists, DJs, and producers pushing its boundaries. The emergence of digital sampling machines led to new beat compositions, Rakim and Big Daddy Kane's intricate flows forced other emcees to sharpen their flows and rhyme patterns, and the debut of *Yo! MTV Raps* introduced a new audience to hip-hop.

Regional lines were also beginning to fade. While New York City remained the primary breeding ground for top talent, the genre expanded beyond the Tri-State area during this period. High-profile acts emerged from the West Coast, the South, and other corners of the country, deepening the talent pool in ways unseen in past years. Let's take 1997, for instance. That year, Busta Rhymes, Jay-Z, Missy Elliott, Scarface, Will Smith, and Wu-Tang Clan all released studio albums. Their voices, production, messaging, and delivery were completely unique and instantly recognizable to an audience. They all evoked a different emotional response, and the same sentiment rings true for most of the 1990s.

This era is also considered a pivotal moment in rap history because of the abundance of socially conscious music. Amid the crack and HIV/AIDS epidemics, which disproportionately affected Black Americans throughout the 1980s and 1990s, artists were conditioned to address social issues at some point in their discography. While groups like Brand Nubian, Public Enemy, and Goodie Mob largely focused on social issues, acts like OutKast did so more covertly on songs like "Da Art of Storytellin."

On the 1998 release, André 3000 delivered a heartfelt verse about a young woman's struggles with domestic abuse and drug addiction. Solo artists like Common, Lauryn Hill, Mos Def (now known as Yaasiin Bey), and others also conjured introspective songs that tackled societal issues with equal success. Even rappers like Jay-Z, who often raps about his past life as a street hustler and drug dealer, acknowledged the lives he affected while immersed in the underground trade. On 1997's "You Must Love Me," he raps about his past regrets selling crack, and how his hardened experiences led him to shoot his brother in the shoulder.

> *As we grew fussing and fighting continued*
> *As I plundered through ya stuff and snuck ya clothes to school*
> *Got intense, real intense as we got older*
> *Never believed it would lead to me poppin' one in your shoulder.*

As significant as these artists and songs were during rap's "Golden Age," the era also birthed gangsta rap. The subgenre was considered harmful by civil rights activists, politicians, and academics, but some of the music proved to have conscious messaging at its core.

From Conscious to Gangsta

In 1988, acts like NWA, Ice-T, Just-Ice, and Too Short brought gangsta rap to the masses, shifting the genre's sonic landscape and broadening its reach within mainstream music. Hip-hop went from the fun and light-hearted sounds of groups like DJ Jazzy Jeff & The Fresh Prince and Salt-N-Pepa, to the ultra-realistic and gritty worlds Ice Cube, Dr. Dre, Eazy-E, and other West Coast artists drew listeners toward.

While West Coast artists introduced gangsta rap to the masses, Philadelphia-bred emcee Schoolly D is considered the father of the subgenre. His record "P.S.K.— What Does It Mean?," an abbreviation for the Park Side Killas street gang, described a lifestyle of sex, drugs, and senseless violence. The record laid the blueprint for gangsta rap music, with Ice-T penning "6 in the Mornin'" after hearing the 1985 track. In a 2023 interview on the Questlove Supreme Podcast, Ice-T stated:

> I heard P.S.K. and it blew my mind. I was in Santa Monica, and at first the track came on, and the track sounded like angel dust. And then Schoolly came on, "P.S.K., we're making that green. People always say" … Now at that time, people were always yelling on records. Who is that fly nigga [saying]

"One by one I'm knockin' you out. K for the way my DJ cuttin' ... Put my pistol up against his head. And said, 'You sucker-ass nigga, I should shoot you dead.'" Then I researched it, and P.S.K. is Park Side Killas. He's repping a set. It's OK. That was the green light like, "Oh, they want to hear this shit."[2]

Years after Schoolly D's landmark single, N.W.A. had a statement project of its own. The group's debut album *Straight Outta Compton*, which boasted singles like "Fuck Tha Police" and "Straight Outta Compton," reflected the anger and rage that urban youth felt during this period. They weren't trying to debunk or conceptualize why police brutality was occurring. They were saying "we've had enough and are going to fight back," even if it killed them.

It wasn't the first gangsta or hardcore rap album, but it was one of the genre's most revolutionary compilations. Backed by DJ Yella and Dr. Dre's unique penchant for jazz samples, doo-wop, and p-funk beats, members Eazy-E, Ice Cube, and MC Ren rapped about the gruesome streets of Compton, which were brimming with street hustlers, prostitutes, and drugs at the height of the crack and HIV/AIDS epidemics.

N.W.A. served as the narrator, describing the issues millions faced in the country's urban enclaves. Unlike Public Enemy, N.W.A. wasn't afraid to bend at eye-level with the criminal-minded. The group embraced the "gangsta" label and boasted about their criminal ways in a manner traditional conscious acts like Public Enemy never would. Shockingly, White teenagers in suburban America were drawn to the group's hard-nosed messaging, which voiced the thoughts of people who lived in a world far different from their own. They yearned for music rebellious in nature, filled with lyrics that disavowed their parents' rules and restrictions. The album went on to sell more than three million copies, becoming the group's biggest and arguably most impactful album. N.W.A.'s success marked the mass production and distribution of gangsta rap, from the hood to the 'burbs.

After the World's Most Dangerous Group dissolved in 1992, the subgenre expanded with its former members. Ice Cube perfected his gruff, ultra-realistic sound on albums like 1990's *AmeriKKKa's Most Wanted* and *Death Certificate* the following year. Dr. Dre went on to pioneer the G-Funk sound with his protege, a 21-year-old Snoop Dogg, and the stockpile of artists at Death Row

Records—most famously 2Pac, The Lady of Rage, and others. Their influence, paired with hardcore acts like Wu-Tang Clan, Mobb Deep, and others that formed, ushered in new forms of gangsta rap throughout the decades.

Rapper LNS, one-half of the Atlanta-based duo Sheesh, said gangsta rap inspired future artists to address the realities they faced. He said this form of gangsta rap, known as "reality rap," drew listeners who lived or could relate to the lifestyles and memories reality rap artists discussed. Rather than glorifying imprisonment, gang warfare, and street violence, artists like DMX addressed their past experiences and mental scars as lessons learned. In this form, LNS said gangsta or reality rap could be inherently conscious, depending on the messenger's intent. LNS stated:

> I think conscious rap and reality rap go hand in hand. When you talk about being conscious, it's about being conscious of the world. My reality is my everyday life, so how can I not rap about my reality?

At the height of gangsta rap in the mid-1990s, politicians and civil rights activists like C. Delores Tucker spearheaded a national anti-rap campaign, which criticized the often graphic and derogatory lyrics depicted in albums like Snoop Dogg's debut project, *Doggystyle*. The civil rights vet, who marched alongside Dr. Martin Luther King in the Selma to Montgomery marches, shifted her focus from race and women's rights to gangsta rap in the early 1990s. She believed the subgenre promoted violence, drug use, greed, and misogynistic views—a venomous cocktail that negatively altered the minds of young listeners.

Among the bevy of artists and label heads she held liable, Tucker said Death Row Records was the biggest distributor of "porno rap" to young listeners. "The pimps in the entertainment industry who distribute gangsta rap are major contributors to the destruction of the African American community," Tucker said in a 1996 *Los Angeles Times* article.[3] In response, former Death Row Records CEO Suge Knight labeled Tucker a false "moral guardian" and questioned her academic credentials. He also claimed she rented slum properties to low-income Philadelphians and was fired as the Pennsylvania Secretary of State for abusing her role for personal gain.

The bitter and hotly contested exchange resulted in further accusations and defamation lawsuits. Tucker also became a lyrical punching bag for rappers like Eminem, Lil Kim, Jay-Z, Lil Wayne, and 2Pac, who took slights at Tucker in songs and interviews. Despite the constant jabs, Tucker continued to voice her disdain for gangsta rap until her death in 2005 at the age of seventy-eight. And while her stance on rap was shared by other activists, political figures, and critics, it didn't stop gangsta rap or hip-hop from topping the Billboard charts or engulfing pop culture.

The Commercialization of Hip-Hop

By the mid-1990s, hip-hop had evolved into a global export. The genre shattered regional barriers from the East and West Coast. Acts like OutKast and Goodie Mob opened pathways in Atlanta. James Prince's Rap-A-Lot Records and the Master P-led No Limit Records turned cities like Houston and New Orleans into expansion points. Uncle Luke and Miami's 2 Live Crew continued to scorch earth in South Florida's searing rap scene.

The development of TV shows like *Yo! MTV Raps*, which was the precursor to popular shows like BET's *106 & Park* and *Rap City*, also aided the growth of hip-hop music and culture both in fandom and access. The crowds grew larger, the money was more abundant, and the lifestyle of a rapper became more enticing. Its growing popularity was welcomed by new consumers, as artists like 2Pac, Snoop Dogg, Jay-Z, and later 50 Cent, Kanye West, and Drake rose to global superstardom.

Before audiences began to cross over globally, pioneers like Kurtis Blow set the path for other global stars to rise. At twenty years old, Blow became the first rapper to sign a major record deal. His signing under Mercury Records, now owned by Universal Music Group, made him one of the first commercially successful rappers in hip-hop history. Thanks to classic records like 1980's "The Breaks" and the Top 5 Billboard R&B hit "If I Ruled the World," Blow's profile elevated to national audiences. His musical success led to the 1986 "Now More Than Ever" Sprite commercial.[4] Blow became one of the first rappers to appear in a national ad for a mainstream brand, and the thirty-second TV spot established a long-standing relationship between hip-hop and Sprite. Blow's ad inspired the 1990 "I Like the Sprite in You" commercials featuring LL Cool J and the Atlanta rap duo Kris Kross, as well as other endorsements by Common, Nas, and Drake.

With Blow's breakthrough in commercialization, other artists shifted their sound and style to appeal to big-name brands. The Queens trio Run-DMC, consisting of Joseph "Run" Simmons, Darryl "DMC" McDaniels, and the late Jason "Jam Master Jay" Mizell, was already blurring genre lines. Rap-rock crossovers like the Aerosmith-assisted "Walk This Way" and "Rock Box" established the group's formative sound, but the 1986 hit "My Adidas" turned the three Adidas Superstar-stomping artists into fashion icons. The song's success and the group's growing hold on youth sneaker culture led to a $1.6 million endorsement deal with the sportswear company.

Acts like Wu-Tang Clan took things further. The Staten Island-bred collective helped strengthen New York City's grip on rap music in the early 1990s, while also expanding the Wu brand outside of music. The group, consisting of the RZA, GZA, Method Man, Raekwon, Ghostface Killah, Inspectah Deck, U-God, Masta Killa, Ol' Dirty Bastard, and later Cappadonna, leveraged the success of classic records like "C.R.E.A.M." and "Protect Ya Neck" to establish one of rap's first clothing lines, Wu-Wear. The group went on to publish a comic book series and other global ventures, broadening the marketability of rap artists and their reach on a global scale.

Artists like Dr. Dre, 50 Cent, and Jay-Z also took note, with all three leveraging their musical stardom to forge business ventures in tech, entertainment, spirits, and TV production. Dr. Dre and record executive Jimmy Iovine founded Beats by Dre in 2006, and the headphone company was acquired by Apple for $3 billion in August 2014. Jay-Z and 50 Cent also parlayed their musical success into multiple independent ventures. Along with co-founding Roc-A-Fella Records in 1994, Jay-Z established everything from the 40/40 sports club, the Tidal Music streaming platform, and the full-service entertainment company, Roc Nation. After launching G-Unit Records and apparel, 50 Cent used his on-screen talents and knack for executive production for a series of films and TV shows.

Materialism Reigned Supreme

Following the success of Run-DMC's "My Adidas," hip-hop music and fashion were at the center of pop culture. Early acts like LL Cool J, Kool Moe Dee, and Slick Rick encouraged fans to swarm nearby retailers to purchase Adidas Superstar shoes and tracksuits, thick or "dookie" gold chains, and Kangol bucket hats. And a Harlem hustler and haberdasher named Daniel Day, better known as Dapper Dan, merged hip-hop couture with luxury-house brands. Like sampling in rap music, Dapper Dan remixed recognizable fashion house logos, threading them into sports jackets, trench coats, and other garments. The Dapper Dan-sewn look was synonymous with street hustlers and gangsta rap during the late 1980s and early 1990s.

The evolution of hip-hop fashion also led to a new turn in rap music. While braggadocio-fueled rhymes still permeated hip-hop channels, rappers began to move away from songs about being the most skilled emcee. Instead, having the flyest clothes, sleekest rides, and an abundance of sexual companions became the new currency. It established luxury rap and the materialism that came from it as early as the mid-1980s.

After Slick Rick name-dropped Gucci, Polo, and Bally on his 1985 song "La Di La Di," it seemed like a legion of artists were mentioning their go-to brands, lifestyles, and riches for all those to hear. Even artists like 2Pac, whose career skyrocketed after his debut album *2Pacalypse Now*, went on to make party records like "I Get Around." The 1993 song emphasized his young bachelor lifestyle. The music video followed 2Pac as he avoided a mansion full of fans and female admirers, who all wanted a piece of the West Coast star.

The same goes for Brooklyn's Biggie Smalls. Songs like "Big Poppa" and "One More Chance" showcased his womanizing ways, even for a big guy with a noticeably lazy eye. He didn't shy away from his player persona, and both he and his friend Jay-Z talked a big game and big wallet, too. Biggie was often photographed wearing Coogi sweaters and Versace sunglasses, and Jay-Z rapped about his international exploits and mafia-style business practices on 1996's "Feelin' It." And on "Imaginary Players" he even convinced owners of the Range Rover 4.0 to sell their rides in exchange for the 4.6, and to toss their Cartier frames if they didn't have a platinum trim. During this era, Philly artist and entrepreneur Chill Moody stated:

Music became glorified commercials in a sense. I remember when 50 Cent used the iPod in the "P.I.M.P." music video. That was a play. Jimmy Iovine asked Apple for $150,000 to make this video better, and we'll put your iPod into it. [50] is the reason we as a culture started fucking with iPods, and I don't he got [paid] what he was supposed to get from that. But it was something. He was driven to do it because there was something behind it.

Record labels and marketing giants were shifting their focus toward similar artists, who reflected the same gangsta, flashy, womanizing or sexualized personas that mirrored superstar artists of the era. The added marketing push helped fuel the careers of the aforementioned artists, as well as rappers like Nas, Lil Kim, Foxy Brown, The Lox, and others. But the more consciously driven and Afrocentric acts from the early 1990s slowly fell from the foreground, leading to fewer radio spins and record sales in the late 1990s.

During the early formation of hip-hop, Moody said there was a time when conscious rap was mainstream. But once music industry giants and label heads shifted their focus, Moody said the sound became less visible and profitable toward the latter part of the 1990s and early 2000s, stating:

There was a time when it was cool to have a message in the music. The powers that be, or whoever's controlling the mainstream messages, it benefited them at that time for some Black empowerment. At the end of the day, that's all this socially conscious hip-hop is. It's finding a way to educate your people.

Instead of bottling rap in its purest form for wider consumption, luxury lyrics and violence-ridden tales were at the forefront. But not everybody was a fan of the genre's newfound direction. Rather than allow rap to lose the essence of its conscious-fueled messages, artists like Common, then known as Common Sense, made a decree with the 1994 song, "I Used to Love H.E.R."

"I Used To Love H.E.R."

"I Used to Love H.E.R." reimagined hip-hop as a woman once imbued with purity, whose exposure to materialism, overt sexualization, and unoriginality altered "her" identity. These elements, and the rise of gangsta rap, were damaging the hip-hop (woman) that Common and others grew to love. Ironically, the 1994 record led to Common's ascension to mainstream rap, but it also caused a rift between the South Side Chicago native and Ice Cube.

Cube, who felt Common blamed the West Coast for rap's dilution, hurled insults at the *Can I Borrow a Dollar?* rapper on the Westside Connection record, "Westside Slaughterhouse." Cube raps on the 1995 track, "All you suckas want to diss the Pacific. But you busta niggas never get specific. Used to Love H.E.R., mad 'cause we fucked a pussy-whipped bitch with no Common Sense." Common responded on the "The Bitch in Yoo," rapping "Now, what the fuck I look like dissing a whole coast? You ain't made shit dope since AmeriKKKa's Most," alluding to Cube's first album.

Years later, the two emcees would resolve their differences at the home of Nation of Islam leader Minister Louis Farrakhan. But the divide between traditional hip-hop purists and mainstays within gangsta and hardcore rap continued to dilate. There was less conscious and politically focused music circulating the airwaves, which reflected the fleeting album sales. Among the top-selling rap albums of the 1990s was Biggie Smalls's *Life After Death*, which deviated from the grounded sound of New York rap during the 1980s. The Diamond-selling project was equipped with glimmering tracks like "Mo Money Mo Problems" and "Sky's the Limit," as well as hard-hitting street records like "What's Beef?" and "Ten Crack Commandments."

While hardcore and gangsta rap were pushing record sales, acts like Scarface, 2Pac, DMX, and Naughty by Nature were still weaving conscious messaging in their music. The Geto Boys' 1991 song "Mind Playing Tricks on Me" was one of the first rap songs to explore the perils of mental health issues. "White Man'z World," a track from 2Pac's posthumous album *Don Killuminati: 7 Day Theory*, rapped about Black people receiving reparations for their hardships in America. And during an unprompted rant at the 1998 Grammy Awards, Ol' Dirty Bastard addressed Wu-Tang Clan's unmistakable target. "I don't know how y'all see it, but when it comes to the children: Wu-Tang is for the children," Ol' Dirty Bastard said to the crowd. "We teach the children, know what I mean? Puffy is good but Wu-Tang is the best."

Conscious rap may have taken a backseat to gangsta and hardcore rap, but there was still an abundance of artists who focused on cultural and sociopolitical issues. Among them were acts like Brand Nubian, Dead Prez, and Rawkus Records heavyweights Talib Kweli and Yasiin Bey.

Rawkus Records Rocks the Bells

As the Brooklyn-bred duo Black Star, Kweli and Bey anchored a new brand of conscious rap in the late 1990s. Their first album *Mos Def & Talib Kweli Are Black Star* was a landmark project that reinvigorated the underground New York sound that had lost its grip with the wave of West Coast and Southern rap stars. Backed by production from Cincinnati transplant Hi-Tek, the two emcees meld their distinct styles over soul-stirring beats and euphoric samples. Bey, who started out as a child actor on the short-lived CBS sitcom *You Take the Kids*, had an offbeat charisma and unconventional sensibility that oozed with stardom. From the fake patois, hand-swaying melodies, and showmanship, Bey was primed to cut through the invisible tape that entrapped most underground acts. Kweli, on the other hand, was more subdued.

Kweli was far less interested in Hollywood entry points. As the son of two academics, he unlocked Afrocentric teachings and rapped about the effects of mass incarceration from an authoritative stance. Lacking the same animation and flair as Bey, Kweli's delivery was fueled by descriptive lyrics that widened a song's margins. He was the perfect yin to Bey's yang, and the duo set the stage for Rawkus Records' brief takeover in the late 1990s.

Rawkus Records was formed by Brown University graduates Brian Brater and Jarret Myer in 1995. The independent label was famously funded by their friend James Murdoch, the son of media tycoon Rupert Murdoch. The label was defined by top underground talent, with Brater and Myer signing rap trio Company Flow, Pharoahe Monch, Kweli and Hi-Tek's Reflection Eternal, and a pre-fame Eminem. In 1996, Rupert Murdoch bought a majority of the label, which landed a distribution deal with Priority Records three years later. And while the now-defunct label folded after a series of short-lived joint ventures, it established an ecosystem of top lyricists who inspired new forms of conscious rap to take shape in the new millennium.

Despite their acclaim as lyricists and rap purists, author, journalist, and NYU professor Kathy Iandoli said their limited commercial success and visibility was a result of the "shiny suit era." It was a time defined by a glossier look and sound that pierced the back-half of the 1990s, and Kweli and Bey were oddly positioned in its uprising. One of the pioneers of the "shiny suit era" was Sean "Diddy" Combs, who Iandoli said manufactured a version of hip-hop that was "hook-heavy and less thought-provoking." And with the genre's commercialization, Kweli and Bey were forced to bear the weight of consciousness—a task that capped their mainstream success. Their world-class lyricism filled the stomachs of hip-hop fans yearning for conscious rap, but Iandoli said their music didn't always translate to platinum plaques:

> It was the world around them that labeled them lyrical gods in the face of what Sean "Diddy" Combs was doing to hip-hop. The hip-hop purists were like, "You are our savior." And for that reason, that prevented them from getting commercialized. If they went into that world they would be looked at as sell-outs. And I think that constant fear of selling out ultimately kept them in one very specific way.

The Shiny Suit Era

After Mase's multi-platinum debut album *Harlem World*, Bad Boy Records was on top of the musical food chain. For a moment, it seemed like rap was becoming glossier in the late 1990s. Thanks to a young, fiery Lil Wayne, the term "bling bling" would make its entry into the world's lexicon, and the music and videos were reflective of a new, brighter age in hip-hop. The songs were backed by the sultry vocals of a popular songbird of the era, and woven into an upbeat song about the finer things in life—plush leather seats, first-class flights, and champagne toasts. The music videos were glimmering with high-priced cars and scantily clad vixens, with visionaries like Hype Williams maxing out production budgets to bring the grand ideas to life.

The metallic suits and blinding lights on Will Smith's "Gettin' Jiggy with It" and Mase's "Feels So Good" flashed a luxurious turn for hip-hop. Fans were drawn to the glitz of the records, which was routinely crafted by Diddy's in-house production team The Hitmen. The group was led by former rapper Deric "D-Dot" Angelettie. Other members included Mario Winans, Chucky Thompson, Steven "Stevie J" Jordan of reality show fame, and later Kanye West. Their collective powers, and Combs' ear for satiny samples and Billboard-topping melodies, created lush hits like Mariah Carey's "Honey" and Faith Evans's "Love Like This."

Artists that originated from a more grounded street sound also took note, adding buzzing instrumentals and soulful R&B samples from the 1960s and 1970s to capture the same sound. Jay-Z's "(Always Be My) Sunshine" toed the same line, which was a notable changeup from his early mafioso style on 1996's *Reasonable Doubt*. But there's no denying it expanded his musical reach and influence. The same was true for Nas, The Lox, and Cam'Ron, who all benefited from the added commercial success and marketability The Hitmen provided.

Two Coasts Divided

Of course, there was a place for the sleek and bold sound The Hitmen crafted on Bad Boy albums like *No Way Out* and *Forever*. But there was also a growing need for conscious music in the years following the East Coast–West Coast rivalry, which placed two of rap's biggest stars at the center of a bi-coastal feud. It was a moment sparked by the shooting of 2Pac inside Manhattan's Quad Recording Studios on November 30, 1994.[5] The "Keep Ya Head Up" rapper was headed to a planned recording session, and was welcomed by Bad Boy artists Lil Cease and Biggie's rap group Junior Mafia. As they approached 2Pac, three men barged into the studio lobby demanding money, eventually shooting the rap and movie star five times and robbing him of $40,000 in jewelry.

2Pac was rushed to New York's Bellevue Hospital Center for emergency surgery. Against doctor's orders, he checked out of the hospital the next day, bandaged, wheelchair bound, and with revenge at the top of mind. Despite years of denial, 2Pac blamed Diddy, Biggie, and Bad Boy Records for orchestrating the near-fatal attack. 2Pac's infamous 1996 song "Hit 'Em Up" took direct aim at Biggie, Junior Mafia, and the New York-based label. On the track, which is among the most hostile diss records in rap history, 2Pac insists Biggie and the group set him up for the Quad Studios shooting. He also hints at a potential affair with Biggie's then-wife, R&B singer Faith Evans, which further fueled the conflict. While Biggie claimed 1994's "Who Shot Ya?" wasn't directed at 2Pac since the song was recorded well before the shooting, rap fans couldn't help but connect the song's lyrics to the ill-timed incident.

Tensions escalated during the 1995 Source Awards at New York's Paramount Theater. While 2Pac was imprisoned at the time, Death Row Records' Suge Knight delivered an acceptance speech that drew further division between the two coasts. "Any artist out there wanna be a artist, and wanna stay a star, and don't wanna—and won't have to worry about the executive producer tryna be all in the video, all on the record, dancin'—come to Death Row," Knight said as he accepted an award for Motion Picture Soundtrack of the Year.

Knight's speech was a perceived jab at Combs, who regularly ad-libbed on his artists' songs and cameoed in their videos. Presenters attempted to defuse the inflamed crowd, including Combs himself, but the moment led to another string of hostile moments throughout the night. As late filmmaker John Singleton presented the award for Producer of the Year, he tried to silence the murmuring crowd to no avail. "We gotta kill all this East Coast, West Coast, South, Midwest dissension in rap," he claimed. And as the winner Dr. Dre approached the stage with Snoop Dogg, the hostility prompted Snoop to launch a tirade that echoed throughout the award show and the hip-hop community. "The East Coast ain't got no love for Dr. Dre and Snoop Dogg and Death Row? Y'all don't love us? Well, let it be known then," Snoop hurled onto the crowd.

The conflict reached its apex in 1996, with *Vibe Magazine* releasing a cover story titled, "East vs. West: Biggie & Puffy Break Their Silence." The rapper and super-producer rejected any involvement in 2Pac's shooting or the killing of Knight's close friend Jake Robles during an Atlanta party. The violent threats led to a handgun-drawn exchange between Biggie and 2Pac at the 1995 Soul Train Awards, and Combs was exhausted from it all. "I'm ready for it to come to a head, however it gotta go down," Combs told *Vibe* journalist Larry

"Blackspot" Hester. "I'm ready for it to be out my life and be over with. I mean that from the bottom of my heart. I just hope it can end quick and in a positive way, because it's gotten out of hand."

The East–West friction met its end by 1997 with the death of the two rap stars. On September 7, 1996, 2Pac was shot four times at a Las Vegas stoplight. While sitting in a black BMW sedan with Knight, a white Cadillac pulled up alongside them and opened fire. 2Pac was struck twice in the chest, and once in the arm and thigh. He died six days later in a Las Vegas hospital. Orlando Anderson, a Crips gang member, was suspected of murdering 2Pac. The two men were in a brawl earlier on the night of the shooting, but Anderson, who died in an unrelated gang shootout in 1998, was never charged for the crime. On September 29, 2023, Anderson's uncle Duane "Keefe D" Davis was arrested for the first-degree murder of 2Pac. And in October 2024, 2Pac's family reportedly hired New York attorney Alex Spiro to investigate an alleged link between Combs and the rapper's death.

Six months after 2Pac's death, Biggie faced a similar fate. The "Warning" rapper was killed in a drive-by shooting in Los Angeles on March 9, 1997—just two weeks before the release of his sophomore album *Life After Death*. Their deaths paralyzed the hip-hop community. The violent lyrics and life-threatening exchanges once criticized by politicians manifested into real, irreversible bloodshed, affecting all those involved in their tragic losses. Fans were left wondering where the once-uplifting genre had gone wrong, and how a redemptive path could be paved. For many, the answer was conscious music.

Consciousness in the New Millennia

Acts like Common, Bey, Kweli, The Roots, Lauryn Hill, and others still carried the same introspection and sharp lyrics of the genre's predecessors. The soulful, reggae and jazz-rap infused album, *The Score*, is a seminal project that lifted the Fugees to iconic status. It also set the stage for Hill's legendary rise as a star, both in music and film. The ultra-talented R&B singer and emcee blazed a solo career with one of rap's best debut albums, *The Miseducation of Lauryn Hill*. The acclaimed project made her the first hip-hop artist in history to secure a Grammy Award for Album of the Year.[6]

While big-name artists like Jay-Z, Eve, DMX, Missy Elliott, Eminem, and others ruled the Billboard charts from the late 1990s to the early 2000s, their music also consisted of socially conscious messaging. Eve's hit song "Love is Blind" addresses the domestic abuse a close friend of hers endured, which raised awareness on an issue rarely discussed in rap. Eminem's "Cleanin' Out My Closet" dove into his tumultuous relationship between him and his mother, his shortcomings as a father, and the difficulties he experienced in his youth.

When you dig deep into Cole and Lamar's catalogs, Philly rapper Chill Moody said conscious acts like Dead Prez and Pharoahe Monch, as well as more commercially successful artists from that era, inspired them to harness the same lyrical powers and messaging. Moody stated:

They found ways to make that their own. You may not have heard a song from Gil Scott-Heron, but then you listen to Chill Moody and you will see I have songs solely dedicated to the messages that Gil Scott-Heron had in his music. You just have to dig a little deeper. Had Nas not gone on this recent run, there are young bouls who may not have known what Nas was doing. But if you listen to Cole's "Let Nas Down," then they are like, "Let me dig more into this." I think that right here is what keeps us going for another 50 years and ensures the music doesn't die.

There was also an unlikely platform that served as an incubator for conscious artists, who benefited from a wider and more diverse audience. Outside of traditional late-night programs and sketch comedy shows like *Saturday Night Live*, Comedy Central's *Chappelle's Show* was hyper focused on conscious acts during its first two seasons from 2003–4.

Chappelle's Show took the culture by storm. The innovative sketch comedy show was hosted and cultivated by comedic giant Dave Chappelle. While often revered for its memorable characters and witty commentary, the show also championed hip-hop artists and culture. *Chappelle's Show* featured live performances and appearances from rappers, but not all were invited to the Comedy Central hit. *Chappelle's Show* featured conscious and thought-provoking lyricists such as Common, Black Thought, Talib Kweli, Yasiin Bey, and several Wu-Tang members. He also showcased a young and hungry Kanye West, who would soon bridge the gap between conscious rap and mainstream music. The move introduced a new generation to the subgenre and helped solidify the careers of budding artists amid its evolution.

Despite their inspiring records, much of hip-hop was beginning to lean further into materialism, overt sexualization, and the unoriginality that artists like Common foreshadowed years before. Conscious artists were still *successful*, no doubt. But they weren't as highly touted as other artists of the time, despite the marginal or often distant talent gap.

The landscape was also vastly different. Bad Boy Records was still assembling top talent, but soon Roc-A-Fella Records, Irv Gotti's Murder Inc., and Dr. Dre's Aftermath Entertainment emerged as rap's most dominant musical forces in the early 2000s. Jay-Z was at the top of his game as a solo commodity. Gotti's signing of Ja Rule and Ashanti proved to be a dynamic one-two punch, and Eminem and 50 Cent's emergence under Dr. Dre yielded more than a decade of consistent hits.

Other regions were also catching steam. Virginians Pharrell, Timbaland, Missy Elliot, and Clipse were cranking out futuristic club and street bangers that played in nightclubs across the country. Nelly's lullaby-based hits "E.I." and "Dilemma" helped put St. Louis on the hip-hop map. Chingy soon followed with a series of sing-songy hits of his own. In Chicago, rapper Leonard Harris, better known as GLC, said the city was a melting pot of hip-hop influences, with artists like Twista, Common, Kanye West, and later Lupe Fiasco emerging on the national stage. "We were embracing the East and West Coast with N.W.A., Too Short, and Spice-1," he said. "We were listening to A Tribe Called Quest, Jungle Brothers, and Native Tongues. And as time went on, people's perspectives began to change." But few regions or collectives matched the height and longevity of the South's takeover.

The South Has Something to Say

The 1995 Source Awards is widely remembered as a point of tension in the East and West Coast beef, but it was a pivotal moment for Southern artists, who felt their music was shunned from major radio stations and award show consideration. After accepting the award for Best New Rap Group, OutKast's André 3000 stood atop the Paramount Theater stage and confronted the contentious crowd head on. "So what's up Dre," OutKast member Big Boy said to André 3000 as he approached the mic. "I'm tired of those close-minded folks, y'know what I'm saying. It's like we got a demo tape, but nobody want to hear it. But it's like this—the South got something to say," André proclaimed.

Years later, André 3000 would be proven right a thousand times over. Southern rap emerged as hip-hop's third coast by the early 1990s with acts like Geto Boys, 2 Live Crew, UGK, Three 6 Mafia, and OutKast penetrating the mainstream. Houston and Port Arthur, Texas were the home of the chopped-n-screwed sound, and early Atlanta influencers like MC Shy-D, Kilo Ali, and Hitman Sammy Sam were pillars of Georgia street rap. Memphis innovators like DJ Spanish Fly established the city's dark and distorted lo-fi signature, and Miami figures like James "Maggotron" McCauley and producer Amos Larkins helped forge the booty bass wave. And years before No Limit and Cash Money Records were in full swing, mix-masters like Mannie Fresh helped shape New Orleans bounce in the Crescent City.

Each region boasted a swath of musical styles and influences, which branched off to create a myriad of popular subgenres. In the mid-2000s, crunk morphed into one of the more dominant sounds of hip-hop and R&B. It was party music at its core. The thudding bass, emphatic riffs, and occasionally melodic vocal tones made for a punchy sound that was tailored for down South nightclubs. The movement in the 2000s was largely carried by Three 6 Mafia and Atlanta artists like Lil Jon, Ludacris, and the Ying Yang Twins. Smash-mouth classics like "Salt Shaker" and "Move Bitch" blasted from the subwoofers of the stretched out, candy-painted cars that Southern rap stars talked about in their music.

Before its arrival in mainstream music, crunk music was played in Miami nightclubs during the city's bass scene in the late 1980s. Partygoers danced to the booming bass, electro-dance instrumentals, and zippy synth lines that blasted from the venue's speakers. But the crunk sound fans were later drawn to didn't come to form until the early 1990s. The term was first used in 1993's "Player's Ball," and three years later, Three 6 Mafia and Memphis rapper Tommy Wright III used the term for their singles "Get 'Em Crunk" and "Getting Crunk." The name was established then, but the sound didn't fully take shape until years later. The first wave of true crunk songs started with 1992's "Tear da Club Up," and that same year, Lil Jon & the Eastside Boyz released "Get Crunk" and "Shawty Freak a Lil Sumtin." A decade later, artists like Usher and Ciara embraced the style, turning the once regional sound into a national mainstay in hip-hop and R&B through the mid-2000s.

Snap Music, Soulja Boy, and Internet Culture

With crunk music's favor in the mainstream, a new subgenre called "snap rap" or "snap music" began building steam in the South. Fun and up-tempo dance music has been an integral part of hip-hop since its inception. While rap evolved into an artform that contained deep, introspective, and heartfelt messaging, house party songs are also deeply ingrained in the genre's makeup. There were some that managed to slip in social and political messages, while others were made to set a block party ablaze. For every boundary-pusher like Public Enemy's "Fight the Power," there was a song like House of Pain's "Jump Around" or MC Hammer's "U Can't Touch This" that set the balance. The same thing happened with snap music.

The traditional party record took a new turn with the emergence of the video-sharing platform YouTube in December 2005; aspiring artists could freely upload their music for millions of viewers without the promotional push of a record label. In 2006, a Chicago-born and Mississippi-raised teenager named Soulja Boy rose to prominence from the online site. He began releasing dance videos and songs to YouTube, and his song "Crank That" took the internet and music industry by storm. The song, produced by the young artist on Fruity Loops demo software in ten minutes, led to a slew of people uploading themselves doing the dance on YouTube. The song shot up to No. 1 on Billboard's Hot 100 charts, selling millions of copies and ringtone purchases worldwide. The Internet sensation is considered the first viral dance trend in hip-hop history, and one that forever changed the music business and media landscape.

The popularity of "Crank That" and the crunk movement in Atlanta led to a bounty of dance tracks that dominated hip-hop radio and filled TV spots on countdown music video shows like BET's 106 & Park. Other songs like DEM Franchize Boyz's "Lean Wit It, Rock Wit It," D4L's "Laffy Taffy," and Young Joc's "It's Going Down" would rise out of Atlanta. Even New York artists joined in on the dance craze. DJ Webstar and Young B's "Chicken Noodle Soup" and Lil Mama's "Lip Gloss" had young kids dancing from the corners of Harlem to Brooklyn. Even with its raging popularity, many traditional rap fans felt the genre was on its deathbed.

While the snap music era provided some catchy tunes, some of which would last the test of time, the songs had little to no social commentary or introspective content. Veteran rapper Ice-T would even go on record saying, "Soulja Boy, I know you're young enough to be my kid but you single-handedly killed hip-hop, man."[7] Some fans labeled Ice-T an old, bitter hater whose best rapping days were long behind him, other hip-hop purists agreed with his sentiments. Kanye West would later express his concerns in the 2010 song "So Appalled," stating "Niggas is going through real shit, man they outta work. That's why another goddamn dance track, gotta hurt. That's why I rather spit something that gotta purp[ose]."

Trap or Die

Along with the arrival of crunk and snap music, trap music exploded in the mid-2000's. Musicians across genres incorporated the rattling hi-hats, heavy sub-bass, booming 808 kicks, and swift cadences that are synonymous with the subgenre. But the word "trap," and its early sound, was embedded in Atlanta from the mid-1990s. The word "trap," which is slang for a place used to produce and sell drugs, was first heard on Goodie Mob's 1995 track "Thought Process" by member Khujo: "All my folks that hang with me. When I was out in the trap. Or when I was goin' through one of our episodes. Only God knows, what I go through."

In a 2020 interview with media mogul DJ Vlad, Khujo talked about his days dealing drugs as a teenager. The streets, he said, were the inception of the word "trap" itself, with groups like Parliament-Funkadelic and others setting the soundtrack for the underground trade market that surrounded him. Khujo denied his role as the first to use the word "trap" in a song. He credited André 3000 with saying the word "trap" on OutKast's 1994 debut album, *Southernplayalisticadillacmuzik*.[8] On "Player's Ball," André 3000 rapped, "So I begin to piece my two and two together. Gots no snowy weather, have to find somethin' to do better, bet. I sets up trap, so shut up that. Nonsense about some silent, silent."

The word "trap" was out in the zeitgeist, and artists like Dungeon Family member Cool Breeze was one of many Atlanta artists that formed its early elements. The subgenre didn't achieve mainstream success until the arrival of T.I., Jeezy, and Gucci Mane. The three artists pioneered a gritty, down-home sound that was anchored by heavy bass drums and drug-slinging tales of Southern street culture. Their music also shed light on the consequences of imprisonment, the loss of cherished friends, and the onset of paranoia that comes with the trap lifestyle.

Journalist A. R. Shaw, the author of *Trap History: Atlanta Culture and the Global Impact of Trap Music*, said T.I.'s *Trap Muzik* was the first major hip-hop album that illuminated the word "trap," and songs like "Rubber Band Man" and "24's" branded the subgenre for hip-hop fans outside the Atlanta region. In a 2017 interview with radio personality and podcast host Angie Martinez, T.I. said he was the first rapper to shape what became trap music.[9] "A lot of people don't know that I created trap music. There was no such thing as trap music prior. No such thing, it didn't exist. It was Organized Noize and crunk."

After a string of independent album releases, and a brief stint at Bad Boy Records as a member of the group Boyz n da Hood, Jeezy's major label debut *Let's Get It: Thug Motivation 101* added to trap music's ascension. The Akon-assisted "Soul Survivor" and the lead single "And Then What" echoed Jeezy's street ties, and the project's raw, rough-cut edge increased Georgia's command even further.

Gucci Mane, who helmed Atlanta's mixtape landscape throughout the 2010s, also laid the ground for trap music's popularity in the mid-2000s with his debut album, *Trap House*. The 2005 release, paired with piano and synthesizer-filled tracks like "Go Head" and the Zaytoven-produced "Icy," placed Gucci Mane atop the list of trap music pioneers next to T.I. and Jeezy. Shaw stated:

The kingpin, street guy, and the middleman. They were all rapping from a different perspective. T.I. was rapping from the perspective of a kid on the corner, who had enough money to put it in a rubber band. Gucci is the same, but he had a slimy way about it. Jeezy was rapping from a distributor's perspective, almost coming from an elevated perspective. That's what you hear on his first album, *Let's Get It: Thug Motivation 101.*

Their music, influence, and collective eye for talent also helped usher in future players of the subgenre. Their music labels' signings and collaborations with future Georgia-made stars like Young Thug, 21 Savage, Migos, and Future helped reinvigorate trap music in the early 2010s.

As crunk music began to taper off in the late 2000s, trap music became the de facto sound in Atlanta and hip-hop during this period. The sound eventually broke outside of Atlanta's musical sphere, and the sonic template was used by artists across genres, including traditionally R&B and pop acts like Beyoncé, Ariana Grande, Rihanna, and Justin Bieber. Country acts like Miley Cyrus, Post Malone, and Shaboozey also benefited from trap's transcendence between the 2010s and early 2020s. And within rap, artists like Travis Scott, Lil Uzi Vert, Lil Yatchy, and others clung to the subgenre to craft their own version of trap music.

J. Cole and Kendrick Lamar were also featured on hit trap songs. On 2017's "Mask Off (Remix)," Kendrick had one of the year's best guest verses. He followed that up with another Atlanta-to-Compton connection on the Metro Boomin and Future collaboration "Like That" years later. And J. Cole's chameleon-like presence easily glided on trap songs with the likes of 21 Savage, Young Thug, Bia and several others.

Drugs, Drank, and Dissension

While the influence of trap music spanned decades, LNS believes the glorification of violence and substance abuse is what made the subgenre harmful to easily impressionable listeners. As hot as it was in nightclubs, stripper joints, and college house parties, the rapper said it was beginning to resonate with the wrong audience. LNS stated:

I love Future, but he changed rap forever when it comes to the consumption of drugs and making it cool to stay a junky. I like his music, but you have to talk about the downside. I've talked about the downsides of wildin' out, going to prison, and being in shootouts. I did all of that.

In the early phases of trap music, Shaw said much of the subgenre, as raw and abrasive as it seemed, was inherently conscious music. "It showed you a problem that existed, no matter how it was disseminated," he said. Up until the 2010s, artists like T.I. and Jeezy used trap music to reflect the harsh realities they faced in their youth. Like the word itself, they felt trapped or cornered by the dangerous and jarring circumstances that surrounded them. With drug dealing appearing to be their only escape, they turned to it, rapped about it, and opened doors for others to do the same. It was reality rap, but as time went on, the music shifted from a hustler's point of view to one of a substance abuser. The transition weakened the quality of trap music and encouraged drug and alcohol addiction at unforeseen heights. It created a generation of rappers who were dependent on the very drugs trap music pioneers served in their youth, a moment Shaw said speaks to the mental health issues that were unaddressed during the era:

> There was a torch that was being passed. The sound didn't stay the same, and the artists didn't stay the same. The messaging didn't stay the same when we went from Jeezy, T.I. and Gucci to a Future. Jeezy, T.I. and Gucci's perspective were, "Okay, we're selling and hustling. This is how we make our money." But Future comes in and switches it, and then you see the mental health aspect where artists are depending on the drugs. His perspective was, "These young brothers are out here hurting, and now they're getting high on their own supply." Or they're getting supplied from other individuals, and it changed the whole landscape. Trap became about popping pills and doing lean, and now we're seeing the impact unfold in real time.

In an effort to garner fame and success, Shaw said a slew of artists were appropriating the lifestyles and backgrounds of these artists. It not only soiled the impact trap music once had, it developed harmful offshoots with even more damning messages. "More people are cosplaying as hood dudes," Shaw said. "Some of these subjects are real. But at the same time, give us something else."

LNS said the audiences this music attracted pushed record labels to invest more into this form of trap music. There was less of a focus on conscious artists, and by the late 2000s, conscious music appeared to evaporate from the mainstream completely. "Labels stopped putting money behind the Commons and the Lupe Fiascos," LNS said. "If we're talking about a timeline, I would say around 2006, 2007, and 2008. After that, there wasn't much conscious rap. That's a big gap. Everything else was getting money behind it, and conscious rap was overshadowed. There wasn't enough space for it commercially."

Throughout the 2010s, drug-related deaths reached unparalleled heights. The deaths of artists like Mac Miller, Juice WRLD, Lil Peep, and others were the result of their lifestyles, much of which was reflected in their music. This made the presence of J. Cole and Kendrick Lamar that much more pressing. The two fixtures rose to stardom at the height of trap music's ascension. And while they dabbled in the popular subgenre, they purposefully avoided celebrating drug use and alcoholism in their music.

Cole's fifth album, *KOD*, highlighted the generational effects of drug use. Ahead of the project's 2018 release, J. Cole tweeted on X, formerly known as Twitter, that the album had three meanings—King Overdosed, Kids on Drugs, and Kill Our Demons. He didn't delve into the connection directly, but records like "Friends," "Brackets," and the title track address the disillusion with drugs as a coping device for emotional pain, stress, and misguided thoughts. And Kendrick's "Swimming Pools (Drank)," disguised as a party record, tackled his long fight with alcoholism. The Compton rapper dove into the dark side of the liquor bottle from one family member to the next. He also discussed how soberness can unlock emotional grief on 2022's "Mother I Sober."

Kendrick and Cole's influence continued to outweigh the ever-evolving changes and trends bubbling up in the genre. They refused to compromise their image, message or likeness to remain relevant in a social media and clout-driven climate. Even when Cole or Lamar embraced modern trends and sounds momentarily, their ability to trickle in conscious messaging was unmatched compared to other mainstream rappers. Still, the rise of violent and drug-fueled messages, paired with the decline in conscious rap, made the essence of hip-hop appear to fade away.

To succeed as a new mainstream act, it seemed like emerging rappers had to be cutthroat gangsters, trap overlords, or make snap songs with an accompanying dance—and even a mixture of all three. Of course, more established artists were exceptions, but even they dipped their toes in other subgenres to garner added favor. But over time, fans wanted the social commentary and complexities of Kendrick Lamar, and the heartfelt and transparent storytelling of J. Cole. They craved a modern version of hip-hop music that reflected their realities and made them think critically about the world around them. The next class of artists would soon fill the void, with Kendrick Lamar and J. Cole at the forefront.

3
The Rise of King Cole

The day was August 4, 2015. Screams from a sold-out crowd at Madison Square Garden shook the iconic arena. The audience stood on their feet as a 29-year-old rapper from Fayetteville, North Carolina, graced the stage. He wore a singular chain across his chest. Dangling from the gleaming necklace was a pendant in the shape of the legendary Roc-A-Fella Records logo. At the time, the chains were only worn by official members of the Roc-A-Fella camp. This included label signees such as Kanye West, Memphis Bleek, Cam'Ron, and Freeway.

During Cole's performance, renowned rapper, music mogul, and entrepreneur Jay-Z emerged from backstage to deliver a surprise performance alongside Cole. After performing his legendary record, "Public Service Announcement," he stopped the music to let the crowd know that the chain Cole was sporting wasn't an ordinary jewelry piece. It was the original Roc-A-Fella chain that Hov once donned himself.[1]

That night marked Cole's "chaining day." Jay-Z and his former business partners Damon "Dame" Dash and Kareem "Biggs" Burke started the ritual for new Roc-A-Fella signees. Bestowing their newly signed talents with a Roc-A-Fella chain symbolized their new membership into the imprint. In hip-hop, it held the same gravitas as an Italian mob boss placing a signet ring onto the finger of an initiated member, or "made man." However, Jay giving Cole his personal chain meant much more than giving him another Roc-A-Fella pendant.

It represented a changing of the guard. Jay-Z, who many consider the greatest rapper of all time, acknowledged Cole as the future of hip-hop. It was a monumental night for Cole and reflective of his personal and musical journey. He was wearing the chain of the very figure who once rejected his CD during his early years as an emcee. That same person would later recognize his greatness on one of the grandest stages in the world. And with Hov's public cosign, it was clear Cole was the next big star in line.

Born into a Cole World

Jermaine Lamarr Cole was born on January 28, 1985, in a military base in Frankfurt, West Germany. His parents, James and Kay Cole, were both enlisted in the US Army at the time of his birth.[2] Shortly after Cole was born, his parents got a divorce.[3] His mother left the military and brought him and his older brother Zach to North Carolina. Cole's discography is unabashedly transparent about his family life and upbringing through his music. It hasn't been Cole's overarching narrative or persona, but he's discussed growing up biracial, with a White mother and a Black father who was absent for most of his life. While he's always maintained a close relationship with his mother, he's expressed how her battle with alcohol abuse impacted his childhood in songs like "Once an Addict."

Cole began rapping around the age of twelve. He was influenced by heralded emcees like Nas, 2Pac, Eminem, Canibus, André 3000, Lil Wayne and Jay-Z early on in his career.[4] This influence can be heard in his storytelling, lyricism, and impassioned delivery. In 2013, J. Cole and Kendrick Lamar had the opportunity to hit the road with Eminem for a string of international concerts on the "Rapture Tour." During an interview with Cole and Kendrick in Australia, Cole said he was attempting to sound like a mixture of Nas and Eminem on his first record.[5]

Cole knew at a very young age that rapping was his passion. Bomm Sheltuh was a hip-hop duo from Fayetteville that gained a following in the underground rap scene. The group consisted of two members named Filthe Ritch and Nervous Reck. The two emcees had elite lyricism and natural musical chemistry, which they displayed on their back-and-forth rhyme schemes. In a 2021 interview with Canadian journalist Nardwuar the Human Serviette, Cole said that Bomm Sheltuh was the first rap group from his hometown that he heard who was releasing the same quality of music that he loved at the time.[6]

At fourteen years old, Cole was confident enough in his rap skills to reach out to the group online. He told the duo he was the best emcee in the city and was ready to prove it. Seeing his persistence, the group invited him to one of their shows at Duh! Skatezone, one of the few venues that held hip-hop shows in the city. They gave him an opportunity to display his talent on stage, in front of their captivated audience. Despite being the only child performer in attendance, Cole impressed both the audience and members of Bomm Sheltuh. The two artists believed in the young emcee, and went on to mentor him and help refine his promising abilities.

Cole began sharpening his skills by collaborating on tracks with Bomm Sheltuh as a part of their camp. Bomm Sheltuh christened him into their team by giving him the name, "Therapist." While he wasn't feeling the moniker initially, he later embraced it out of respect and admiration for the duo. He went on to drop the name "Therapist" in college because it felt more like a character than his true self. In a 2013 interview with Ryan Seacrest, Cole stated:[7]

It started to feel like wrestling, or like a character. I didn't like it, so I need a better name. My homeboy in middle school used to say, "Hey, J. Cole," so I just went with that.

He decided to use J. Cole, a simple abbreviation of his real name, moving forward. But in honor of his mentors, Cole went on to open a recording studio in North Carolina called the "The Sheltuh in Raleigh." This is the same studio where the artists signed to Cole's Dreamville Records recorded some of their signature records.

Along with the mentorship of Filthe Ritch and Nervous Reck, Cole's mother played a pivotal role in supporting his musical aspirations. While he was connected with Bomm Sheltuh, Cole knew he wouldn't get the best beats among the crew. They secured those for their own projects.

Without cash to buy beats elsewhere, Cole decided to learn how to craft his own beats. Cole often went to a store called McFadyen Music in Fayetteville, where he played around with different production equipment. His mother saw his interest in beat-making machines and was determined to get her ambitious son the machine he had his eye on, the ASR-X Pro. She put it on layaway, and after a year of making payments, Cole had his first beat machine.

Cole would go through his mom's CDs to find music to sample. Her collection ranged from artists like Mary J. Blige to acts like Eric Clapton, Steely Dan, and Dire Straits. Once Cole mastered the ASR-X Pro, he elevated his hip-hop profile from rapper to rapper-producer. This gave him free range to create and hone in on his own style and sound.

Once his mother remarried and they moved in with his stepfather Edward on 2014 Forest Hill Drive, he had a bedroom where he could practice his rhymes in the mirror.[8] He had the privacy and space needed to fully explore his gifts. While their family became more financially stable, it came with other burdens. He addressed the ups and downs of his family's financial situation in 2010's "Before I'm Gone."

> *See, me, I lived it all, from dirt-poor in a trailer*
> *Worried about my mother and never trustin' my neighbors*
> *To middle-class with a backyard and my own room*
> *To bein' the only Black kid in my homeroom.*

Within his music, Cole often reflects on his traumatic experiences with his stepfather, and the abandonment he felt from his biological father. On "3 Wishes," Cole details the domestic violence his mother faced by the hands of his stepfather, and the guilt and pain he had after witnessing the abuse at age twelve.

> *And I heard rumbling from struggling and rolling on the ground*
> *Could never get used to that sound, my mama saying "Get off me!"*
> *My tears is tumbling now, I wish that you never saw me, 'cause I*
> *Felt like a coward, so powerless I was only 12.*

In a track called "Can I Holla at Ya," which samples Lauryn Hill's "To Zion," Cole delves deeper into his relationship with his stepfather. He details how close he and his stepfather were, and how they had more of a rapport than Cole and his biological father. He also expresses how he watched his mother crumble once his stepfather left their family behind.

Amid the dysfunction during this time, Cole's outlets were music and sports. Basketball played a large role in Cole's adolescence. Like many inner-city kids, a young Cole thought his pathway to riches would be through music or basketball. Cole played basketball and was a first-chair orchestra violinist at Terry Sanford High School in Fayetteville. While he says he was a good player, he admits he wasn't a star on his high school squad. "I was always in love with basketball as a kid, but I thought I was way better than I really was," Cole said to *Sports Illustrated* in 2013.[9]

He was cut from the team freshman year, but instead of quitting, he became the team's manager in hopes of making the roster the following year.[10] To his dismay, he was cut again in his sophomore year. Yet, his determination never wavered. He continued to work on improving his game, and his hours in the gym eventually paid off. He made the team during his junior and senior year, and was praised by his teammates for his stout defense and shot blocking. Cole tried to walk on at the St. John's University basketball team his freshman year, but didn't show up to the second tryout, coming to grips with the fact that his hoop dreams were now over. He had brief stints in the Canadian Elite Basketball League and the Basketball Africa League, but his main job continued to be music. The trials and tribulations he faced on the court inspired the name of Cole's mixtapes and debut album, *Cole World: The Sideline Story*.

College Boy

J. Cole enrolled at St. John's University in 2003.[11] He entered as a computer science major, but switched after meeting what he described as a "miserable professor."[12] After Cole met the programmer-turned-educator, one thing was sure—he didn't want to do whatever it was he did for a living. Instead, he became a communications major with a business minor.

Going away to college was a major feat for him. Cole was attempting to become the first person in his family to graduate from college. He was also moving from his small hometown to one of the biggest cities in the world. He didn't know anyone in New York City, which made the transition challenging. What he did know was that NYC was booming with legacy record labels and music industry connections. For the first time in his life, the opportunities seemed endless.

Cole found himself immersed in the campus culture at SJU. He was heavily involved in organizations such as Haraya Club, which was the university's pan-African student coalition. He later became the organization's president and was even invited back to perform at the campus by the student group. While in college, Cole continued to write and record music. He carved out time to reach out to record label executives, with hopes his music would lead to a deal. While most of his attempts were unsuccessful, Cole didn't allow it to deter him. He knew he had skills. All he needed was the rest of the world to see it.

Carolina's Finest

When people think of J. Cole, most don't associate him with Southern hip-hop. He's never flashed a Southern drawl, leaned into the rugged aesthetic, or crafted music popularized by other Southern acts. Cole has broken the traditional mold, but he's very much a Southern artist.

Although hip-hop is a product of Black American culture, it's a genre that's been consistently dominated by artists from specific major cities. Musical hubs such as New York, LA, Atlanta, Houston, Memphis, and Chicago have undoubtedly been at the forefront of the genre. Other cities like St. Louis and Detroit have also made their mark with Nelly, Eminem, Big Sean, and other artists rising to stardom. Other Southern cities have influenced the sound of the genre, but there's still a bevy of cities, regions, and states that haven't been properly represented in hip-hop. This sentiment rings true for the Carolinas.

Greenville, North Carolina native Petey Pablo had a brief moment of fame with the club hit "Freek-A-Leek" and the hard-hitting North Carolina anthem "Raise Up," but the two records didn't immediately lead to other Carolina acts breaking into the industry. The region was still lacking a mainstream emcee who was respected and heralded as a lyrical powerhouse. That was until Cole emerged from Fayetteville.

To truly understand an artist's story, it's essential to look at where they came from. Fayetteville is known as the home of Fort Bragg, the largest military installation by population in the world. With its large military presence, the city is racially diverse. However, it also has a long history of racism. While the city's Market House in downtown Fayetteville is considered a historical landmark for tourists, it was once a site for enslaved people to be auctioned and sold as property. Even in post-slavery, the Black plight in Fayetteville has consisted of a segregated business district and schools,[13] racial land restrictions, violence, and police brutality.[14]

Being raised in a city with this history and a noticeable lack of hip-hop representation, Cole was motivated to take on the industry as an underdog. That mentally led to a series of No. 1 albums, top 10 Billboard hits, Grammy awards, and a bankable musical label. Now, when people think of Fayetteville, he's likely the first name that comes to mind. Fayetteville Mayor Mitch Colvin said Cole is undeniably the biggest rapper to emerge from the Carolinas:

> He's become a global staple that represents Fayetteville in a positive way. Here, of course, we look at him like that locally, but the world has an even larger appreciation for him. And when he comes home … you see the effects of his work, rather than him taking the shine for it.

Mixtape Ascension

In the 2000s, an era often referred to as the "blog era," digital media exploded and uprooted the music business as we knew it. Signed and unsigned artists began using the internet to cultivate and grow organic fanbases through internet-based platforms without the backing of recording companies and traditional marketing tactics. The term "blog era" stems from the online news sites and forums that were helping spark the careers of musical talents during this period.

Some of the most recognizable blogs were Fake Shore Drive, 2DopeBoyz, HotNewHipHop, and Pigeons & Planes. They drew young rap fans to obscure or lesser-known artists because of journalists promoting and discussing their new projects. Artists with standout mixtapes were gaining momentum, and J. Cole was among the new crop of rappers benefiting from the trend. Former HipHopDX editor and hip-hop journalist Justin Hunte said the "blog era" emerged during a reshuffling of the music industry, which allowed new or established underground artists to develop a fanbase on their own terms. And Hunte said Cole benefited greatly from the era, stating:

> Overall, you saw record labels acquiring other record labels, and now we're down to basically three—Sony, Warner, and Universal. You saw the same thing on the radio side. Most companies are Cumulus or iHeart, or whatever. What that did was for people in my generation, kids I went to college with who moved to different places, we all heard the same songs on the radio. We saw all the same videos, regardless of region. You lost a lot of regionality. A lot of the variations that we love in hip hop were gone on the mainstream level. The blogs were where you found that diversity. That's where most people found MF Doom. If you don't have the blog era, you don't really get to see MF Doom because he was nowhere near mainstream. You didn't get artists like Rhymefest, Lupe, J. Cole, Kendrick or TDE at the onset. The blog era showed you what was going on.

By 2007, Cole was fully invested into making it to the top as a producer and rapper. While still enrolled in college, Cole got the opportunity to meet his idol Jay-Z.[15] He caught wind that Jay was working on his upcoming album *American Gangsta* in a nearby New York City studio. He immediately produced beats with pre-recorded hooks that he thought could fit on the album, and loaded them onto a CD.

Cole and his friend waited outside the studio for three hours until Jay-Z appeared. Jay-Z finally arrived in a Rolls Royce Phantom, and Cole nervously told him that he had a beat CD for *American Gangster*. The rapper responded, "Man I don't want that shit, give that to one of those guys." The moment discouraged the 22-year-old rapper, who described the disappointment in the 2013 track, "Villimunati."

> *With a burned CD full of jams that was up in my hand.*
> *When he said he didn't want it it was fuck him again.*
> *One day, he gon' regret playing me.*
> *Little did I know in a year he'd be fucking paying me, what could you*
>   *say to me?*

Cole was discouraged, but he didn't let the disappointment stop his musical pursuits. On May 4, 2007, Cole released a standout project that separated him from his peers. Just before graduating college Magna Cum Laude, Cole uploaded his debut mixtape *The Come Up* to the digital music platform DatPiff.[16] Hosted by DJOnPoint, the mixtape consisted of original songs and freestyles over classic hip-hop tracks like Jay-Z's "Dead Presidents," Kanye West's "My Way Home," Nas's "You're da Man," and Beanie Sigel's "Mom Praying."

Cole spoke from an inherently unique perspective that captivated a new audience. It veered away from the braggadocio that many of his peers rapped about. His early music was filled with introspective, vulnerable, and transparent messaging. He rapped from the perspective of a young man, who rose above poverty, went to college, and was now struggling to chase his dreams. Grammy-nominated engineer Ben Thomas said Cole's ability to connect with everyday people through his music is what sparked his momentum and eventual stardom, stating:

> I think J. Cole follows that lineage of speaking to the average Black person. J. Cole was talking about things like single mom stuff. He's not talking about [things] like, "Damn, I had to steal to eat." He also wasn't talking about, "Hey, I'm in a gang or I was shot." He's speaking to the middle to lower middle class Black community, which, sadly, is the majority of Black people in this country. I think that's why he appeals to Black people. He speaks to a very easily digestible and understood version of Blackness.

While some of Cole's material appeared juvenile in nature, the mixtape showed his versatility at his young age. Songs like "College Boy" reflected his life of partying, sex, and struggles to keep up with his college classes, but that was only the tip of the iceberg. In a heartfelt record called "Can't Cry," Cole addresses the obstacles he felt were impacting the Black community. He tackled the impact of systemic racism, gang violence, pedophilia, unemployment, and other social issues. He delivered these lyrics in a manner that was empathetic to the conditions many people face in the inner-city and reinforced his disdain toward the current state of America at large.

This compassion and vulnerability toward social issues is what helped him galvanize a loyal fanbase early in his career. The mixture of conscious messaging and witty punchlines on *The Come Up* helped gain this mixtape recognition. Cole was now getting recognized for the skills he spent years refining, and the tape was downloaded and streamed over half a million times upon release.[17] Justin Hunte credits this to his story's relatability:

> *The Come Up* hit hard because J. Cole really represented a lot of things that were missing in the mainstream. J. Cole had a very familiar and tangible story. Here's a guy that grew up in Fayetteville, his dad was in the military, and he went to college—St. John's. He loved basketball, he loved rapping, and he loved hip-hop. That's a very common story.

"Sometimes I Brag Like Hov"

Riding the high of his debut mixtape's success, Cole immediately started producing, writing, and recording a plethora of new tracks that he hoped would land him a record deal. One of the tracks was 2009's "Lights Please." The record was centered around his conversations with a woman he was seeing intimately. While she was more invested in their sexual connection, Cole was more interested in discussing the systemic issues facing the Black community.

Label executive and artist manager Mark Pitts heard the song and set up a meeting with Cole.[18] Pitts then played the record for Jay-Z, and Cole's wishes were eventually granted. Jay was so impressed that he signed Cole, who became the first official artist under his revitalized record label Roc Nation. The dreams of the budding star were now becoming a reality. He wasn't signed because of a fleeting club record with a viral dance. He was recognized for his thought-provoking storytelling and introspective messaging—elements he would integrate even further on his later releases.

With the cosign from a hip-hop giant, Cole's second mixtape *The Warm Up* drastically changed the trajectory of his career. The 2009 project showcased a much more polished storyteller and lyricist. The tracklist contained original songs and another mix of his rendition of classics by Jay-Z, Nas, and Kanye West. While tracks like "Grown Simba" and "Dead Presidents II" showed off his lyrical prowess, songs like "Can I Live" and "Hold It Down" gave his fans the ultra-realistic depictions and pain-filled stories his core audience would grow to love.

A track called "Losing My Balance" would become a fan favorite. Each verse of the song carries a different tale. The first is a story about a woman trying to find acceptance through men who mistreat and use her for sex. The second verse details the struggles of everyday life in Cole's hometown. He highlights the trauma that stems from inner-city violence, and encourages young people to pursue something outside the dangers of street life. In the third verse, Cole explains how his infatuation with a woman forced him to spend less quality time with his family. This song—and the larger project— displayed Cole's depth, complexities, and ability to connect with the human experience on different levels. Critics and fans marveled at the 22-track offering, which cemented the young Roc Nation signee as one of rap's next big stars.

With the success of *The Warm Up*, Cole received several awards and acknowledgments. He won Underground Music Awards (UMA) Male Artist of the Year,[19] was included on MTV's Hottest Breakthrough MCs of 2010 list,[20] and was nominated for Rookie of the Year at the 2010 BET Awards.[21] He was also one of ten artists selected for XXL's Freshman Class in 2010.[22] The annual list has highlighted rising rap artists since its inception in 2007. The 2010 class is considered one of the publication's best lists, with Cole joining household names like Big Sean, Nipsey Hussle, and Wiz Khalifa on the cover. Artists like Freddie Gibbs and Jay Rock also went on to have strong careers.

Cole was waiting for Roc Nation to give the green light for his debut album, but he didn't want to lose the momentum or the new fanbase he had built. During a 2014 performance at Irving Plaza in NYC, he took a moment to discuss the pressure of getting a release date from his label. "Every interview, and when I see fans, they're saying, 'Yo, where is the fucking album at?'" Cole didn't want his fans to think he wasn't taking his career seriously.

One day in the studio, he wrote and recorded a freestyle over Kanye West's "Devil in a New Dress," which he called "Villematic." In the verse, he expressed how he knew everyone was eagerly waiting for the album. It was on that day that Cole decided to release a full project that he labeled a "mixtape." He knew the songs he had stashed were album quality, but he wanted to give them to his fans for free as a thank you for their patience and support. This decision led to the creation of *Friday Night Lights.*

Released on November 12, 2010, *Friday Night Lights* featured twenty songs with guest appearances from Wale, Kanye West, CyHi The Prynce, and Drake. Almost entirely self-produced, the tape is widely revered as one of Cole's greatest bodies of work. It weaves layered autobiographical stories, taking listeners into his life after signing a deal and gaining fame. Tracks like "Too Deep for the Intro" and "Before I'm Gone" showcased emotional depth, lyrical growth, and a perfected flow.

Critics and fans alike gave the project rave reviews. It marked a coming-of-age moment for Cole, demonstrating a matured sound and elevated emcee. As a bonus, he included "Looking for Trouble," a posse cut from Kanye West's *Good Friday* series. Along with Kanye, the track featured respected lyricists like Pusha T, CyHi The Prynce, and Big Sean. Cole's ability to stand out among these seasoned emcees further solidified his status as a star. Cole's momentum was fueled by a pair of critically acclaimed mixtapes, and the anticipation for an official album at its peak. The pressure was on, and he would soon be faced with a major choice. Go commercial or stay true to what got him here.

Go Commercial or Stay True

To be deemed a commercial success in the eyes of a record label, artists typically need at least one hit single on their album. The project needs a song that can garner the attention of the masses, and draw anticipation for an upcoming release. In hip-hop, this has historically been a record that largely appeals to female consumers, or is an undeniable club joint that resonates with a broader audience.

While unconventional records like Kanye West's "Jesus Walks" and Eminem's "Lose Yourself" amassed great success, they were the exception and not the rule. The tried-and-true formula for modern hip-hop acts has been to get the party going, or collaborate with an R&B artist to appeal to women listeners. Even if the song contains misogynist messaging, it still needs to sonically appeal to a female audience.

The formula forces many hip-hop artists to be faced with a very difficult choice: Should I stay true to the messaging and style that built my core fanbase, or make the kind of music that will take my career to the next level? The pressure to remain relevant often consumes artists who have a desire to reach the masses. While they are passionate about making music that contains powerful messaging and intricate storytelling, they are simultaneously introduced to the tempting success that comes with dumbing down their lyrics and sound. In many cases, it's the difference between an artist propelling to superstardom, or "falling off" like many of the conscious rappers of the past.

Cole's profile was elevated by his mixtapes, his affiliation with Jay-Z, and his presence on popular blog sites. By the summer of 2010, it was finally time for him to tease a debut album under the Roc Nation imprint. In May 2010, he kicked off the rollout with the release of a song called "Who Dat." The song was well received by hip-hop fans but it barely reached Billboard's Hot 100, peaking at No. 93. Neither the Billboard placement nor buzz the song generated warranted the release of his anticipated project.

After "Who Dat" failed to become a chart-topper, Cole dropped a self-produced track called "Work Out." The song contained a more melodic hook and simplistic lyrics that people could sing along to. While it lacked depth, it was a fun song that became a favorite for casual music fans. It was a huge commercial success, peaking at No. 13 on the Billboard charts and widening Cole's reach beyond hip-hop circles.[23]

It would go on to reach multi-platinum status and become the lead single for Cole's 2011 debut, *Cole World: The Sideline Story*. While the masses enjoyed the record, it left a bad taste in the mouths of hip-hop fans who championed Cole as a conscious emcee. The record didn't feel like the same Cole whose heartfelt and complex stories engulfed them in his music. Among them was another one of Cole's musical heroes—Nas.

Let Nas Down

After the release of "Work Out," Cole received a surprise phone call from legendary hip-hop producer No I.D. The renowned hitmaker told Cole that when he was in the studio with Nas, the "N.Y. State of Mind" rapper said he hated Cole's new hit single "Work Out."[24] The news devastated Cole. Nas was one of the emcees who inspired him to pick up the pen and pad. Nas's opinion meant more than that of just a casual fan who didn't vibe with a record. It was equivalent to a young filmmaker finding out Spike Lee disliked their project. Even worse, Cole felt he was being judged for a track that wasn't his best work.

His idol's disapproval motivated him to respond on wax. While working on his next album, *Born Sinner*, Cole released a self-produced song called "Let Nas Down." On the record, Cole conveys how he idolized Nas so much growing up that he posted his verses on his wall for inspiration. He also pointed to the hypocrisy of Nas's critique, as Cole felt Nas also made commercial songs that lacked depth, like "You Owe Me." By the end of the track, Cole conceded that he sacrificed his artistry to chase what the industry preferred, hence letting the legendary Queens rapper down.

Two days after recording "Let Nas Down," a moment of divine fate occurred. While boarding a plane in Houston, Cole let his manager Ibraham "Ib" Hamad listen to the track. As Ib played the record, a familiar face was boarding the same plane. It was Nas himself. While he was caught off-guard by the chance encounter, Cole knew it was a fateful moment he had to seize. He walked over to Nas, and asked him to listen to the record. "Bro, I know this is gonna sound fucking insane. I just made this song fucking two days ago. I can't even explain to you how crazy it is that I'm seeing you right now, randomly on this flight. But I have to play you this song." Cole explained in his 2024 audio series *Inevitable*.

Nas agreed and listened to the record on the flight. After listening, he didn't give Cole a response in real-time, which left him wondering what his thoughts were of the lyrics. Nas would later respond to this track with a record of his own. He penned a mature and sincere track called "Made Nas Proud." He spit a compelling verse over Cole's song, giving his perspective on the situation and the pressures he himself faced with adapting to industry standards. Like Jay-Z, Nas acknowledged Cole in a way that further cemented his impact within the industry, and Cole fully understood his intentions.

Cole was now secure in his positioning within the rap game. It was solidified, and he knew it. He flexed this confidence by releasing *Born Sinner* the same day as Kanye West's *Yeezus* and Mac Miller's *Watching Movies with the Sound Off*. On the 2013 album, Cole decided to take a different approach with promotions and singles than his debut. While the lead single "Power

Trip" was a unique R&B-leaning love record with Miguel, Cole was sure to feed his core audience with other introspective records.

A song called "Miss America" led the rollout for the new album. The record unapologetically swayed as far away from a traditional single as possible. It contained a dark, grimy, and almost eerie beat produced by Cole himself. The song contained rhymes that challenged the American system of capitalism, racism, and societal norms.

> *Fuck the man, Uncle Sam I won't sell your crack*
> *I won't fight your wars, I won't wear your hat*
> *I'ma pass your classes, I'mma learn your craft*
> *I'ma fuck your daughters, I'mma burn your flag,*

While Cole appeared to go out his way to make a non-traditional single, "Miss America" still garnered attention. It became the theme song for the video game *Splinter Cell: Blacklist*'s trailer, a video game franchise that Cole used to play in college.[25] In a 2012 interview with *Billboard*, Cole said he purposefully shifted the idea of what elements encompass a lead single.[26]

> "Miss America" shifts things a little bit, it changes the conversation it takes it in a more aggressive direction, more raw, more social commentary. Any type of commentary is good compared to what a normal single is these days. That's my aim is to shift culture slightly, change the conversation ... nobody expects that for your first single.

On this album, Cole also rolled out "Crooked Smile," a single that would become a staple in his catalog. This song is a transparent record that sees Cole reveal the insecurities he faced growing up with an imperfect smile. He spun this testimonial into an inspirational song that encouraged people to love themselves unconditionally. The record also tackled how social media sets unrealistic beauty standards, which negatively affect people's psychology. He dove even deeper on the song's final verse, addressing racial oppression, poor policing, and systemic racism.

Born Sinner was a pivotal point in Cole's career. He fully embraced his position as a musical and cultural figure, one unafraid to break away from popular norms. Instead of rapping about money, cars, and beautiful women on his singles, Cole was driven to address social issues. He didn't shy away from them for mainstream acceptance or approval. He addressed them head on with hopes of inspiring, educating, and generating dialogue amongst his listeners and Black America. He was taking control of his career and decided that being a "conscious rapper" would inevitably be a part of that identity, and a driving force for his success.

Choosing Consciousness ... Consciously

Being a "conscious rapper" is an identity that many mainstream artists have either intentionally or subconsciously strayed away from. This is primarily due to two reasons: it limits them financially and/or artistically. From a financial standpoint, many believe that pro-Black music that tackles social issues can stifle an artist's reach and marketability. There is an ongoing debate that this content could lead to a cognitive dissonance that dissuades the largest music audience in America—White fans—from wanting to engage with protest records.[27] The thought leads some artists to alter their music to fit the palate of their intended fanbase.

The same limitations are placed on musicians who claim to be conscious artists. There are a social responsibility and expectation for your messaging to be progressive. But once they veer away from their traditional sound, or fall short of the expectations of consciousness, they are often left without the same commercial success or fanbase they once had. In a 2024 interview on the podcast *Earn Your Leisure*, Common discussed his issue with being labeled a conscious rapper early in his career.[28] Not only did it limit the music he made, Common said it partly stifled potential collaborations with other big-name emcees, stating:

> I went through a journey with being called a conscious artist. When they first said it I was like, "Man, why they calling me that?" It did put me in a box. I like women and I like drinking. Automatically, if you're put into a conscious box, they expect you to only be talking about Assata Shakur, or the [Black] Panthers, and Malcolm X, and you have to always be serious.

Author, journalist, and NYU professor Kathy Iandoli said these restrictions are even tighter for women rappers. Throughout the 1990s, conscious female emcees were expected to mute their appearance, avoid records that promoted parties and sex, and strictly focus on social issues. Anything else was a point of criticism. Despite the conscious music she contributed as a solo artist and member of the Fugees, Iandoli said Lauryn Hill was "dragged" for posing for the November 1998 cover of *Details* magazine in red shorts and a black tank top, stating:

> She was so happy about her curves, and everyone was like, "This is [her] selling out. What about 'Doo Wop (That Thing)?'" And it was like, "Wow, you can't celebrate your beauty? In order to be conscious as a woman, you can't have sex? You can talk about injustice toward women, but not to the point where you challenge men?" The restrictions for a conscious female rapper versus a conscious male rapper is definitely different.

Even with the limitations placed on the back of conscious artists, Cole embraced the duality of being vocal about social issues, while still revealing his flaws as a human. Even when featured on songs with other prominent artists in the industry, Cole used the moment to raise awareness on societal issues, even if the subject matter wasn't congruent with that of the song.

Miguel's song "Come Through and Chill" is a mellow record set around romance and sex. During the final minute of the song, Cole inserts a left-field verse about systemic racism, similar to his shift on "Lights Please." Amid the conversation with a woman, he addressed what was really on his mind. He used this instance to call out the US President Donald Trump for insensitive remarks, and discussed the prevalence of police brutality in America.

While Cole has tackled issues like this directly through song, his storytelling has been the superpower that has separated him from other conscious artists. Many rap fans and artists simply define conscious records as protest music, but Justin Hunte said Cole is among the few who have redefined what consciousness looks like in modern times, stating:

> I think that introspection is something that fills a conscious void in this space. Being honest about your insecurities, being honest about your challenges, [and] things that are holding you back. There's not as much macro conversation on big topics that I'm seeing at scale that are hitting the

masses. You might find a song on an album that talks about the conditions people might have come up in, but you don't necessarily see as much conversation about how we make our community better. I look at conscious rap as more introspection. It still happens, don't get me wrong, but outside of major artists, you don't necessarily see those songs on the charts in the same kind of way.

"They'll Never Feel My Pain"

Modern music is often critiqued for the lack of substance and creativity within songs and albums that are thrust into the mainstream. Many attribute this occurrence to the pressure placed on artists by record labels and streaming companies, who have their own formulaic methods to make records that will generate the most income. A capitalistic approach to music has been increasingly prevalent in the digital age, which has stifled artists' creativity and weakened the messages conveyed in their music.

In an era where "fast food" music is abundant, Cole and Kendrick Lamar have established a blueprint and foundation for modern artists to achieve mainstream success while making culturally impactful and progressive music. Given the shift in the music industry, hip-hop professor and attorney Timothy Welbeck said Cole and Kendrick's presence has become even more valuable. He believes they were able to set a new standard:

> There's an entire generation of people coming up after [Cole and Kendrick], who view them as someone who says that I can talk about more than gross material, misogyny, and how good of an artist I am. That's part of the legacy that they've left.

Honesty is an integral part of Cole's messaging and impact. He has chosen to place his real life on display for the world to see. From his pain-filled adolescence to his success in college, he's bared it all within his music. Many modern hip-hop artists today choose to embellish, or flat out lie, about their upbringing to convey a tougher street image. Cole refused to follow suit, even while believing that it would've made it easier for him to excel if he did it.

In a 2013 interview with *The Wall Street Journal*, Cole was asked if his journey of making it as a rapper would've been easier if a criminal background was a part of his narrative. In his response, he said, "*Scarface* is a lot of kids' favorite movie for a reason. There's an appeal about the edginess of, 'Yo, I was in the streets and I sold drugs.' When you have that story, and it's real and authentic, and you can mix that with a real skillful way to tell it, of course. It would have been way easier for me."

Instead of leaning into fictitious stories of a criminal past, Cole focused on his lived reality as much as possible. He also deliberately decided that songs like "Work Out" would not become his identity as an artist. Although the song was a hit, it was apparent that he had much more to offer his audience than a club record. Instead, Cole continued to pour out his innermost thoughts, beliefs, and convictions in his future projects without hesitation. He was done chasing hit records. He was making music that would inspire, uplift, and emotionally connect with his listeners. He wanted to be revered as one of the greatest rappers to ever live.

While on the rise to the top, Cole was not alone as a musical giant. Other notable emcees shined throughout the 2010s and 2020s, but Cole was consistently mentioned alongside another mainstream emcee who kept conscious messaging at the forefront of his music. This artist is Kendrick Lamar.

4

From K.Dot to West Coast Savant

Riding the momentum of his debut album *Section.80*, a 24-year-old Kendrick Lamar took the stage at The Fonda Theatre on August 19, 2011. West Coast legends Snoop Dogg, Kurupt, and the Game joined the budding star in front of the roaring crowd, with "Westside" chants echoing throughout the 1,200-seat venue. The moment was more than a random assemblage of coast-bound ambassadors on LA soil. It was the crowning of a new West Coast king, and Snoop was the man to hand over the reins:

> We've been watching you rock like a motherfucker, right? And we're watching Game pass the torch to you, and we're watching all this love. It's a beautiful thing, my nigga, you're great at what you do, you're not good. You're great at what you do … Imma say this, and Imma mean this … Nigga, you got the torch, and you better run with it. This is yours.[1]

As his musical heroes wrapped their arms around him, Kendrick tucked his head to conceal the unexpected burst of emotion. The journey to his coronation was riddled with past failures, spells of self-doubt, and close brushes with death. Those memories poured out of a teary-eyed Kendrick, who dreamed his music would touch the very artists and people who inspired him. And that night it was apparent it did. "My tears is all on the internet," Kendrick recounted in a 2024 interview with R&B singer SZA.[2] "And now I look back and I love that moment. I love that that happened. Because it showed me in real time expressing myself and seeing all the work that I put forth actually come to life in that moment."

The night at The Fonda marked the first time Kendrick shed a tear on stage. Snoop's words stamped his presence in the West and signaled his path to become one of rap's most heralded voices. And since his fateful crowning, Kendrick has proved Snoop's beliefs were rightly held.

Soul Flows Inside His DNA

Long before the multi-platinum albums and record-setting world tours, Kendrick Lamar Duckworth was born on June 17, 1987, at Dominguez Hospital in Compton, California. His parents, Kenneth "Kenny" Duckworth and Paula Oliver, met as teenagers in the South Side of Chicago. The couple moved to Compton in 1984 to break away from the war-torn streets in the Midwest city. Kenny was affiliated with the Gangster Disciples, a notorious street organization founded by former Chicago rivals David Barksdale and Larry Hoover in 1968. Fearing Kenny would seep too deeply in the lifestyle, Paula made an ultimatum: "I can't fuck with you if you ain't trying to better yourself," Kendrick recounted in a 2015 interview with *Rolling Stone*.[3] "We can't be in the streets forever." Months later, Kenny's hustling days in Chicago's Bronzeville neighborhood were over. The couple stuffed their belongings in two black garbage bags and boarded a train to California with $500 to their names.

Three years later, their first of four children was born in their new city. From infancy, Kendrick was surrounded by soul and hip-hop music. His parents named him after the Temptations lead singer Eddie Kendricks, and as a newborn, Kendrick was transported from the hospital nursery as his father blasted Big Daddy Kane's "'Cause I Can Do It Right" on their way home.[4] His first time hearing gangsta rap was at one of his parents' house parties. He snuck in the living room, and danced to Snoop Dogg's "Who Am I (What's My Name)?" until he was tucked back into bed.

Kendrick's family nicknamed him "ManMan" for his precocious and stoic nature. His temperament served him well through most of his childhood, with drugs and senseless violence within an arm's reach. While his family moved from Chicago for a better life, "Compton was just as rough," Kendrick said in a 2012 interview with *Spin*, "but they didn't know that."[5] At eight years old, Kendrick saw a man get shot and killed at Tam's Burgers, a local joint just six blocks from his childhood home at 1612 137th Street. That was the second murder he witnessed. The first was at age five, when a teenage drug dealer was gunned down outside his apartment unit. With Kendrick's uncles firmly planted in the streets, there wasn't much separation. If he veered too far left, he could have easily been on either side of a gun barrel.

For decades, Compton was ruled by street hustlers and gang bangers. Kendrick's parents tried to shield him from the city's dangers, but exposure was inevitable. They were at too close range. "You just get numb to it," Kendrick said. He needed an outlet to untangle his reality, or else it would consume him. Naturally, he gravitated to hip-hop and began writing his own rhymes in seventh grade. He was introduced to creative writing and poetry by his English teacher Regis Inge at Vanguard Learning Center. When tensions flared or students were faced with at-home challenges, Inge encouraged them to "cuss the paper out," stating:

> I told them they could take their pen and paper and be angry at the police. They could be angry at their daddies for telling them he ain't going to go back to jail anymore, and then his ass went back to jail the next week. They could write it out and get it out, and not hurt anybody.

Inge taught students the basic elements of poetry, from alliteration to assonance and onomatopoeia, and they performed their work in front of the class. Kendrick was a shy, bright-eyed student, who imbued pages with reflections that were advanced for someone his age. But occasionally, Inge circled words or phrases he felt weren't up to par. He pointed Kendrick and his classmates to a thesaurus on the class bookshelf, motivating them to expand their vocabularies. And if that didn't work, Inge told them to use their favorite rapper's lyrics for inspiration. "I told them if they listened to N.W.A., all they're doing is poetry over music," Inge said. "I had to give them the vision of what poetry is, and then I made it competitive."

Inge turned his classroom into a slam poetry stage, and Kendrick shined as a natural performer. With each stanza, an avalanche of excitement came over him, and suddenly his minor stutter momentarily disappeared. The poems helped Kendrick unravel the complexities of his upbringing, and each composition allowed his other thoughts to freely roam. With Inge as his hype man and his friends as his audience, the foundations of Kendrick's emcee skills were formed. "Kendrick was a solid student, but when he started poetry, I could see the talent," Inge said. "And as he tells it, he really started getting into it when he went to high school and met other artists. That's how his career later transpired."

By the time Kendrick arrived at Centennial High School, his future as a rap star was already in his sights. He turned his early poetry and cafeteria freestyles into rap songs, with hopes he could follow the same path as Eazy-E, Dr. Dre, DJ Quik, the Game, and other Compton legends. But at age sixteen, the straight-A student was beginning to fall for the same traps that landed his family members behind bars. "My uncles and all my cousins was doing it on a daily basis—shootouts, running in my momma house, trying to hide somewhere, selling dope," Kendrick said in a 2012 interview with The Fader.[6] "So for a while, I thought that was how it was supposed to be, until I ventured out into other spaces and people didn't know about what was going on where I was from."

It was a path his tough, militant father urged Kendrick to avoid. While the rapper admitted Kenny's approach was brash on 2022's "Father Time," he steered him away from the dangers that surrounded him. That guidance, as raw as it seemed, was ultimately his saving grace. "The cats that's in jail they never had father figures. I had one," Kendrick said. "He wasn't perfect but he was there to pull me out and let me know when I'm about to bump my head." Kendrick briefly considered studying psychology and astronomy in college, but the confidence he and his parents had in his abilities fueled his musical ambitions. His mother let him borrow the family van for studio sessions, even when the gas tank was near empty. His father was more skeptical at first, but eventually he came around to support Kendrick's dreams as an emcee.

The Hub City Threat

Decked in an oversized black T-shirt and Washington Nationals fitted cap, a teenage Kendrick covered his first mixtape, *Youngest Head Nigga in Charge (Hub City Threat: Minor of the Year).*[7] Little is known about the make-shift project or the label that distributed it. The demo was pieced together by Kendrick and his long-time collaborator David "Dave Free" Friely, who released it sometime between 2003 and 2005 under "Konkrete Jungle Muzik."[8] The mixtape features a compilation of freestyles over Jay-Z's "Hovi Baby," Snoop's "Drop It Like It's Hot," Lil Wayne's "Go DJ," and other classic beats.

The young rapper, who went by "K-Dot," flashed his raw lyricism and storytelling ability over Jay-Z's "Hova Song (Intro)." "No man can withstand the nights I slept, under my sheets with no life thinking 'bout death," Kendrick rapped over the intro. But he hadn't yet separated himself from his early influences. It was clear he studied Jay-Z and Lil Wayne's flow and cadence, and his attempts to mirror the two heavyweights on their songs came off a bit clumsy. His lyrics were solid, but they weren't nearly as focused as his subsequent releases. He was in early development with little guidance. All he needed was a big brother figure in the music industry to point him in the right direction, and he found that when he found Top Dawg.

It was Kendrick's early mixtape that grabbed the attention of Anthony "Top Dawg" Tiffith, who founded the label Top Dawg Entertainment in 2004. By then, it was a local independent label operating out of Tiffin's home studio in Carson, California, fighting to get off the ground. He built the dimly lit studio in 1997, and equipped it with enough room for a battered couch, Pro Tools rig, and vocal booth.

After establishing the TDE brand, Tiffin started opening the studio, which he called the "House of Pain," to aspiring LA artists. At first, Tiffith wanted to manage R&B groups, but a friend convinced him to stick with the genre he knew best (though he would later add SZA and other R&B artists to the TDE roster). He left his street hustling days behind to enter the music business. He was inspired by his uncle Mike Concepcion, a founding member of the Crips gang who went on to produce for artists like MC Hammer, Blackstreet, and other big-name acts. "I was out here dodging bullets and the police, and he had Bentleys and a big house. I thought, 'Shit, I can't go to jail doing music—let me try that,'" Tiffith told *Billboard* in 2014.[9]

In his search, Top turned to familiar roads. The Watts neighborhood product was molded by the streets of Nickerson Gardens, known as the birthplace of the Bounty Hunter Bloods gang. He managed to escape the violence-ridden area to become one of hip-hop's most recognizable music executives. But before he cultivated a stable of platinum-selling stars, Top needed a flagship artist to spark the momentum.

The Top Dogs at TDE

In 2005, Jay Rock became the first signee under TDE. Before meeting Top, the "Blood Niggaz" emcee was actively avoiding the man, fearing that he would discipline him for something he did in the street. What Top really wanted to talk about was music. After hearing Rock on one of his friends' mixtapes, he was intrigued by the young rapper. He eventually hunted him down while Rock was getting a haircut on a friend's porch, and invited him to record at his Carson studio. He went on to sign him to TDE, and two weeks later, Top introduced Rock to K.Dot. But Kendrick met Top through far different circumstances.

Before Dave Free became the co-president of TDE in 2007, he worked as a computer technician. By fate, he received a call from Top, who was in need of a computer fix. He drove to his Carson home and knew there was no salvaging Top's computer. But there was an opportunity to play Kendrick's music to important ears. Free decided to play songs from Kendrick's *Y.H.N.I.C. (Hub City Threat: Minor of the Year)* to draw his attention. The stunt left Top's computer in disarray, but it proved to be a savvy move. Top was blown away by Kendrick's promising skillset and invited the young rapper to an in-person audition.

When they met, Kendrick freestyled for Top and fellow TDE founder Terrence "Punch" Henderson for two hours. His multi-layered flows and fiery delivery impressed the pair, who knew they could mold Kendrick into one of rap's most prolific spitters. After landing Jay Rock, Top signed Kendrick to a deal.[10] The agreement sparked Kendrick's musical career, and eventually changed the fate of the hyper-local imprint. Like NBA Hall of Famer Kobe Bryant, Kendrick was a young phenom looking to make an impact in the big leagues. All he and Jay Rock needed were mentors with keen musical ears and savvy business practices, and Top and Punch fit the bill. They were built to lead a musical powerhouse, with Kendrick and Jay Rock serving as TDE ambassadors.

The six years between Kendrick's TDE signing and his debut album in 2011 was his true education. As K.Dot, he released four mixtapes in that span. Each project was necessary coursework, preparing him to graduate from amateur rapper to full-fledged musician. Through countless nights locked in Top's studio, Kendrick and Jay Rock forged a brotherhood. They worked on solo and joint records together until the early hours, then woke up the next day on Top's couch to do it again with fresh ears.

Kendrick's first mixtape under TDE was 2005's *Training Day*. Based on the 2001 film of the same name, which starred Oscar-winning actor Denzel Washington in the role of corrupt LA cop Alonzo Harris, the project addresses the same subjects seen in the motion picture. Kendrick rapped about the implications of street violence and poverty in his hometown, while giving listeners a snapshot into the mind of an eighteen-year-old artist. "Everybody want to know why my gameplan so strong. That's because I don't have to think with a lightbulb on. Nigga, I eat, sleep, and shit rap. I never relax," Kendrick raps on "Blame God."

On "Good Morning America," Kendrick declared himself a West Coast star on the rise, who embodied the spirit of 2Pac, Snoop, and Dr. Dre, with a mix of Lil Wayne, Eminem, and André. His ambitions, as high or unrealistic as they seemed, were backed by hard work. Kendrick and Jay Rock joined forces on 2007's *No Sleep 'Til NYC*, which heavily featured a freshly. signed Ab-Soul. And with "Fear" and "K.Dot" Photoshopped over his eyelids, Kendrick's 2009 mixtape, *C4*, was an unapologetic tribute to Lil Wayne's *Tha Carter III* at the peak of his powers.

Despite the jabs from music critics, Kendrick and TDE were fully behind the Weezy-approved project. Like Wayne at Cash Money Records, Kendrick was a young protégé, who signed to a small independent label that evolved into a talent hub. The signing of Schoolboy Q in 2009 rounded out TDE's supergroup Black Hippy. Kendrick, Rock, Ab-Soul, and Q built a bond over years of rotating spots on Top Dawg's couch, splitting Jack in the Box orders, and pulling stomach-turning pranks on each other (mostly at Ab-Soul's expense). While no album spawned from the collective, the four emcees placed their differing hoods and gang affiliations aside and became a musical force.

The four emcees had their distinctive styles. Q was the in-house comedian, whose loud personality matched his extraordinary skill. Early on, he did more shit talking than actual rapping. But after seeing Kendrick, Soul, and Rock at work, he picked up the tools of the trade. Ab-Soul was the nerdy conspiracist from the "ghetto suburbs" of Los Angeles, who Kendrick later credited for pushing him as a lyricist in 2024's "heart pt. 6." "His words legendary, wishin' I could rhyme like him. Studied his style to define my pen," Kendrick rapped on the *GNX* release.

Jay Rock was the bedrock of the label, whose scorching rhymes reflected the very grind he and Top shared as Watts natives. Then there was Kendrick—the over-thinker, whose mind was filled with musical concepts and strategies to stretch his artistry as far as he, or anyone else, could take it. That drive made him one of the more dynamic of the four artists, but his ascension wouldn't have happened without Top, Punch, the "House of Pain," or Black Hippy.

From Hype Man to Hype Machine

As Kendrick cut his teeth in the mixtape circuit, Punch and Top were pushing for Jay Rock's ascension. The Watts rapper secured a recording contract with Asylum Records, and later a joint venture deal with Warner Bros. Records in 2007. While some industry execs were interested in Kendrick, long-time music executive and A&R Richie Abbott said Jay Rock was drawing the most buzz at the time. "I've worked with Snoop, DJ Quik, and MC Eiht, you name it," Abbott said. "To me, Jay Rock was what had been missing in LA." Abbott, who was running urban publicity for Warner at the time, started working with Jay Rock when he first signed with the label. Whether it was Top Dawg's home studio or Warner's California headquarters, Abbott said TDE moved like an army. Anywhere Jay Rock went, he was accompanied by Top, Punch, Schoolboy Q, Ab-Soul, and a "quiet little dude" in the corner named Kendrick. But after Punch passed him Kendrick's song "Bitch I'm in the Club," Abbott began looking at the reserved guy in Jay Rock's crew a bit differently.

After Jay Rock landed a deal with the Kansas City-based label Strange Music in the fall of 2010, co-founder and flagship artist Tech N9ne invited Rock and Kendrick on the "Independent Grind Tour." Throughout the 43-city tour,

Kendrick served as Jay Rock's hype man. If he was lucky, he performed one or two songs of his own on stage. Abbott said it was a transformative time for both Kendrick and Jay Rock. By closely watching Tech N9ne and fellow artist Krizz Kaliko on stage, they learned how to command an audience, and carry that same energy and showmanship to every tour stop. When they weren't performing, Kendrick and Jay Rock recorded music with E-40 in his hotel room. And by the end of the tour, Abbott said the duo gained their "stage lungs," expanded their fanbase, and were ready to headline tours of their own, stating:

> When I'm seeing Kendrick smash all these arenas, I'm like, "Okay, he paid attention." He was always taking notes and calculating, and I always respected and appreciated that about him. He pays attention to every aspect of the business—down to the merch, security, the crew, and sound. And when you see his show now, you see all the elements he learned.

Once the tour wrapped in October 2010, Jay Rock's long-delayed debut *Follow Me Home* was slated for a release the following year. Kendrick was cooking up new music, and a new artistic identity that felt a bit closer to home.

Hello World ... Kendrick Here

While some rappers never meet their musical heroes, Kendrick was seventeen when he met Jay-Z. He signed an artist development deal with Def Jam Recordings in the early 2000s, and was introduced to the rap legend, and then-Def Jam president, during a meeting with the label. "I don't think even Jay remember that," Kendrick said in a 2012 interview with MTV.[11]
This was when I like first turned 17. And I remember coming out here for a meeting and I was too excited, man. And all I remember was Jay walking in the room, "Yo, what's up?" And walked back to the elevator and we was like "Damn, that's Jay." So he doubles back, goes back to his office next door and he's playing my music. Put me in the studio and that was just one of those situations where I wasn't ready.

Kendrick's deal under Jay-Z dissolved shortly after their brief encounter. The disappointment would have shaken most artists in his position, but

Kendrick took it on the chin and delved deeper into his craft. At twenty-two years old, Kendrick was on a path of reinvention. With four mixtapes under his belt, and a debut EP in the works, K.Dot's name was beginning to transcend regional barriers. He was looking to shed his old artistic profile for a new, more authentic one.

Months after releasing C4, Kendrick decided to drop the name K.Dot for his birth name, Kendrick Lamar. His re-introduction came with an epiphany. If he wanted to become a generation-defining artist, he had to peel back the layers and reveal more of himself. While the name "K.Dot," or "Dot," was long-held by his homies back in Compton, Kendrick wanted his identity—and the emotional and spiritual wounds that came with it—to be fully displayed. From then on, there would be no more questions on who Kendrick Lamar was, or what he represented. Everything he was (and wanted to be) was going to bleed on every song, feature, and album he produced under the new moniker he carried. In a 2009 interview on the TDE YouTube channel, Kendrick stated:

> A nigga just felt like I needed people to know my story. I came in the whole shit just wanting to rap. If you heard all the mixtapes and what not, then you'd know I'm just rapping and spitting, all bars. I'm mature now. I want to let people know that I'm an actual artist who does music, so why not start, if you want to know who I am as a person first and then get into the music, why not start with my real name.[12]

The name change was established with the release of 2009's *The Kendrick Lamar EP*. While his previous work showcased his lyrical prowess, the new project fully revealed the man and artist his fans would grow to admire. "Human music. That's what we got going at Top Dawg Entertainment," Kendrick said. "You can't classify it as one thing or the other and all that. If you're a real person, you're going to relate to it." His past mixtapes were fragmented by his influences, not yet reflective of the artist that would bloom on albums like 2012's *good kid, m.A.A.d city* or *DAMN.* years later. But the self-titled release was the true step forward.

Rather than freestyle over other people's radio hits, Kendrick locked in with Q-Tip, Black Milk, Jake One, TDE in-house producer Sounwave, and other beat-makers to craft his most resonant project to date. On "Wanna Be Heard,"

Kendrick details the fight to be recognized among the growing list of emcees that spawned from rap's blog-era, and the swarm of critics who blasted his past projects for unoriginality. Instead of folding under the unfavorable judgment, *The Kendrick Lamar EP* was the response and *growth* he needed as a rapper and songwriter.

He wanted his music to serve as a vehicle for the vulnerable and unheard, who shared his past struggles and life experiences. He addressed the widespread effects of mass incarceration on "Uncle Bobby & Jason Keaton" and the hazards of mindless materialism on "Vanity Slaves." Kendrick hadn't yet mastered the ability to weave these concepts into palatable hits or club records, but the tracks showed his willingness to address heavy topics with intricate rhymes. All he needed was time, and *The Kendrick Lamar EP* was the embrace of a new sound and artistic metamorphosis. A new Kendrick Lamar. "I think I was put on this Earth to do music," Kendrick said. "I think everybody has their mission to set out what they want to do, or what they're supposed to do in life. I think God made me to spread my voice to the world, straight up."

From Momma's Kitchen to the World Stage

With the release of *The Kendrick Lamar EP*, the rapper was long past his days writing rhymes on his mother's kitchen table, hoping the freshly inked verses translated to hit records. Kendrick was knocking on the industry's door, positioning himself to seize everything the rap game had to offer. The new project and self-realized moniker marked a new era for Kendrick, and his subsequent releases were proof of his evolution. Once looking to prove he could out-rap fans' favorite rapper, he was determined to prove he was the full package—an elite lyricist and musical artist.

Kendrick carried his rising momentum into the new decade with 2010's *Overly Dedicated*. His songwriting was sharper, the music was better produced and sequenced, and Kendrick was rapping on astronomical levels. He was fully capable of bottling conscious raps into head-nodding records like the g-funk homage "Average Joe." On "Ignorance Is Bliss," Kendrick pushes back on the "conscious" rapper tag. Instead, suggesting he's somewhere between a West Coast street artist and lyrical philosophers like 2Pac and Ice Cube. "The critics are calling me conscious. But truthfully, every shooter be calling me Compton." Kendrick also revealed his internal battles with alcohol on "P&P 1.5," and the sinful allure of drug-dealing on "R.O.T.C (Interlude)." But "Ignorance Is Bliss" grabbed the attention of his future mentor and legendary music producer Dr. Dre.

Following *OD*'s release, Dre saw the music video to Kendrick's "Ignorance Is Bliss," and decided to give the rapper a phone call. Kendrick picked up the phone while eating at Chilli's with his sound engineer Derek "MixedByAli" Ali. At first, he brushed it off as a fake call. He didn't believe one of rap's most prolific figures would reach out to him directly, so he ended the call without warning. "We got a call, like, 'Yo, Dr. Dre likes your music.' And we're like, who the fuck is this on the phone? Fuck outta here, boy," Kendrick revealed in a 2017 interview with Howard Stern. "We hung up. We might've blown it. But another call came in from somebody else, then another call came from somebody else like, 'Yo, they tryna reach out and figure who you with.'"[13]

The next week, Kendrick was in the studio with Dre to record songs for the producer's long-awaited and since scrapped album, *Detox*. While "Ignorance Is Bliss" may have led to their first official sit down, Kendrick remembered seeing Dre on the set of "California Love" in 1995. At eight years old, Kendrick sat on his father's shoulders to watch Dre and 2Pac in the *Mad Max*-inspired video, and now he was in the studio recording music with the mythical figure. "That moment right there, whether I know it or not, subconsciously … eventually branched me off to what I'm doing now," Kendrick told The Recording Academy in 2013. "It was already designed and destined. Fifteen years later I meet Dr. Dre and I explain that story to him when I seen him, and he remembered that exact same moment."[14]

For their first recording session, Dre provided a beat and asked Kendrick to write to it. The challenge, as intimidating as it was, forced Kendrick to string a series of concepts and verses together in close succession. After their session wrapped, Dre's questions were answered. Kendrick was ready for a mainstream push. The fellow Compton native, who propelled the careers of Eminem, 50 Cent, Anderson .Paak, and other big-name artists, signed Kendrick to Aftermath Entertainment in 2012 through a joint venture with TDE and Interscope.

Years later, an unlikely connection between Dre, Kendrick, and J. Cole was revealed. The "Love Yourz" rapper admitted to nudging Dre to sign Kendrick in a 2021 interview with Nardwuar the Human Serviette.[15] While he may not have been the first person to direct Dre's attention to the would-be star, Cole felt it would help Dre wrap up the decade-long production of *Detox*. "I'm not gonna say I was the first to tell him … When I brought him up to Dre, I was like, 'You know what you gotta do,'" Cole said. "You gotta sign this kid from Compton!" Ideally, Cole would have liked to sign Kendrick himself, "but we ain't have our business intact," he said. The two met at producer No I.D.'s home and soon developed a friendship. A record contract never came to form, but their first of many collaborations happened on Kendrick's debut album, *Section.80*.

A Symbol of HiiiPoWeR

Months before signing to Aftermath, Kendrick's TDE projects and breakout features on Game's *The R.E.D. Album* and Drake's *Take Care* elevated his profile. He joined Meek Mill, Big K.R.I.T., Cyhi the Prynce, YG, Mac Miller, and others on XXL's 2011 Freshman Class, and was ramping up promotion for *Section.80*. The project, released on July 2, 2011, was sewn from the grounds of Compton, and crafted through the lens of an evolved Kendrick, who was beginning to see how the people he grew up with were repeating the harmful cycles inherited from the crack era.

With effervescent flows and stripped-down jazz production, Kendrick's *Section.80* visualized the gang violence and drug use that permeated South Central at the height of the epidemic. On songs like "Ronald Reagan Era," Kendrick addressed the former president's role in breeding a generation of broken families and war-torn sections in Black America. The concept for the album was developed from a memory Kendrick had of an old friend, who was sentenced to twenty-five years to life at age seventeen. The pain and the confusion he felt, knowing his friend would spend most of his formative years behind bars, inspired the rapper to delve into the madness that ensued in the decade. Rapper LNS stated:

Who got me to rap is 2Pac, but Kendrick inspired me the most. The first time I heard him I was in prison. I was listening to him in big ass headphones and was thinking, "Who the fuck is this dude?" He was lyrical and creative, and what impresses me about artists most is when they're themselves. Nobody sounded like Kendrick on his first album.

The lead single "HiiiPoWeR" marked the first collaboration between Kendrick and Cole. The North Carolina native crafted the beat with samples from Pharoahe Monch's "Simon Says," Kanye West's "So Appalled," and vocals from singer Alori Joh. Already aware of Cole's prowess as an artist, Kendrick was blown away by his talents as a beat-maker. "His production is crazy, man," Kendrick revealed in a 2011 interview with Canadian music site The Come Up. "The first time we locked in, he played about 10 beats. I wanted 11 of 'em." In the studio, the first instrumental Cole played was "HiiiPoWeR," and Kendrick sat in twenty-five mixing sessions to perfect the first official lead single of his career.[16]

Shortly after, Kendrick and Cole began working on a joint project together, which sparked years of fan-made demos and stitched collaborations. Rumors of a surprise album resurfaced when Cole and Kendrick released *Black Friday* on November 27, 2015. Unreleased songs were previously leaked by obscure sources, but *Black Friday* was the first dual project confirmed by the two artists. Kendrick rapped on Cole's "A Tale of 2 Citiez" and Cole rapped on "Alright" from Dot's jazz and funk-infused album, *To Pimp a Butterfly*. But to fans' dismay, a full-fledged project never came together. On rapper Lil Yatchy's podcast, *A Safe Place*, Cole said "time" and "life" soon put the grand idea to rest in the 2023 episode:

This was after we was already building this relationship, and I had these beats at the time and I was playing them for him … In that moment, we talked about, "Yo, bro, we should do a project." We ain't ever got the chance to go in and do it correctly, because that would take time, bro. For us to do something that's full of our potential, that meets our real potential, you're gonna need time … At least a year. [17]

The planned album was nixed, but "HiiiPoWeR" became the first of many subsequent releases between the two artists. The duo exchanged verses on Cole's "Forbidden Fruit," and they were featured together on Jeezy's "American

Dream," DJ Khaled's "They Ready," and other records. Their first collaboration also hatched Kendrick's HiiiPoWeR movement. Like 2Pac's social and cultural campaign "Thug Life," an acronym that stands for The Hate U Give Little Infants Fucks Everybody, Kendrick launched a similar crusade he hoped would transcend gang and street culture. The three i's in HiiiPoWeR represented heart, honor, and respect. "That's how we carry ourselves in the streets, and just in the world, period," Kendrick said. Being of HiiiPoWeR meant being a symbol of dignity and standing above a world brimming with hate, vitriol, and destruction.

On "HiiiPoWeR," Kendrick chronicled a spiritual awakening. He references social activists and thought leaders like Huey P. Newton, Malcolm X, and Martin Luther King Jr. throughout the track, but the song itself was inspired by a half-delirious dream of 2Pac. In his vision, the late rapper walked up to him and said, "Keep doing what you're doing. Don't let my music die." "It scared the shit out of me," Kendrick said in a 2011 interview with Home Grown Media Group. "And I'm really big on shit like that, like when someone comes in your dream and relays a message, you got to listen to that." Kendrick detailed the vision at the start of the "HiiiPoWeR" music video, and just before the credits rolled, he shouted out 2Pac's famed social movement, "Thug Life."[18]

The song and movement were timely given the state of hip-hop in the early 2010s. Kendrick and Ab-Soul felt the genre had deviated from its conscious-driven roots and was in need of redirection. On the second to last track of *Section.80*, Ab-Soul crystalized the movement's purpose. "Started HiiiPower because our generation needed a generator. And the system made to disintegrate us." The movement was supported by Schoolboy Q and Jay Rock, who shouted "HiiiPoWeR" on "There He Go" and Soul's "Black Lip Bastard Remix."

While "HiiiPoWeR" didn't capture the attention of listeners en masse, it showed Kendrick's desire and ability to forge a unifying message. It was everything he intended to trigger on *Section.80*, but he was prepared to take a more personal approach. After signing to Aftermath Entertainment, he wanted his major label debut to focus more directly on his own upbringing in Compton. From the peer pressure of gang culture, the cycles of gun violence, to his early dreams of rap supremacy—he wanted to capture it all. And by fully chronicling his story, he was confident his message would reach hip-hop fans more broadly. "I always said *Section.80* was just a warm-up for the story I'm trying to tell. *Section.80* was more about the people, my debut album will be more about me," Kendrick told *Billboard* in 2011. "I know what I have to do and what I have to talk about, so there's really no pressure."[19]

good kid, m.A.A.d. Industry

On October 22, 2012, Kendrick released *good kid, m.A.A.d city*, a project widely considered his magnum opus. Temple University professor and attorney Timothy Welbeck said *Section.80* was a broad view of Compton's dissension in the 1980s, but *GKMC* was a heightened account of Kendrick's life amid the madness. Welbeck stated:

> *Section.80* is his manifesto of a child growing up in the crack era of Compton, and then *good kid, m.A.A.d city* is a cinematic overview of it. It's him delving deeply into the traumas that he's experiencing, but also the intergenerational trauma of his community—and the toll it's having.

The album cover is a grainy snapshot of an infant Kendrick, dangling from his uncle's knee in front of a small kitchen table, with a forty-ounce of malt liquor and Lamar's baby bottle resting on top. The image was a peek inside his childhood home, and by the end of the project, listeners felt like they experienced Kendrick's life from the passenger seat.

GKMC kicks off with a seventeen-year-old Kendrick, whose infatuation with a girl named Sherane leads to a surprise attack outside her home. The sex-obsessed teen had hoped their lustful conversations would lead to physical touch. Instead, he's confronted by the less blissful elements of his neighborhood. "I pulled up a smile on my face, and then I see. Two niggas, two black hoodies, I froze as my phone rang." What follows is one of several voicemails throughout the album, which tie the concept together with sleek precision, and highlight the experiences that birthed Kendrick Lamar—the man and the artist. Before GKMC's release, Kendrick stated this in a 2011 interview with *Billboard*:

> I'm a good kid in a mad city. When you think of Compton, you think of the stigma of gangs and gang culture. That's something I've been around my

whole life. I was always that one individual in my neighborhood who was always trying to escape the influences rather than being oblivious to it. But I also had my head bumped a few times to finally know what I was doing. The only thing that separates me from my friends in jail is the fact I had a father. He gave me the balance I needed. I put that same balance in my music—the balance of knowing the gang culture from my cousins, uncles, and pops. And at the same time, my mother and father gave me the idea of being a dreamer. They taught me the world is bigger than Compton and to go out and explore it.

From floating in mental suspension on "Don't Kill My Vibe," to freestyling in the back of his homie's white Toyota, succumbing to the pressure of Henny shots, Remy Wine sips, and home invasions, Kendrick tackles these topics in seamless form. His slick quotables and piercing delivery is elevated by production from Hit-Boy, Pharrell, Terrace Martin, Dr. Dre, Just Blaze, and killer features from MC Eiht, Drake, Anna Wise, and Jay Rock. All parties helped conjure a musical cocktail that was palatable to the masses.

In the years since its release, *GKMC* has proven to be one of Kendrick's most influential bodies of work. The album remained on the Billboard 200 for twelve consecutive years, making it the longest-running project to ever reach such a milestone.[20] It also established TDE as a musical powerhouse and revitalized West Coast rap in ways unseen since 2005's *The Documentary*.

To Pimp a Prophet

A year after the release of *GKMC*, Kendrick was on top of the world. He had released one of the decade's most memorable debut albums, and reignited rap's competitive flame with his verse on Big Sean's "Control (HOF)." "I got love for you all but I'm tryna murder you niggas. Tryna make sure your core fans never heard of you niggas. They don't want to hear not one more noun or verb from you niggas." Lamar challenged artists like Drake, J. Cole, Big KRIT, Wale, Meek Mill, Tyler, The Creator, Jay Electronica, and even Sean. The draw for lyrical arms triggered responses and accompanying diss records, servicing rap fans who were longing for rap battles amongst the new class of emcees.

Heading into the 56th Annual Grammy Awards, Kendrick's profile was among the hottest in music. He was favored to win for Best Rap Album, but on January 26, 2014, another rapper shockingly snagged the highly coveted award. Fresh off smash hits like "Thrift Shop" and "Can't Hold Us," the Seattle-based duo Macklemore & Ryan Lewis took home the golden gramophone. The ruling by the Recording Academy sent shockwaves throughout the industry, with hip-hop fans, radio personalities, and music journalists questioning the decision, including Macklemore himself.

After winning the award, and three others on the night, Macklemore sent an apology to Lamar. "You got robbed," Macklemore texted Kendrick minutes after the main show ended. "I wanted you to win. You should have. It's weird and it sucks that I robbed you." Ironically, this very moment wasn't even televised. Macklemore and Lewis won during the pre-show five hours before his message was delivered. The rapper went on to screenshot and post the text on Instagram, hoping it would silence critics and soften the backlash. But Macklemore's public apology backfired, with artists like Drake calling the move "wack as fuck." "You won. Why are you posting your text messages? Just chill. Take your W, and if you feel you didn't deserve it, go get better—make better music," Drake told *Rolling Stone* weeks after the award show.[21]

Despite opposing reports, Kendrick graciously accepted Macklemore's apology, later calling him a "genuine person" who deserved the honor. Two years later, Kendrick and his fans were redeemed. His sophomore album *To Pimp a Butterfly* landed eleven Grammy nominations, the most for any rapper in a single night and second all time behind Michael Jackson.[22] On February 15, 2016, the annual award ceremony was back at the Staples Center, now named Crypto.com Arena, with more than twenty million viewers tuned into the live broadcast. Only this time, Kendrick was hoisting the gramophone for Best Rap Album.

The award was presented by West Coast legend Ice Cube and his son O'Shea Jackson Jr., which added to the momentous occasion. "And the Grammy goes to," Cube said as he opened up the envelope. "*To Pimp a Butterfly*, Kendrick Lamar." The rapper immediately embraced his long-time partner Whitney Alford, then walked to the stage to deliver a speech dedicated to his parents, mentors, and the woman who had supported him since their early days in high school. Kendrick looked up the crowd, stating:

First off, all glory to God. That's for sure. My foundation, my root to me being on this stage, Kenneth Duckworth and Paula Duckworth. Those who gave me the responsibility of knowing and understanding, accepting the good with the bad, I'll always love you for that. Whitney, I will always love you for supporting me and keeping me motivated into being the best person. Top Dawg, my top dog brother, Top Dawg himself. We were eating you out a house and home, we'll never forget that. Taking these kids out of the projects, out of Compton, and putting them right here on this stage to be the best they can be. We'll never forget that ... Hip-hop, Ice Cube. This for hip-hop. This for Snoop Dogg, Doggystyle. This for Illmatic. This for Nas. We will live forever, believe that. [23]

Kendrick went on to win four other Grammys that night for an album filled with jazz, funk, and sonically rich soul. The lead single "i" may have drawn mixed reactions from fans, who diminished the inspiring song down to a preachy after-school jam upon its release, but the message of Black unification set the tone for the album.

TPAB is a symphony of spoken word and a poetic chronology of Black oppression. Songs like "Complexion (A Zulu Love)" address the devastation of colorism, "How Much a Dollar Cost" delves into the misguidance of materialism, and "Hood Politics" decodes the destructive powers of US politics—from Compton to Capitol Hill. And with an uptick in Black deaths by the hands of law enforcement in the 2010s, "The Blacker the Berry" and "Alright" were sounding boards for Black America. The latter became a universal protest anthem for those setting the picket lines, hoping their demands and long-fought freedoms were finally granted.

And we hate po-po. Wanna kill us dead in the street fo'sho. Nigga, I'm at the preacher's door. My knees gettin' weak, and my gun might blow. But we goin' be alright

The album, which featured an unheard 2Pac interview on the outro "Mortal Man," was new artistic territory for the 27-year-old artist. A 2014 trip to

South Africa was the source of *TPAB*'s musical direction. As he roamed the streets of Durban, Johannesburg, and Cape Town, he ventured to historic sites like Nelson Mandela's jail cell on Robben Island. His long-time friend and in-house producer Mark "Sounwave" Spears said the expedition widened his and Kendrick's eyes. "We felt it from deep in our hearts, and to have it be seen like that was a blessing, that's all I can say," the Grammy-winning producer said in a 2020 interview with *Billboard*.[24]

Kendrick was no longer speaking to the poverty-struck citizens of Compton, or others throughout the country, his music was for everyone who wrestled with the same struggles. He wanted to illustrate the beauty of Blackness, and the magnificence of a world few are able to fully absorb. In a 2016 interview with Grammy.com, Kendrick recounted the trip:

> I saw all the things that I wasn't taught. Probably one of the hardest things to do is put [together] a concept on how beautiful a place can be, and tell a person this while they're still in the ghettos of Compton. I wanted to put that experience in the music.[25]

The journey led to a road of Grammy glory, which was capped off with an electrifying performance. Kendrick walked to the stage, decked in a blue prison uniform with his hands mangled in chains, and opened the performance with a verse of "The Blacker the Berry." "I'm the biggest hypocrite of 2015. Once I finish this, if you listenin' sure you will agree. Been feelin' this way since I was 16, came to my senses. You never liked us anyway, buck your friendship, I meant it." As the song progressed, Kendrick and his dancers broke from their chains, and skimmed to the other end of the platform to perform "Alright." With African dancers surrounding him, Kendrick drew in the cheering crowd with feverish intensity, switching from acapella back to the saxophone-fueled instrumental. He closed the performance standing center stage, with a glowing image of Africa and the word "Compton" flashing behind him for all the world to see.

What Happens on Earth, Stays on Earth

Following his Grammy-winning achievement in 2016, Kendrick was gearing up to make another monumental splash. He teased a new project on "The Heart

Part 4," a blistering five-minute track that warned of his imminent return two years after *TPAB*. "You know what time it is, ante up, this is in forever. Y'all got 'till April the seventh to get y'all shit together." And on April 7, 2017, the iTunes preorder link to Kendrick's fourth studio album, *DAMN.*, was released. The official artwork, tracklist, and release date was unveiled just days later.[26]

Originally titled "What Happens on Earth, Stays on Earth," the highly anticipated project was released on April 14, 2017. Kendrick returned to more modern instrumentation but also leaned more heavily on pop-inspired compositions. Kendrick's collaborations with Rihanna on "LOYALTY.," U2 on "XXX." and "LOVE." with TDE vocalist Zacari showcased his dexterity as a soul-baring lyricist and gifted songwriter. While the album was more pop-inspired compared to *TPAB*'s more fervent sound, *DAMN.* wasn't short on conscious messaging.

Grammy-nominated sound engineer and producer Ben Thomas said the collaborations with Rihanna, U2, James Blake, Steve Lacey, and others struck sonic and conceptual balance, but *DAMN.* still weaves commentary on the mishandlings of the 2016 presidential election ("XXX.") and personal stories that still resonate today. "He did multiple rap songs that are pop songs. 'HUMBLE' and 'DNA' have strong hooks that are very short and digestible on the surface. But we know there are layers underneath," Thomas said.

Among Kendrick's most enriching tales is "DUCKWORTH." The outro unveiled the chance meeting between Top Dawg and Kendrick's father, nicknamed "Ducky," who worked at the KFC Tiffith intended to rob. Instead of sticking up the talkative, curly topped attendant at the drive-thru window, Top took the free chicken and two extra biscuits Ducky made for him and left. That decision, as Kendrick detailed on the song, changed both of their lives in ways they never imagined. "Whoever thought the greatest rapper would be from coincidence? Because if Anthony killed Ducky, Top Dawg could be servin' life. While I grew up without a father, and died in a gunfight," he rapped.

After *DAMN.* dropped, fan conspiracies began to spiral on social media. Some conjured references to Jesus's resurrection and *The Matrix* films, while others were convinced a second and more politically charged album called "Nation" was on the horizon. The only theory Kendrick confirmed was that the song "BLOOD" and "DUCKWORTH" were interchangeable intros and outros, and the poignant stories wedged between the two songs were intended to be heard both forward and reverse. Listening in either direction reveals different sides of the same Kendrick—a man wrestling with the wickedness of fame, and the power of self-realization ("DNA.") and restraint ("ELEMENT."). He even re-released the album with a reversed tracklist. In a 2017 interview with MTV News, Kendrick stated:

> It plays as a full story and even a better rhythm. It's one of my favorite rhythms and tempos within the album. It's something that we definitely premeditate while we're in the studio. The initial vibe listening from the top all the way to the bottom is … this aggression and this attitude. You know, "DNA," and exposing who I really am. You listen from the back end, and it's almost the duality and the contrast of the intricate Kendrick Lamar. Both of these pieces are who I am.[27]

DAMN proved Kendrick's rightful place in the conversation for rap's biggest star. The album surpassed Drake's *More Life* "playlist" in album sales, with *DAMN* racking in 603,000 first week sales compared to Drake's 505,000.[28] The triple-platinum album earned Lamar a second Best Rap Album award at the 2018 Grammy Awards and a Pulitzer Prize for Music. It was the first time a recipient outside of classical music and jazz was given such an achievement, a sign that Kendrick's music and cultural contributions were recognized beyond the world of entertainment. Grammy-winning rapper GLC, who collaborated with Kendrick on "Poe Mans Dreams (His Vice)," stated:

> I think everything he's done—all the accolades that he's gotten over the years—he's earned it because he's very consistent. He may not put out a whole lot of music, but when he does, it's going to be some gas. I respect him for that.

Reigniting Black Soul

After *TPAB*, Kendrick had nothing left to prove but his staying power. The jazz-funk jams and multicolored flows on *TPAB* showed how far his artistry could reach. It was a sonic think-piece for generations of hip-hop fans and music lovers to seep into. *DAMN* was an exercise in dazzling rhyme and storytelling, complemented by top-billed hits and a timely message for Black America.

As much as he juggled on *DAMN*, Kendrick's political conscience was well within balance. It was necessary in a post-Barack Obama administration, with newly elected president Donald Trump peeling back on climate change initiatives, healthcare policies, immigration programs, and other Obama-led actions. The business mogul and former reality star nestled his way into a presidential race few thought he could win. And despite receiving nearly 2.9 million less total votes than Democrat nominee Hillary Clinton, Trump won enough key electoral states to secure his place in the Oval Office. It was the most votes any losing presidential candidate received in US history at the time, and the cost proved pivotal.[29]

Within a year of his presidency, Trump pulled out of the Paris Climate agreement, an international treaty that aims to cut greenhouse gas emissions. He altered the Affordable Care Act, which was designed to expand health insurance coverage to millions of uninsured Americans, and attempted to repeal the Deferred Action for Childhood Arrivals (DACA) program. The Obama-era policy granted legal status to child immigrants who were illegally brought to the US and by no choice of their own. Trump also propagated false conspiracies about the former president. He claimed Obama was born outside the US, and was the founder of the terrorist organization, ISIS—among other things.

While one faction celebrated the return of a white, conservative leader, Trump's victory shocked millions of left-leaning voters. Trump shattered the old, primitive mold of political figures. He was big, brash, and unafraid to ruffle the feathers of niche minority groups. Trump's actions in his first term revealed the true ugliness of America, and proved Obama's presidency wasn't indicative of a new, refined country. Its blemishes were only concealed.

Obama's place as the country's first Black president didn't eliminate racism or dismantle the long-standing effects of systemic oppression. The support Trump received for his sexist, xenophobic, and racism-fueled soliloquies on his 2016 campaign trail, and his eventual actions after taking office in January 2017, was a dangerous turn in the nation's political sphere. It empowered far-right, neo-fascist militant organizations like the Proud Boys, and other harmful groups who follow Trump's misguided lead.[30] While *DAMN* was a more self-realized project, Kendrick was compelled to point out Trump's political misfires and take physical action in the wake of the 2016 election. In a 2017 interview with *Rolling Stone*, Kendrick stated:

> On and off the album, I took it upon myself to take action in my own community. On the record, I made an action to not speak about what's going on in the world or the places they put us in. Speak on self; reflection of self first. That's where the initial change will start from.

Kendrick's coronation at The Fonda Theatre in 2011 wasn't solely about being the next-best West Coast rapper. It was indicative of a new cultural figure, who was undefined by album sales or Grammy wins. The power of his music and voice spoke volumes. As respected as Kendrick and Cole are as emcees, their greatest attributes are their principles as social leaders. Through their music and charitable actions, they have educated fans on social and cultural issues, and inspired them to take their own measurable steps toward progression.

With their combined releases, Kendrick and Cole have reached unparalleled heights. Alongside multi-platinum artist Drake, they took over the rap game as the three leading voices of their generation. Artists like Future, Chance the Rapper, Wale, Big Sean, Nipsey Hussle, Joey Bada$$, and others were also major contributors, but Cole and Kendrick's mainstream success, longevity, and cultural impact is unmatched. When all three elements are considered, Temple professor and attorney Timothy Welbeck said no other two names should be considered atop the list of all-time greats. "If neither one of them ever makes another song again, they are two of the greatest rappers of all time. And they have substantially influenced and shaped the culture in tremendous ways, both in terms of their influence, their impact, and even their skill level. It's something that will span generations."

5
Policing, Politics, and Pens

To be among the best rappers of all-time, addressing social issues is a prerequisite. The genre's most prolific artists have made inspiring or eye-opening records that have tackled racial injustice, mass incarceration, politics, and gun violence. An elite crop of emcees have woven these themes into generation-defining hits. Among this list of musical supernovas are J. Cole and Kendrick Lamar. They have consistently amplified social justice movements and soundtracked global protests just as easily as they have filled concert arenas. All they needed was the right hook, bridge, or message to galvanize an entire fanbase. Their ability to craft socially and politically charged songs is reflective of the iconic artists that came before them.

With her sonorous voice and blues-inspired hits as an instrument of change, Nina Simone was a civil rights activist of equal measure. "The High Priestess of Soul" penned protest anthems that expressed her frustration and anger with racial injustice and inequality. Her song "Mississippi Goddam" is among her most resonant works.[1] The 1964 release lamented the bloodshed that transpired at the peak of the Civil Rights Movement. Over an upbeat show tune, Simone pointed to the 16th Street Baptist Church bombing that killed four Black girls in Birmingham, Alabama, as well as the assassinations of Dr. Martin Luther King Jr. and fellow activist Medgar Evers.

In the decades since Simone's "Mississippi Goddam," an elite class of hip-hop artists have struck similar chords, attuned to issues plaguing Black Americans and the larger diaspora at moments of civil unrest. One such moment came with the killing of Mike Brown.[2] On August 9, 2014, the eighteen-year-old was walking in the middle of a two-lane street in Ferguson, Missouri, a predominantly Black suburb a few miles north of downtown St. Louis. Police officer Darren Wilson drove by and told them to use the sidewalk. After words were exchanged, the White officer confronted Brown, and the heated exchange led to a scuffle between the two. The officer then shot and killed an unarmed Brown, leaving his body in the street for four hours in the summer heat.

Brown's death spurred thousands of Ferguson residents to come outside their apartments in protest, and soon a nation of community organizers and social activists followed their lead. The racially charged shooting was reminiscent of several unjust killings of Black civilians. Two years before Brown's death, a South Florida teenager named Trayvon Martin was shot and killed while walking back from a convenience store. The seventeen-year-old was targeted by neighborhood watch organizer George Zimmerman, who was acquitted for murder charges in 2013. A year later, a 43-year-old man named Eric Garner was killed on a Staten Island sidewalk by police for being suspected of selling loose cigarettes.[3] During the encounter, Garner raised both hands in the air and pleaded for the officers not to touch him. Seconds later, then New York Police Department officer Daniel Pantaleo choked the 350-pound man from behind, then pulled him to the sidewalk. Garner's dying words, "I can't breathe," became a national rallying cry.

"All We Want to Do Is Take the Chains Off"

With Brown's death just three weeks after Garner was killed, cities across the country joined Ferguson residents in protest. What began as a peaceful dissent ended with smashed car windows and a torched convenience store. Police in armored vehicles responded with tear gas and rubber bullets, which drew even more advocates and national news sites to Missouri. Brown's death also kindled a national conversation on police brutality, with many campaigners pushing for police reform, and other left-wing leaders and libertarians advocating for the defunding of law enforcement agencies.

Six days after the Ferguson protests began, Cole uploaded the somber track, "Be Free." The SoundCloud upload circulated the country in what felt like a matter of hours. By late afternoon, the song had more than 250,000 listens, with fans, music blogs, and other media sites discussing the new release.[4] Cole's emotional lyrics added to the discourse that spread across social media and national airwaves. The same reactions were happening within hip-hop circles. Like the responses drawn from Trayvon Martin's death, Cole's "Be Free" reflected the frustration and mourning felt by Black Americans.

All we want do is be free
All we want do is be free
All we want do is take these chains off
All we want do is break the chains of pain

In a blog post unveiling the song, Cole wrote a candid message about Brown's death. "That coulda been me, easily," he wrote. "It could have been my best friend. I'm tired of being desensitized to the murder of black men." The original cover art featured a widely circulated image of Brown's body on the street, but it was later changed to a photo of the late teenager's mother, Lesley McSpadden. The record included a written message: "Rest in Peace to Michael Brown and to every young black man murdered in America," Cole wrote. "I pray that one day the world will be filled with peace and rid of injustice."[5]

After penning the tribute, Cole flew to Ferguson to join protestors on the ground. The Dreamville CEO gathered other members of his crew along for the trip, where Cole spent hours connecting with advocates pledging for justice in the Missouri suburb. "We didn't come down here to do any interviews. We didn't come down here to talk to any press," Cole told Complex while standing outside the QuikTrip store on West Florissant Avenue. "We came here to feel it. This is history, and we want to be a part of this just like everybody else wants to be a part of this. That's why we're here."[6]

The trip to Ferguson aligned with Cole's larger mission as an artist and musical activist. The song "Be Free" wouldn't be enough to unbind the wrongs faced by Brown and his family, or the injustices endured by generations of Black Americans. Cole was determined to engage with the people directly affected by Brown's death, while wrestling with his own thoughts on police brutality by walking the same path as protestors. Artists like Young Jeezy also traveled to Ferguson to show their support.[7]

Cole's presence in Ferguson and his subsequent performance of "Be Free" on the *Late Show with David Letterman*, which followed the St. Louis County grand jury's decision to clear Wilson of Brown's killing, further placed police brutality at the forefront of the American conscience. His efforts drew more eyes to the problem, but it didn't slow the rate of Black people dying by the hands of law enforcement. Ten years after Brown was killed, documented police killings in the US continued at nearly the same rate. Between 2013–24, Mapping Police Violence tracked 13,987 police killings in America. The data showed that Black people were nearly three times more likely to be killed by police than White people in the US.[8]

Despite Cole and other artists' outrage, Kendrick didn't always bear the message regarding police brutality. The Compton rapper received criticism for toting the social justice line. On 2015's "The Blacker the Berry," he rapped, "Why did I weep when Trayvon Martin was in the street, when gangbanging make me kill a nigga blacker than me? Hypocrite." His statement in a 2015 interview with *Billboard* drew even harsher criticism from activists and fellow artists. "I wish somebody would look in our neighborhood knowing that it's already a situation, mentally, where it's fucked up. What happened to [Michael Brown] should've never happened," Kendrick said when asked about Mike Brown's death.[9] "Never. But when we don't have respect for ourselves, how do we expect them to respect us? It starts from within. Don't start with just a rally, don't start from looting—it starts from within." While fellow rapper Azealia Banks didn't mention Kendrick by name, she directly quoted the Compton native on Twitter, now known as X, and wrote, "dumbest shit I've ever heard a black man say."[10]

"We Gon' Be Alright"

Ironically, another police-connected killing drew global outrage, and placed Kendrick at the spear tip of a social movement. On May 25, 2020, 46-year-old George Floyd was handcuffed and pinned to the ground under the knee of Minneapolis police officer Derek Chauvin.[11] The White officer held his knee on Floyd's neck until he took his last breath at the scene, an act for which Chauvin was later charged and sentenced to 22½ years in prison for executing.

Disturbing videos of the incident led to global protests and a racial justice movement.

The backdrop of the movement was a song Kendrick released five years before Floyd's death. The *To Pimp a Butterfly* standout, "Alright," reflected the long-held frustrations of Black Americans, who have been among the biggest victims of police killings in America. Like "Fight the Power" during the LA riots, "Alright" served as the anthem for protestors and social justice crusaders. "And we hate po-po. Wanna kill us dead in the street for sure," Kendrick rapped. Along with Childish Gambino's "This Is America," Kendrick's "Alright" skyrocketed up the US Spotify charts weeks after Floyd's murder.[12]

Aside from the song's boost in streaming numbers, Kendrick took silent action after Floyd's death. He attended a "peace walk" through Compton in June 2020, covered in an all-black outfit with his face concealed. He seemed to let his presence and solidarity speak more broadly than words could muster. He declined to comment on the uptick in "Alright" streams, but offered fans insight into his silent approach on 2021's "Family Ties" with artist Baby Keem. "I been duckin' the social gimmicks. I been duckin' the overnight activists. I'm not a trending topic, I'm a prophet," he rapped.

In the years that followed, both Cole and Kendrick have made broader and more informed proclamations. They grew to become more effective activists and advocates, both in music and in action. Their perspectives on racism, mass incarceration, drug culture, and gun violence evolved as their own experiences shifted. For Cole, one unexpected run in with law enforcement opened his eyes that much further.

"So Much for Integration. Don't Know What I Was Thinking"

Profiling based on implicit or explicit bias remains a prominent issue in America. Consequently, subjugated groups within the country are often judged and mistreated based on misconceptions and stereotypes about their race, culture, or religion. While America champions its diversity, the lived experiences and treatment of many citizens with the populace remain subpar.

As Cole's career continued to blossom, so did his record label Dreamville. Cole's North Carolina studio "The Sheltuh" was becoming a staple for the Dreamville signees and other rising stars. Acts such as Ari Lenox, EarthGang, Bas and JID often used this studio to record songs that would later become fan favorites. Outside of utilizing the studio for the creative process, Cole would sometimes have friends over at the studio who weren't emcees at all. He would hang out at the studio with friends who were simply proud of his success and wanted to spend time with him and catch up.

On March 18, 2016, The Sheltuh was forcibly raided by SWAT. Neighbors in the suburban area reported that they believed drugs were being distributed from the studio owned by Cole. Upon arrival, a team of at least twelve officers kicked in the door and entered the home with guns drawn as helicopters circled the property.[13] Thankfully, Cole and his team were out of town during the raid. Nonetheless, Cole's experience with racial profiling inspired him to record and release a song called "Neighbors." The melancholy record details Cole's feelings after the incident. Unlike other conscious records by Cole, the song doesn't offer much hope for change. It simply highlights how Cole's optimism about equality and integration was fading, and how living in a predominantly White neighborhood makes him a target as a Black man. He ends the record with one somber message. "So much for integration. Don't know what I was thinking. I'm moving back to southside," Cole rapped.

Exactly four months after the release of 2016's *4 Your Eyez Only*, Cole released a visual for "Neighbors." Instead of releasing a traditional music video for the song, he dropped the raw footage of SWAT raiding his studio with the song underscoring it all. Cole gave people a chance to see the excessive force used to raid his studio. It shone a light on how even at this level of success, fame, and wealth, he was still subject to the racial oppression that Black men still face within the country and his own home state.

4 Your Freedoms

From the early stages of their careers, mass incarceration has been an integral theme in Cole and Kendrick's music. On 2009's "The Get Up," a 24-year-old Cole delivered a momentary ode to his loved ones locked behind bars. The song largely addresses his upbringing in Fayetteville, North Carolina, which he refers to as "Fayettenam." He manages to slip in a motivational message to the people who succumb to the harsh conditions of his hometown. He rapped:

For all my niggas doin' time, man, up in prison (hold your head)
Felt you had to resort to crime, man, fuck the system
We raisin' babies up in Hades where it ain't no hope
Ain't no fathers, don't take no scholarship to slang no dope (hell nah).

On 2015's "Caged Bird," Cole and Dreamville-signee Omen delved far deeper into the ill conditions that lead many people to a life of crime, or worse, imprisonment.

Friends that's doin' years
Prison tats on they backs like souvenirs
We wish that you was here

On "Uncle Bobby and Jason Keaton," Kendrick seeps into the mind of a man trapped in imprisonment. He describes the emptiness of excommunication, the rotting smell of solitary confinement, and the paranoia that comes with having your toughness constantly tested. He draws the experiences from his own family, who wrestled with the lasting effects of institutionalization. Despite the expiration of his uncle Bobby's sentence, a string of bad decisions on the outside landed him back in a prison cell. On the third verse, the rapper broadens the conversation. He addresses the alarming number of Black men in jail, the effects it has on generations of Black families, and the US government's role in the anarchy for financial gain.

Sitting on the couch, thinking bout the ratio of blacks in prison.
It's compact in prison when Blacks packed with minorities.
System grab more of these eighteen-year-olds,
eighteen-year sentence with no parole, the state won't oversee

The two artists continued to address mass incarceration in their later projects. On "Poe Mans Dreams (His Vice)," Kendrick scrolls back to his days of adolescence. As a kid, Kendrick said he dreamed of following his uncles' footsteps, even if it meant planting his feet in a 6-by-8-foot cell. Kendrick rapped on the *Section.80* track:

> *I used to want to see the penitentiary, way after elementary*
> *Thought it was cool to look the judge in the face when he sentenced me*
> *Since my uncles was institutionalized*
> *My intuition had said I was suited for family ties*

As his misguided thoughts vanished with maturity, Kendrick details a new kind of motivation. He wants his music to uplift the minds and fill the pockets of those he lost to the justice system. Through his music, he intends to capture the hardships and emotional toll brought on by their imprisonment, while offering feelings of hope. "I want you to know that I'm so determined to blow. That you hear the music I wrote. Hope it get you off Death Row."

Kendrick continued to question the views of people from the outside. On "Mortal Man," he asked listeners if he were arrested and placed in jail, whether he would be viewed as a "criminal" or the same "K. Lamar." On "untitled 05" from his 2016 compilation album *Untitled Unmastered*, Kendrick confronts how his anxiety and alcohol addiction has nearly pushed him to test his freedoms. He details past brushes with death and other occurrences that could have easily landed him in the same place his family and close friends are currently resting—a jail cell or casket. As bleak as the songs appear, they offer a 360-view of incarceration. They demonstrate what effects imprisonment has on the convicted, and how his faith, family, and musical ambitions helped him escape mental and physical entrapment.

J. Cole took further steps to address mass incarceration. Following the success of *2014 Forest Hills Drive*, Cole followed up the multi-platinum and Grammy-nominated project with another deeply personal album. Only this time, he was rapping from the perspective of a close friend, who was killed in a shooting at age twenty-two. Cole identified the man as James McMillan Jr. His tragic death left his daughter Nina without a father, but Cole's *4 Your Eyez Only* didn't leave McMillan's story untold.

The album captured the elements McMillan intended to share with Nina before his death. The intro "For Whom the Bell Tolls" refers to the bells often heard during funeral services. "Change" directly reenacts McMillan's funeral, and Cole describes what it was like seeing his murder reported on the news. The end of "Ville Mentality" features the voice of a young girl, presumed to be McMillan's daughter, describing the frustration she faces in her father's absence. "I get mad and I slam my door, and I go in my room. And then I get mad, and I wish my dad was here," she explains.

The grim and somber theme wasn't made entirely clear until the final track, "4 Your Eyez Only." Cole's lyrics describe the thoughts of a man split between street hustling and turning a new leaf to support his newly formed family. The man has since accepted death, and the song is a reminder that his love, admiration, and support for his daughter will remain, even if he's not there in physical form.

You probably grown now so this song'll hit you.
If you're hearing this, unfortunately means that I'm no longer with you
In the physical, not even sure if I believe in God. But because you still alive
He got me praying that the spiritual is real.

In the final minutes of the track, Cole left a profound message for other listeners who wrestle with a similarly gut-wrenching reality. "I dedicate these words to you and all the other children. Affected by all the mass incarceration in this nation. That sent your pops to prison, when he needed education. Sometimes I think this segregation would've done us better," he said.

The thought-provoking project, which delves into the cyclical effects of gun violence, drugs, and imprisonment, was partly inspired by Michelle Alexander's book *The New Jim Crow: Mass Incarceration in the Age of Colorblindness*. During a panel discussion in honor of Dr. Martin Luther King Jr., Cole described how the 2010 book shaped the "4 Your Eyez Only" tour.[14] Cole decided to don an orange prison jumpsuit and shackle his hands in chains on stage after a friend gifted him the book by the civil rights litigator and legal scholar. Since Alexander's seminal project was released, it's become a referential text in Africana Studies and a resource for fellow civil rights scholars. The book addresses the dysfunction of the US criminal justice system, and how modern-day systems of racial control have plagued generations of Black Americans since the days of the War on Drugs in the early 1970s.

During a discussion with acclaimed filmmaker Ryan Coogler, Cole said elements of *The New Jim Crow* illustrated the frustrations he and others felt growing up in the South.[15] It also crystallized a new musical pathway for him to explore. "So much of my career, my art was, like, storytelling from my own perspective. I would always give you little branches of somebody else's perspective, but so much of it was my personal journey, my personal growth, my personal flaws, this, that, and the third," Cole explained to Coogler at the 2020 event. "And it was a time period when I was like, that was not interesting to me."

After reading the book and venturing back to North Carolina, Cole said it broadened his perspective. He began looking at music—and the world—with a wider lens. Through the story of McMillan, he aimed to chronicle the pain and anguish caused by White supremacy. Instead of showing fragments of his own hardships, he used someone else's story (and struggles) as a medium to convey a larger message that resonated with his listeners.

The *4 Your Eyez Only* album, the 62-date tour, and the orange jumpsuit symbolized a personal awakening. Alongside Kendrick, Cole became a rap dissident who willingly used his platform to address issues untouched by most mainstream artists. "I had a whole different perspective of the landscape and the situations [that] the revolving door had some of them in," Cole later told Coogler.

Kids on Drugs

Alcohol and drug use has been prevalent in the lyrical content of music for over a century. While the popularity of specific substances shifts generationally, the battles of addiction remain a human experience that is often reflected through song. However, there is a key difference in expressing battles with drug use and glorification. One key difference lies in omitting the negative consequences that accompany the behavior. In hip-hop, many point the blame for drug glorification in different directions. Some blame Southern hip-hop's promotion of lean or "syrup," a mix of prescription grade cough syrup, soft drinks, and candy, as a key point of the glorification of hard drugs becoming more prominent within the culture. Others point to excessive marijuana use from emcees like Snoop, Wiz Khalifa, B-Real, and Curren$y. Regardless of who's to blame, substance abuse is a part of everyday life for many people. As long as people are indulging in the behavior, the music will reflect it accordingly.

In the 2010s, the amount of drug overdoses in America was on the rise. According to the CDC, the age-adjusted rate of drug overdose deaths had increased substantially from 12.3 per 100,000 people in 2010 to 16.3 in 2015.[16] Furthermore, in 2016 around 29 percent of all overdose deaths involved fentanyl, a synthetic opioid drug approved by the U.S. Food and Drug Administration that's used to relieve pain.[17] Despite this tragic reality, the glorification of alcohol, opioids, and lean became even more prevalent in the 2010s, with acts such as Future, Young Thug, and Lil Wayne consistently detailing their rockstar lifestyles and promoting drug use in popular hit records. In contrast, Cole and Kendrick have intentionally highlighted the dangers of substance abuse and addiction in uniquely different ways, both through their music and the visuals that have accompanied their records.

On April 16, 2018, Cole shocked his fans by announcing on Twitter that he would be hosting a free event at Gramercy Theatre in New York City in a few hours.[18] It was a first-come, first-served event, and the rules were "no phones, no press, and no cameras." As fans entered the music venue, their phones were immediately taken and locked away to prevent leakage of the event. The tight-lipped event ended up being a listening party for Cole's newest album *KOD* that would release in just four days. Fans gathered in bliss as Cole played the entire album to the audience while explaining the themes of the record.

According to Cole himself, *KOD* has three meanings: Kids on Drugs, King Overdosed, and Kill Our Demons. The album's artwork was designed by Detroit-based artist Kamau Haroon, professionally known as Sixmau.[19] The cover features Cole as a regal king with his eyes white, possibly signifying himself being under the influence. Above him reads, "This album is in no way intended to glorify addiction." Underneath the image of Cole lie the disturbing illustrations of children using different drugs.

KOD emphasized the complexities of addiction throughout its tracklist. On the record "Friends," Cole delivers an empathetic plea for both his peers and the youth to veer away from drug use. He manages to address the trauma that leads to addiction, while simultaneously educating listeners of the dangers of succumbing to the temptation of narcotics. He raps, "You running from yourself and you buying product again. I know you say it helps and no I'm not trying to offend. But I know depression and drug addiction don't blend." In addition to drug addiction, he tackles the addiction to money ("ATM"), social media validation ("Photograph"), and sex/intimacy ("Kevin's Heart").

KOD was a massive success, hitting No. 1 on the Billboard Hot 100 list without any promoted singles beforehand. The album furthered Cole's desire to speak to more than just his own perspective and issues that he faced. He wanted to tackle broader social issues through storytelling, and *KOD* accomplished that goal.

Kendrick has also been vocal about the struggles of addiction on record. While Cole often tackles issues head-on, Kendrick's genius as a songwriter lies in his ability to mask conscious messaging in mainstream music. This was a gift that a prolific singer-songwriter named Sam Cooke executed generations earlier. Cooke, who was associated with progressive figures such as Malcolm X and Muhammad Ali in the 1960s, sought to address social issues in his music during a time where racial segregation was prominent and it was dangerous to do so as a Black man in America. In 1960, he released a single called "Chain Gang." On the surface, it was an upbeat, fun, and extremely catchy record about laborers singing while working. However, the song resonated with many Black Americans differently. While created to be radio friendly, the lyrics of the song shed light on the inhumane forced labor that many Black men were subjected to in Southern prisons. The song became a huge hit, peaking at No. 2 on the Billboard Hot 100 and proving that veiled protest songs could make it to the mainstream.[20]

On the album *good kid, m.A.A.d city*, Kendrick used a similar strategy on the record "Swimming Pools (Drank)," which remains one of the more resonant tracks on the album. The T-Minus-produced song became a club hit, peaking at No. 17 on the Billboard charts, and drew fans across other musical genres. At its core, it's a record about the deadly effects of alcoholism and peer pressure. Kendrick camouflaged the message over rattling hi-hats and an ambient bassline. "Some people like the way it feels. Some people want to kill their sorrows. Some people wanna kill their sorrows. Some people wanna fit in with the popular, that was my problem," he rapped. The transparency of the song and larger project garnered praise from critics and Grammy voters.

It would be nearly impossible to quantify how many people's lives have been saved because of Kendrick and Cole's messaging about drug abuse and addiction. How many people were listening to "Swimming Pools (Drank)" and decided that they need to cut back on alcohol? How many people heard Cole's "Friends" and decided they needed to choose a better way to cope with their everyday struggles? Their potential impact is immeasurable. The same is true of their efforts concerning political issues.

'Demo-Crips and Re-Blood-icans'

Cole and Kendrick's political views haven't always aligned with mainstream thought. While over 120 million Americans cast their ballots for the 2012 Presidential Election, Kendrick stood firm on his abstention. Instead of voting for then-President Barack Obama or Republican nominee Mitt Romney, he opted to skip election day altogether. "I don't do no voting," he said in a 2012 interview with Alternative News. "I will keep it straight up real with you. I don't believe in none of the shit that's going on in the world."[21]

Kendrick's anti-voting stance contrasts the messages many conscious artists have conveyed over the years. Acts like Rhymefest, The Roots, Jeezy, Chuck D, and Killer Mike have been outspoken about their political views, and pushed for voter education and accessibility through their music and actions. Chuck D has voiced Black Americans' frustrations as far back as the Ronald Reagan era, and encouraged his listeners to visit their local polling locations to enact change. Throughout the 2010s and 2020s, Killer Mike evolved into an electoral influencer. The Atlanta rapper has galvanized community residents in his hometown, pushing them to become voter eligible and to march toward the electoral lines when the moment arises.

Killer Mike has joined another exclusive group of emcees who have vied for a political seat.[22] While Kanye West attempted to shake the political sphere with a 2020 campaign for president, the Chicago rapper collected just 60,000 votes out of an estimated 160 million total votes.[23] Other artists have attempted to make similar leaps into politics. No other rappers have aspired for the presidential seat, but legendary rapper Scarface sparked a campaign for Houston City Council in June 2019.

Luther "Uncle Luke" Campbell, formerly of the hip-hop group 2 Live Crew, announced his plans to run for mayor of his native Miami-Dade County. While he was eliminated from the race during a special election on May 24, 2011, his focus on redeveloping the infrastructure in Miami's inner-city reflected his passion for community-building. 2Chainz also alluded to running for College Park mayor in 2015, and fellow Atlanta native Killer Mike also considered running for Georgia's 55th District and as a member on a local school board.

Despite other artists' efforts, Kendrick and Cole both retained the same stance. On 2009's "I Get Up," Cole dismissed the idea of voting or leaning too heavily into politics. "Politicians hollerin' 'bout problems, but I ain't gon' vote. Keep talkin' 'bout change, still, we floatin' in the same old boat. So tell me how I'm supposed to feel when the President spoke. When he ain't never had to struggle, ain't never been broke," Cole rapped.

In time, both artists changed their tune. In 2015's "Hood Politics," Kendrick compared Compton gang leaders to elected officials in Congress. The same people wanting to clear the dangers of the street are the very people equipping low-income neighborhoods with tools of destruction—guns, drugs, and a survivalist mentality. Those same tools are used to fuel the actions that lead to the very deaths Kendrick referenced in the song's first verse.

> Ain't nothin' new but a flu of new Demo-Crips and Re-Blood-icans
> Red state versus a blue state, which one you governin'?
> They give us guns and drugs, call us thugs, make it they promise to fuck
>   with you
> No condom, they fuck with you, Obama say, "What it do?"

In delving further into politics, the cover of Kendrick's 2015 album *To Pimp a Butterfly* features an image of the rapper's friends posed in front of the White House. The digitally altered image, taken by photographer Denis Rouvre, depicts a group of Black men and children in a celebratory display. Kendrick is posed at the center with a child in his hand. Below the group's feet is a White judge with his eyes crossed out, presumed to be dead.

The image, as Kendrick described in a 2015 interview with Mass Appeal, represented "taking people from my neighborhood, and taking them around the world. And letting them see things that I've experienced."[24] The picture's lighting and exposure showed the group's worn scars and burned skin, and placed liquor bottles and cash at the foreground. The colors imbued in the artwork represented the joining of Black Americans and the White House.

It was a poignant message during President Barack Obama's administration, who just six years before made his monumental step into the Oval Office as the nation's first Black president. The President-elect didn't shy away from critiquing the genre, but opened the White House doors to Black artists of all disciplines. Under his leadership, the historically White male-run space was suddenly occupied by the likes of Jay-Z, The Roots, De La Soul, Chance the Rapper, Killer Mike, Common, and other artists who Obama felt embodied the essence of hip-hop.

Both Kendrick and Obama confessed their shared admiration. In a 2016 interview with *The Independent*,[25] Obama declared Kendrick as the hypothetical winner in a rap battle between him and Drake. "I think Drake is an outstanding entertainer, but Kendrick's last album was outstanding. Best album I think last year." The album, *TPAB*, and the song "How Much a Dollar Cost," caught the former commander-in-chief's ear, and he became an avid fan of Kendrick's music and cultural standing.

A year after the release of *TPAB*, the two men met at the very White House depicted on the cover of the Grammy-winning album. Kendrick flew to DC, and sat down with the president for Obama's My Brother's Keeper initiative.[26] Reflecting on the moment during a 2016 PSA in support of the president's mentorship program, Kendrick said: "I sat down with President Barack Obama and shared the same views. Topics concerning the inner cities, the problems, the solutions, and furthermore embracing the youth, both being aware that mentoring saves lives."

Cole tells the story of meeting President Obama on the surprise track "High for Hours," but the rapper's recollection wasn't quite as favorable. On the 2017 MLK Day release, Cole dove into the hypocrisy of a country built on the idea of freedom, when the blood and sweat of enslaved Black Americans are the source of its development. The same laborers—both enslaved and freed—built the White House, the United States Capitol, and other early government buildings, despite initial plans to import European workers.

On "High for Hours," Cole also detailed his meeting with Obama. While he was nervous to raise his hand, he brushed off the hesitation to ask the world leader a glaring question: "Does he see the struggle of his brothers in oppression?" Cole rapped. The rapper explained the president's reaction, while explaining his frustration with Obama and the snail-like pace of the political world. "As the President, what's keepin' you from helpin' niggas out?" As Obama broke down the issues plaguing the lives of Cole's close friends and loved ones, the rapper determined he was "sincere," and was stuck juggling the challenges of the political world, even as the highest-ranking leader of the nation. "But dawg, you in the chair, what's the hold-up? He said, 'There's things that I wanna fix. But you know this shit, nigga: politics," Cole divulged.

The answer, as transparent as it seemed, wasn't to Cole's satisfaction. The rapper called for a revolution to enact the change he and others wanted to see. Cole was tired of waiting for policies to flip, and for resolutions to be met. "Change is slow, always has been, always will be. But fuck that, I'ma bust back until they kill me—feel me?" It would be years before Cole discussed the political world so assertively. Eight years after "High for Hours," Cole released another political temperature check, but this time it was aimed at US President Donald Trump.

When Politics Trump Humanity

Just weeks into his second presidential term, Trump delivered several of the promises he made to millions of voters. He signed dozens of executive orders to secure the US border, a territorial boundary that was riddled with illegal crossings under the Joe Biden administration.[27]

Trump assigned fleets of Immigration and Customs Enforcement (ICE) officers to round up and deport undocumented migrants from the Southern border and other US regions, striking fear in various communities across the country. The president's migrant crackdown resulted in the wrongful detainment or deportation of several US residents, who were mistakenly targeted as illegal residents.[28] One such case involved nineteen-year-old Jose

Hermosillo. The New Mexico resident was visiting Arizona, and was held by border patrol officials in Nogales, a city roughly an hour south of Tucson, Arizona. Despite his pleas of innocence, Hermosillo was held at a privately run ICE facility in Florence, Arizona for nearly ten days. After his family tracked him down, and provided his birth certificate and social security card, federal charges were dismissed and he was released to his family. The Department of Homeland Security also mistakenly sent alarming notices to US citizens, urging them to flee the country before they faced legal repercussions. "It is time for you to leave," the notices stated.[29]

Along with deportation errors, Trump encouraged high-profile companies to strip, or completely remove, their diversity, equity, and inclusion initiatives. He also placed Tesla and SpaceX CEO Elon Musk at the head of a new government program named the Department of Government Efficiency, billed as a federal cost-cutting initiative. Two months into the Musk-led campaign, tens of thousands of federal workers lost their jobs, seemingly with no direction. The job cuts slowed the delivery of essential government services like social security, Medicaid, and veterans' benefits, destabilizing the US stock market and local economies.[30]

A month after Trump took office, Cole released the song "cLOUDs" through his Algorithm blog.[31] He tackles the experience that's come with age, the AI and streaming-obsessed generation of consumers, and the assassination attempt on Trump's life while the president was deep into his 2024 electoral campaign. "I'm that bass in your trunk, the bullet that missed Trump. The gun that jammed, Cause it seemed God had other plans," Cole proclaimed. Although Cole's mention of Trump was light, the record highlighted a fairly controversial moment in the president's campaign.

On July 13, 2024, Trump narrowly survived an assassination attempt during a campaign rally in Butler, PA.[32] Shortly after taking the stage, a lone gunman outside the security perimeter opened fire on the then-Republican nominee. One bullet hit Trump in his right ear before he ducked down. Instead of immediately fleeing the scene, Trump stood up, with blood smeared across his face, and pumped his fist yelling, "Fight," before he was rushed off the stage. The gunman was a twenty-year-old Thomas Matthew Crooks, who was killed by a sniper seconds after opening fire at the event. His failed assassination attempt of Trump resulted in the killing of one spectator, who was shot dead while protecting his family from the gunfire. Two others were critically injured. A reported second assassination attempt was made on Trump's life at the Trump International Golf Club in West Palm Beach, Fl on September 15, 2024.

Despite the life-threatening attempts, Trump was standing victorious on election night in November 2024. He secured the win against Democratic nominee Kamala Harris, who stepped in Biden's place with hopes of being the first Black woman president in the country's history.

Cole's "cLOUDs" was released after Trump's inauguration on January 20, 2025, a moment that sparked a series of questions from political pundits, reporters, and the American public. Tech billionaires such as X owner Elon Musk, Amazon founder Jeff Bezos, TikTok CEO Shou Zi Chew, and Meta's Mark Zuckerberg were just a handful of billionaires seen supporting Trump.

The inauguration stirred a bevy of think pieces, with Biden's warnings of a "dangerous" oligarch flashing in front of the nation.[33] Cole's track addressed the wealth-concentrated administration head on. "Served on a plate with sirloin steak to billionaires who don't care, the world's gon' break. Long as they make money off it, pain brings profit," he rapped.

Nonacceptance … from the Heart

As far back as Trump's first presidential term, Cole and Kendrick expressed their disdain for the political leader. Despite the millions of voters who elected Trump to presidency, Kendrick averted any and all support for the billionaire in 2017's "The Heart Part 4." "Donald Trump is a chump, know how we feel, punk. Tell 'em that God comin," he rapped on the one-off single, which featured samples from Faith Evans' "I Love You" and James Brown's "Don't Tell a Lie About Me and I Won't Tell the Truth on You." The "Heart Part 4" didn't make it onto his next album, *DAMN*, but the record served as a prelude to a masterwork that struck a balance between Kendrick's own personal dealings, and the challenges America would face under Trump's presidency.

Kendrick's peripheral mentions of Trump are scattered throughout the Pulitzer Prize-winning album. He took jabs at Fox News and described the shock of the 2016 election on "LUST." "We all woke up, trynna tune to the daily news. Lookin' for confirmation, hopin' election wasn't true. All of us worried, all of us buried, and our feelings deep. None of us married to his proposal, make us feel cheap," he rapped.

Months after the release of *DAMN*, Kendrick's interest in talking about Trump began to wane. In a 2017 interview with *Rolling Stone*, the then thirty-year-old rapper said criticizing the current president was like "beating a dead horse."[34] Instead of continued discourse, he challenged opposers to take action, rather than lie dormant while Trump conspired to enact policies and executive orders that, Kendrick felt, disproportionately affected Black communities. "You just get to a point where you're tired of talking about it," he said. "It weighs you down and it drains your energy when you're speaking about something or someone that's completely ridiculous."

Cole decided to call out the source of his frustrations by name. Before headlining Rolling Loud Festival 2018, Cole sat down with legendary radio host Angie Martinez at producer Salaam Remi's studio in Miami, Florida.[35] Cole rejected Trump's ideals and political views as his first presidential term was in full swing. He didn't show favor toward liberal or far-right agendas. Instead, he called for more grassroots movements that were at the center of empowering everyday people, no matter the political affiliations or ties. "I know what resonates with me and what don't," Cole said to Martinez. "I just use him as an example of somebody who's like … Those people are dangerous to me, they [are] dangerous. [They're] manipulative."

Along with the throes of the political world, Kendrick and Cole have said sociopolitical imbalance often leaves Black families most vulnerable. The two rappers often reflect on their own upbringings as proof. Kendrick addressed the pressures and long-term effects of violence, drugs, and gang culture in his hometown of Compton. Cole pointed to his single-parent upbringing in the Sandhills region of North Carolina, and how the domestic violence and verbal abuse he witnessed shaped him as an artist, husband, and father. They hearken back to these experiences to show listeners how common these issues are in other households, while highlighting Black women's roles in maintaining the nucleus of the Black family.

Empowering Sistas and the Black Family

Mainstream rap records throughout the years have perpetuated a level of misogyny. While there is now a resurgence of popular women in hip-hop, female emcees such as Nicki Minaj, Glorilla, Cardi B, Doechii, and Meg Thee Stallion have launched misandrist takes of their own. Historically, it has been an overwhelmingly male-dominated genre. This is both in the booth and in the boardroom. Due to this occurrence, the perspective of male emcees has often been the dominant narrative being conveyed.

In rap music, a "bitch" here or "hoe" there is common. Women are often hypersexualized and utilized as merely props within rap music. Record labels constantly flood the market with music that demeans women without any regard for the cultural climate or progression of women in society. "Every generation has misogyny, but others have it in more profound ways," Temple University professor and attorney Timothy Welbeck said. "Somewhere between the late 1990s and the early 2000s it hit its apex."

While Cole and Kendrick are not completely exempt from dropping a misogynist bar here or there within their rhymes, they have each made a conscious effort to empower and highlight the narratives of Black women within their works. J. Cole has built a large fanbase of women, partially by highlighting the struggles and pain they face within his music. On Cole's debut album, he released a powerful record called "Lost Ones." The song is framed around the conversation between a young man and woman dealing with an unplanned pregnancy. Instead of Cole solely rapping from a male perspective, he conveys the perspective of the young woman as well.

In the first verse, Cole raps from the viewpoint of a young man who finds out a woman who he had been intimate with is pregnant. He expresses how he feels unready and unprepared to raise a child and encourages her to have an abortion. In the second verse of the song, he switches to the woman's perspective, who is angry and insulted by both the proposition and the thought that it was his decision to make. The song was thought-provoking and highlighted the reality that many young men and women face in these circumstances.

Kendrick Lamar has also been intentional about advocating for the often-muzzled perspective of women within hip-hop. In the age of social media, the pressure for women to look "perfect" is having a real impact on society. Social media often promotes unrealistic beauty standards by frequently highlighting edited images of women, which predominantly emphasize specific body, hair, and skin types. Research suggests that exposure to this over time can likely lead to serious issues such as body dysmorphia and low self-esteem.[36] In a verse on Kendrick's hit song "HUMBLE," he confronts these issues directly. He references "afros," "stretch marks," and "natural bodies" as attractive and desirable elements of a woman. He also shames the use of Photoshop on social media pictures, to combat this new trend.

Both Cole and Kendrick have amplified the careers of important women in hip-hop through their collaborations and features. One of them includes fellow conscious artist Rapsody. Many casual rap fans discovered Rapsody on Kendrick's song "Complexion," a song that highlighted the deep roots of colorism in the Black community. Cole also collaborated with the heralded emcee on her record "Sojourner," a song that shined a light on her 2019 project called *Eve*. Spotlighting a skilled female emcee with a progressive message like Rapsody emphasizes the importance of women in hip-hop, especially those with poignant stories and messages to share.

Morale in the Black Family

On April 18, 2022, Kendrick tweeted out a link to the website called Oklama. com. Many theorize that he used this word due to its origins in the language Chahta Anumpa, which is native to the Choctaw Indigenous people.[37] In this language, the word Oklama means "my people," and in the Choctaw translated bible, it's often used by prophets or poets when addressing God's people. This is potentially Kendrick believing that the messaging to come was bestowed upon him by the most high. Kendrick used this website to give his thoughts and updates about new music, but most memorably release the name of an upcoming album called *Mr. Morale & the Big Steppers*, along with the release date of May 13, 2022.

Mr. Morale & the Big Steppers was released digitally as a double-disc project with eighteen songs. The Black family is a central theme of this project. The album presents itself as a therapy session for Lamar and centers around issues and trauma that can sometimes plague communities. In possibly Kendrick's most transparent album, both his own family trauma and narratives he witnessed in his youth are displayed with full transparency. On "Mother I Sober," he discusses generational trauma and pertinent issues such as molestation, including a moment when his own mother asked if he was ever abused.

In the song "Father Time," Kendrick talks in depth about fatherhood, masculinity, and his own relationship with his father growing up. He details how his father was extremely tough on him in an effort to prepare him for the world, and how he had to suppress his emotions as a young man to avoid appearing weak. The song presents a full scope of the trauma that Black men often face, and how that trauma impacts their children, creating a cycle of emotional suppression.

> *Daddy issues, hid my emotions, never expressed myself*
> *Men should never show feelings, being sensitive never helped*
> *His momma died, I asked him why he going back to work so soon?*
> *His first reply was, "Son, that's life, and bills got no silver spoon."*

Kendrick also tackles the harsh realities of some dysfunctional relationships on this album. On "We Cry Together," he presents a hostile and heated back-and-forth argument between a man and a woman, where they discuss everything from infidelity to the use of verbal blows aimed at hurting one another. This extreme display of dysfunction highlights how a lack of communication and broken individuals can cause pure chaos. This album's strong focus on maturity, growth, mental health, and interpersonal relationships intentionally seeks to start important conversations about how Black people can move forward together through healing. Its emphasis on mental health, therapy, and self-reflection makes it a thought-provoking project with a clear goal of progression

I Am Not Your Savior

Among the many rare qualities they bear, the mark of Kendrick and Cole's greatness is their ability to capture all of these themes, and channel them into radio-friendly hits, block party anthems, and club bangers. Songs like "Mask Off (Remix)" elevated what would have been another drug-inspired Future hit, and turned it into a record that explored fame, success, and the complexities of the Black American experience. The same can be said for Cole's "ATM," a song that glorifies the endless drive for riches and materialism at first listen. The final verse dispels the blinding effects of such a lifestyle—one that can be far more detrimental than helpful if placed in the wrong hands.

By addressing politics, mass incarceration, and the splintering of the Black family, Kendrick and Cole have become social and cultural leaders. While it would be wrong to narrowly categorize them as sociopolitical artists, there's no ignoring the impact their music and messaging have made on music fans, community leaders, and civil rights advocates. They have owned their positions as ambassadors of hip-hop, while also revealing their imperfections as men, romantic partners, artists, and social leaders.

On songs like 2022's "Savior," Kendrick unraveled all of his personal flaws and past failures. And along with criticizing younger "mumble" rappers, Cole's "1985" acknowledges his own complicity in certain negative hip-hop tropes. Their transparency is what makes Cole and Kendrick prolific artists and changemakers. They have never positioned themselves as "saviors," or the single source for societal change. The two rappers simply place a mirror to America as a call for urgency, and take matters into their own hands. How it's perceived, and the actions taken in the months and years to come, is ultimately up to the listener. But they understand that more can and should be done for Black progression.

When people reference an activist, they often envision community organizers. They think of advocates who lead protests, boycotts, and actively disrupt systems to combat the injustices that oppressed communities face. When it comes to thought leaders, people may acknowledge academics or writers such as James Baldwin, W. E. B. Du Bois, or Cornel West as activists within their own right.

Kendrick and Cole, as well as the conscious acts who have come before and after them, serve as artistic activists. They move the needle as thought leaders and shift cultural and societal norms through their messaging. They use their platforms of millions to shed light on serious world issues ranging from poverty to mass incarceration. In a nation where readership is down in record numbers, they serve as a crucial catalyst for critical thought.[38] They challenge the status quo through potent lyrics as their form of activism, as artists such as Marvin Gaye, Sam Cooke, Nina Simone, Billie Holiday, Bessie Smith, and Michael Jackson chose to do within their respective genres.

6

College, Capitalism, and Religion

The foundation of hip-hop was first predicated on emceeing, breakdancing, DJing, and graffiti, with knowledge serving as the fifth element of a genre and culture that's expanded exponentially over time. Knowledge was once defined by understanding hip-hop history, values, and social impact, but in time, the world of academia began knocking on hip-hop's door.

It didn't take long for the genre to trickle into the world of higher education. In 1991, Howard University, a historically Black university in Washington DC, became the first college to offer hip-hop courses. The implementation of hip-hop studies later expanded to institutions such as Harvard, New York University, and Duke. In 2021, Loyola University New Orleans became the first institution to offer a full hip-hop and R&B bachelor's program in 2021, and schools like Johns Hopkins soon followed suit.[1] Hip-hop studies became interdisciplinary, and universities would begin offering hip-hop courses in departments such as African American Studies, English, Communication Studies, Musicology and Political Science.

While traditional scholars were implementing the genre and culture into a variety of disciplines throughout the academy, there were also several emcees and producers taking on roles at academic institutions themselves. Hip-hop legends like Lupe Fiasco (MIT and John Hopkins),[2] Bun B (Rice University),[3] and 9th Wonder (North Carolina Central University, Duke University,

Harvard University)[4] would go on to teach a variety of unique hip-hop and rap-centered courses. This occurrence added even more validity to hip-hop studies as a discipline, and brought attention to the plethora of ways in which hip-hop can be used as a tool to enlighten the youth.

While more educational institutions began to embrace hip-hop as a powerful force within media and society, conservative pundits like Candace Owens, Jason Whitlock, Ben Shapiro, and others still choose to spotlight the genre's less profound elements as a way to demonize the culture. While conscious rappers have existed since hip-hop gained prominence as a dominant genre, the rap songs that glorified behaviors perceived as dangerous or inappropriate were used to stereotype the entire genre and label it as inherently "bad." This occurrence further divided the culture, placing artists in boxes where they are either creating music that seeks to educate and enlighten, or creating music that is purely entertainment with no redeemable qualities.

As rap music continued to entertain and influence culture, it also continued to be used as a tool for knowledge and was intertwined within the educational system. The connection between Black movements and education is one filled with tales of resistance and the constant desire to move the Black community forward.

Bars and Social Justice

It's no surprise that many hip-hop groups, particularly those with politically charged messaging, were formed at academic institutions. Black intellectuals were able to connect at colleges to learn, share knowledge, and discuss solutions to issues directly impacting their communities. That's how civil rights organizations like the Student Nonviolent Coordinating Committee, or SNCC, and the Black Panther Party were sparked. After four Black college students protested at a segregated Greensboro, North Carolina lunch counter in 1960, veteran civil rights organizers Ella Baker invited all the students who participated in the sit-ins to a conference at Shaw University in Raleigh. Nearly 200 students showed up between April 16–18, 1960, thus creating the leading channel for student activism during the civil rights movement.

A similar connection was formed between future Black Panther Party founders Huey P. Newton and Bobby Seal. The two men met in 1962 at Merritt College in Oakland, California. They joined the Afro-American Association, which was founded as an African history study group by graduate and law students at the University of California, Berkeley. Newton and Seal participated in the group's readings, open forums, and other traditions centered on Black nationalistic rhetoric expressed by Malcolm X, Robert L. Williams, and other historical figures.

Four years later, Newton and Seal left the organization to start the Black Panther Party for Self-Defense in October 1966, taking on a more militaristic approach to combat discrimination and racism-fueled police attacks. The revolution also launched social programs that gave Black Americans access to free education, food, and healthcare services.

These movements were critical at a time when employment opportunities and avenues to higher education were increasingly difficult for Black Americans in the years following World War II.

Organizations like SNCC, the Black Panther Party, and other socially charged factions stepped in to challenge oppressive powers. As evidenced by their launch points, college campuses became a central point for Black intellectualism, and the grounds for future change-makers to join others in pursuit of racial equality. With hip-hop later becoming its own vehicle for social change, rap artists would soon follow the path of Newton, Seal, Kwame Ture, and other civil rights leaders.

Several artists and legendary rap groups emerged while balancing their college coursework. Conscious rap duo Dead Prez was founded at Florida Agricultural and Mechanical University (FAMU) where the members M-1 and stic.man first met.[5] Legendary hip-hop figures Chuck D and Flavor Flav met at Adelphi College in New York, where they would begin curating the legendary group Public Enemy.[6] While attending Adelphi University in Long Island, New York, rapper Chuck D met Flavor Flav in 1982 while studying graphic design at the small private institution. Between designing posters for up-and-coming artists, Chuck D became a DJ at the campus radio station, WBAU 90.3FM. His show was called "The Super Spectrum Mix Hour," and it was created for members of his group, Spectrum City.

That's how he met his other future collaborators Bill Stephney and Hank Shocklee, two members of the acclaimed production team, The Bomb Squad. Chuck D, Stephney, and Shocklee convinced Flav to start his own one-hour show for Saturday nights, and soon the group used their combined musical powers and charisma to start their own group. Once Chuck D put his voice on Shocklee's "Public Enemy No. 1," one of rap's most dynamic and seminal groups was born. If it weren't for the campus radio station at Adelphi, the collective power of Chuck D, Flavor Flav, and The Bomb Squad may have never come to fruition. Like the revolutionary pioneers that preceded them, these artists would go on to push political and social boundaries and rhetoric through their musical contributions.

Some prolific acts even come from a lineage of professors. Talib Kweli was raised by two college professors. His mother was an English instructor at Medgar Evers College, and his father was an administrator at Adelphi University. Kanye West's mother, Dr. Donda West, was also a professor and Department Chair of the English Department at Chicago State University. The marriage between hip-hop and education is longstanding and complex. Poetically, a fictitious sitcom would also play a major role in this union.

A Different World United

In many ways, the connection between hip-hop and higher-ed bloomed at Hillman College, a fictional historically Black university that was the setting of the popular TV sitcom, *A Different World*. Following the success of the hit series *The Cosby Show*, fan favorite Denise Huxtable (played by Lisa Bonet) became the lead of the Bill Cosby-developed spinoff. *A Different World* premiered on September 24, 1987, with Bonet's independent and wildly stylish character moving from her parents Cliff (Bill Cosby) and Clair Huxtable's (Phylicia Rashad) Brooklyn brownstone to Hillman College's Virginia campus. The fictional site was modeled after Spelman College and Clark Atlanta University in Atlanta, Georgia, and the actual exterior shots of Hillman were of Spelman campus.

The original premise for *A Different World*, which ran from 1987 to 1993 on NBC, was to follow a White student as they navigated college life at an

HBCU.[7] In a 2001 interview with the Television Academy Foundation, late TV director Jay Sandrich said the "preliminary cast" originally had Golden Globe-nominated actress Meg Ryan in the lead role, with Bonet's Denise character playing one of her roommates. After Ryan's agents turned down the role, deciding "she shouldn't go into television," the series was reimagined with Bonet at the center of the show.

The original format of the series didn't last long. Bonet—then married to musician Larry Kravitz—left the show after becoming pregnant with future actress and director Zoë Kravitz, and co-star Maria Tomei's character was written off the series after the inaugural season. The show kicked into stride with Kadeem Hardison and Jasmine Guy's characters "Dwayne Wayne" and "Whitley Gilbert" stepping in as the leading characters, creating what many consider to be one of the most iconic romances in sitcom history.

Along with its deep ensemble of characters, *A Different World* is far more remembered for its general promotion of HBCUs and special guest appearances from hip-hop stars like 2Pac and Heavy D. It drew connections between college life and hip-hop culture—from the style of characters' clothes to the dialogue exchanged between them. There was a substantial effort to keep *A Different World* attune with the trends, cultural moments, and social issues directly impacting Black Americans, and hip-hop occasionally served as the backdrop. The show inspired Black Americans from all corners to pursue their education, without fear of being ridiculed, or forced to conform to be viewed positively by non-Black students and administrators.

While few rappers explicitly credit *A Different World* for their college journeys, there's no denying the influence of the show. It opened people's eyes to college life.

It inspired generations of minorities to pursue higher learning, and several rappers are among those who filled college applications, packed their bags, and ventured to college campuses. The list of college attendees-turned-rap stars includes Common, Wale, Megan Thee Stallion, Chuck D, Logic, Lecrae, and J. Cole, who regularly referenced *A Different World* on his early mixtapes.

On 2010's "The Last Stretch," the North Carolina native rapped, "I showed you love, I brought you through, I gave you pounds right? Aye, in my face, you knew your place and so you smile, right? So why I'm here, and now you talking like a little girl? You sound like Whitley, nigga. Me? I'm from a different world." And on "Best Friend," Cole rapped, "Know we be arguing, but ain't you riding with me. We breaking up, we making up like Dwayne Wayne and Whitley. You throw things, you broke things, use both hands and hit me. And right when you call the law, I'll tell my boy to come get me."

While some hip-hop acts credit their college experience for their emergence, another artist said dropping out of school was the source of his success. While Kanye West's late mother, Dr. Donda West, was a well respected academic, his debut album, *The College Dropout*, could easily be considered *anti-college*.

The College Dropout

While shows like *A Different World*, Spike Lee's *School Daze*, and other media encouraged Black Americans and hip-hop fans to pursue higher education, Kanye West's landmark debut took aim at the college lifestyle. Instead of following the path of other rap stars, and his own mother's guidance, West, known as "Ye," made an album that celebrated his decision to drop out of Chicago State University to pursue the highest level of rap stardom.

From the album's second track, "We Don't Care," the pink polo-wearing and backpack-yielding rapper dove into his infatuation with the crack dealers, robbers, and street hustlers that surrounded him in his youth. Criminal activity was the most lavish form of success that many of them witnessed, which made the pathway to college and the middle class far less appealing. With the pressures of the South Side Chicago streets, the music industry, and his own expectations, West delves into how he and others across Black America wrestle with similar societal issues, economic obstacles, and other challenges. Being in college wasn't the ultimate goal for him. Rap stardom was his top priority.

> *My freshman year I was going through hella problems. 'Till I built up the nerve to drop my ass up out of college. My teacher said I was a loser, I told her, "Why don't you kill me? I give a fuck if you fail me, I'm gonna follow. My heart, and if you follow the charts, to the plaques or the stacks. You ain't gotta guess who's back,"* West rapped on "Get 'Em High."

Throughout *The College Dropout*, West maligns the idea that college is where dreams are transformed into reality. Those moments, he contends, happen outside the confines of a higher-ed institution. On "School Spirit," West said the same person who graduates at the top of their class could end up serving him at a Cheesecake Factory. And on "Lil Jimmy Skit," he ridicules the capitalistic side of college life. The people securing college degrees, he claims, are the same ones leaving an endless trail of college debt behind, and fewer opportunities for their families to follow their own ambitions.

While this sentiment may have been true for some, research would call the claims made by West ignorant at best, and irresponsibly detrimental at worst. According to the U.S. Bureau of Labor Statistics in 2004, the year of *The College Dropout*'s release, high school graduates with no college experience earned $562 a week, while college graduates holding at least a bachelor's degree earned a median income of $996 per week.[8] When looking specifically at the Black workforce, this same outcome was sustained. Research indicates that Black professionals with a bachelor's degree earned approximately $18,298 more annually than those with only a high school diploma.[9] While West was able to achieve the rare outcome of becoming wealthy as a rapper and producer without graduating from college, the fact still remained that Black youth at the time had a better chance of achieving a level of financial success and stability with a college degree than without one.

On his sophomore project, *Late Registration*, West continued the same rhetoric. Skits highlighting the fictional fraternity, Broke Phi Broke, were dispersed throughout the project. Ultimately, the two albums are about perseverance. Through poverty, violent-ridden streets, unconvinced record execs, or his own miscalculations, West was determined to fulfill his dreams— college or not. Whatever stigma was attached to being a dropout, he wasn't letting it slow his momentum. And with the success of his college-linked trilogy—*The College Dropout* to 2007's behemoth *Graduation*—he certainly worked his magic. "From the streets to the league, from an eighth to a key. But you graduate when you make it up outta the streets. From the moments of pain, look how far we done came. Haters saying you changed, now you doing your thing," West rapped on "Good Morning."

West wasn't alone in his stance. J. Cole also criticized the predatory methods taken by college institutions and student loan companies. On "Blow Up" from

Cole's *Friday Night Lights*, he rejected other people's inclinations, deciding the path he's chosen as an artist is the one that best suited him. He was far less interested in garnering additional federal student loan payments for graduate school. "Mama say I should reconsider law school. That means I wear a suit and bend the truth and feel awful. Hell naw, got a degree, but what cost you? You make a good salary just to pay Sallie Mae," he rapped. However, that didn't deter Cole's feelings about his college experience, nor the advantages he felt after obtaining his degree in 2007.

"Immediately, I feel like those kids in college can feel my story, just because they feel like I was just in their shoes, which I was," Cole said in a 2010 interview with DJ Vlad.

> And I just feel like it allows me to be smarter business-wise, and it just gave me a whole different experience talking about what most rappers don't even get to really talk about. It doesn't make me better than any other rapper, there's a bunch of rappers who never went to college, like Nas or [Jay-Z], that are geniuses. So, it doesn't necessarily make me better, but it gives me a whole other aspect of life to pick from.[10]

The College Dropout was the first widely respected mainstream hip-hop album to place college at the forefront of the project's subject matter, for better or worse. This project paved the way for normalizing hip-hop records that were delivered from the perspective of a college student. While Kanye West presented the perspective of a college dropout, J. Cole entered the industry and furthered the conversation by conveying the perspective of a recent college graduate.

One key element that Cole homed in on was the survivors' guilt that many Black first-generation students face in college. While presented with a golden opportunity to advance by going away to school, many leave behind friends and family who are left to less optimal circumstances. On the outro of a song called "College Boy" on his debut mixtape, Cole would talk at the end and express this feeling, while still encouraging the community to consider college as an option. He stated:

> *I'm tryna tell y'all niggas, man, college is a good look*
> *A real good look, my nigga*

For more reasons than one, man
Know they try to keep us out of that shit, though

On the intro of the same song, he also shouted out local Carolina colleges and universities. Cole entered into hip-hop using his platform to raise awareness of college and normalizing being a graduate himself. His transparent storytelling and testimonials came across as genuine, unlike many of his peers who appeared on the scene with rhymes filled with luxury living and tales of a criminal past. Former HipHopDX editor and hip-hop journalist Justin Hunte touched on how Cole's story was one that allowed him to resonate with a large listener base.

> I mean, J Cole had a very familiar, tangible story, you know. I mean, here's a guy who grew up in Fayetteville. He went to college. He went to St John's, he loved basketball, and he loved rap and he loved hip hop. I mean, that is a very common story. I look at a lot of these artists as following the Kanye umbrella in the sense that he was going by his real name. You know that Kanye worked at the GAP, and that J Cole went to St John's.

While some rappers speak about college from a lighthearted and party-filled standpoint like Asher Roth did in his hit song "I Love College," some choose to address it differently. Many emcees have rejected and spoken against the institution of college in their lyrics. Some do it subtly by bragging about how they have obtained riches without ever attending a college or university. "I done made a million dollars, and I ain't even go to college," is an example of this from the late artist Rich Homie Quan. These types of lines are a common braggadocious way for artists to convey that they were able to amass great success without higher education, either by choice or due to it not being a feasible option for them.

Other artists have taken much more constructively critical stances on educational institutions. Several have criticized the price of attending college and how it doesn't promise economic success. In America, the rising cost of education and predatory lending practices has led to a student loan crisis. With less inherited wealth on average, this dilemma is increasingly detrimental for the Black community. According to the National Center for

Education Statistics, in 2020 Black graduates held the highest average debt after graduations, averaging $58,400 of debt just four years after completing a bachelor's degree.[11] This occurrence can disrupt many milestones that young Black adults hope to reach after graduation. Buying a home, starting a family, and advancing economically can often be hindered by this starting point.

While often advocating for college as an option for inner city youth, J. Cole also criticized the American educational system by emphasizing the burden of student loan debt. On the song "Villematic," Cole starts the record by expressing how after college many students are left to fend for themselves. He rapped:

To the college kids, no scholarships, startin' your semester
Unpacking your suitcases, fillin' up your dresser
Enjoy it while you got it, after that, it's God bless you
Life is your professor, know that bitch is gon' test you

While Cole was able to speak about the importance of education in the Black community from his own undergraduate experiences, Kendrick entered the game articulating his messages from a different viewpoint. His knowledge of Black history, activism, and resistance was evident since one of his first cult classic records "HiiiPoWeR" referenced Black activists such as Malcolm X, Huey P. Newton, and Marcus Garvey. While he didn't emerge in the industry with a college degree, he did step into the game with knowledge based on his own studies and experiences as a Black man from Compton, California. For listeners, it was clear that he was intelligent and knowledgeable about the systemic issues around him. His lyrical brilliance and intricate perspectives mirrored that of prodigies like Nas, an emcee from Queens, New York, who dropped out of school in the 8th grade.[12] They both rapped about their inner-city experiences with complexity, nuance, and a level of wisdom beyond their years.

Ironically, despite entering the industry without obtaining any secondary education, one of the largest critiques of Kendrick's music throughout the years is that it is too complex and lyrical. His often layered storytelling, intricate wordplay, and advanced vocabulary is sometimes scoffed at by casual music fans who find it hard to follow along with his rhetoric. This same display of brilliance as a writer is what propelled him to legendary hip-hop status and encouraged academics to study and teach his works in latter years.

Higher Learning

Artists like Kendrick are proof that sheer knowledge and wisdom can be obtained outside of a classroom. Like other rap savants before his ascension, Kendrick took a non-traditional route to higher education. At eighteen, he briefly considered studying psychology or astronomy. The straight-A student graduated from Centennial High School in 2005, but later decided to bypass college to pursue his musical career full-time.[13] In a 2012 interview with *FUSE*, Kendrick opened up about his decision. "Not experiencing college, at least for a semester, that was my biggest regret, doing it while I was in my teens," he said. "Now, all these years have passed, I done got deep into a musical career, it's gonna be hard to find time unless I really put my focus into it."

Kendrick actually put his past regret into action. He noted that college was always in the back of his mind. Little was known about his own academic pursuits until a TikTok post in February 2025 showed the superstar sitting in a class on the campus of the University of California, Los Angeles. The images, which dated back to 2022, garnered millions of engagements in a matter of days. "pov: just a normal day at UCLA," the caption read. The TikToker described the feeling of disbelief when he saw Kendrick. "He was incredibly kind and humble," the TikToker user wrote. "I didn't realize who he was at the time—I just saw people asking for photos, and I took some too. It wasn't until later that someone told me who he was."[14]

While he doesn't have a known college degree under his belt, Kendrick has taken up intellectual arms in other ways. Rather than books, Kendrick said most of his wisdom derives from studying the rhetoric of other musical artists and civil rights leaders. He's drawn life lessons from the cerebral poetry of Nas, the unrelenting passion of 2Pac, and the calculated mind of Malcolm X. In navigating the world, and reflecting on his evolving insights, Kendrick has also looked to his own family, friends, and others for guidance. "For me, it's about communicating with people," Kendrick said in a 2014 interview with *The Madd Hatta Morning Show*.[15]

> I was one of them kids that was in the house [at] six, seven years old, having full conversations with grown people that was at the party. So, taking that lifestyle and going across the world and talking to other people from other different cultures and walks of life, it gives you a little bit more wisdom. I had to see things the way you see it and make sense of everything that's going on around you.

Despite not graduating from a formal secondary school himself, Kendrick's art inspired college professors to form entire curricula based on his work. In 2025, Temple University professor Timothy Welbeck announced that he would be teaching a Fall course on the emcee and his contributions to the society, culture, and genre. Welbeck states:

> Beyond the spellbinding technical proficiency he wields, the legions of adoring fans who sing his every praise and massive critical acclaim he has amassed, Kendrick Lamar's riveting content has presented the complex dimensions of the lived experience of Africans who live in urban centers across the US, particularly those hailing from his native Compton. His impressive work exhibits the wide-ranging scope of Afrocentric thought in contemporary mediums and thus is worthy of scholarly interrogation.

A Spiritual Journey

Through close observations and one-on-one conversations, Kendrick's ideas about race, culture, and religion have taken on new shapes. As his thoughts or past declarations have shifted, so has his music. The way people interpret his messaging has also changed throughout his discography.

Following the release of *To Pimp a Butterfly*, some listeners painted Kendrick to be a zany "hotep." In ancient Egypt, a hotep means "to be satisfied" or "at peace." It can also be referred to as an "offering," presented to a deity or the deceased as a form of sacrifice. In recent decades, Hotepism has been used to describe Black Americans who lean on ancient Egyptian history and mythology as a source of pride. Some historians consider it a subculture that celebrates pseudohistory and the appropriation of Egyptian culture, while followers of the Hotep movement see it as a social justice campaign focused on reclaiming the diminished power, knowledge, and history that was stripped from African American communities.

Criticism of the Hotep movement has evolved into social media fodder. Internet memes depict Hotep followers as baseless conspiracists who spew inaccurate ideas about history, disrespect women, denounce homosexuality, and disapprove of interracial marriages. Given this misdirection, it's easy to conflate the ideals or misconceptions of Hotepism. There are countless offshoots and more radicalized groups of Hotepism that don't effectively represent the movement. Despite growing speculation, Kendrick's *To Pimp a Butterfly* doesn't symbolize or reflect any of the doctrine or teachings.

While *To Pimp a Butterfly* leaned into themes of societal exploitation and penned stories that reflected the struggles endured by the African diaspora, it doesn't draw from Hotepism. Neither the word nor hotep rhetoric is present in the project. However, Kendrick's follow up, *DAMN*, rightly drew attention to a new religious turn for the artist. On the song "YAH," Kendrick sheds the same messaging blared by members of the Hebrew Israelites, a religious organization largely made up of African Americans who claim an ancestral connection to the Israelites in the Bible. "I'm an Israelite, don't call me black no more," he rapped on the 2017 track. "That word is only a color, it's not facts no more."

Along with referring to Jesus by his Hebrew name, "Yeshua," Hebrew Israelites also claim Black, Native, and Latin American people have been "punished" racially and systemically because of their disobedience of God. Some Hebrew Israelite subgroups believe Native and Latin Americans are among the twelve lost tribes of ancient Israel, while others differ in ideology and messaging entirely under the same banner.

Kendrick has never declared a direct connection to the religious organization, but he has fairly close ties to the Hebrew Israelite movement. The rapper's cousin Carl Duckworth, who goes by Karni Ben Israel, was connected to a Hebrew Israelite group based in New York.[16] Duckworth appeared on "FEAR," where he was heard delivering a voice message telling Kendrick he would continue to suffer in this world until he recognizes he is "an Israelite according to the Bible."

Beyond the two moments on *DAMN*, and several images of Kendrick and Duckworth together, Kendrick hasn't been connected to Hebrew Israelite doctrine since. Instead, he's continued to parse a wide range of religious themes in his music, leaving his listeners and fans to interpret the meaning behind certain symbols, verses, and music video moments.

What's always been clear is that Kendrick—like so many of his listeners—is figuring it out as he goes. He's continuing to educate himself on different ideologies, doctrine, theories, and political injustices. Whether it's music, religion, race, culture, or fatherhood, he calls back to his imperfections as a source of transformation. As he and Cole have transformed their lives, and sought to further educate themselves on the world they have grown to see, they have supported other people's journeys. Not only among their loved ones, but the journeys their fans have embarked on as well.

It's in the Scripture

For decades, hip-hop artists have weaved religious themes into their music. Artists like Kanye West and Chance the Rapper have infused Gospel music and Christian messaging into their albums. Other artists such as DMX incorporated raw and intensely spiritual moments with songs like "Prayer (Skit)," and Grammy-winning Christian rap star Lecrae Devaughn Moore, or simply Lecrae, has lifted the subgenre to mainstream audiences.

Kendrick has talked about his faith extensively throughout his discography. He's revealed the complexities of navigating the entertainment industry (and life) as a man of God. No better example is 2009's "Faith." The song was from Kendrick's self-titled EP, the first project he released under his birth name. The track is interlocked by three verses about people whose belief in God dwindles as their life conditions grow harsher. The first verse draws from the real devastation Kendrick faced following the real-life murder of a close friend.

I'm giving testimonies to strangers I never met. Hopped on the pulpit and told them how I was truly blessed. Felt like I was free from all my sins when the service was over. Walked out the church, and got a call that my homie was murdered. Then lost my faith again.

After hearing the song, Lecrae reached out to Kendrick for the theodicy-themed record. "It touched me and I reached out to him like, 'Hey, can I talk to you about it?'" Lecrae recalled in a 2015 interview with BuzzFeed. The two sparked a friendship in the years since, with both men communing about life as imperfect Christians who love rap.[17]

Kendrick has talked openly about his Christianity, even proclaiming his musical career as divinely inspired. "I got a greater purpose," Kendrick said in a 2014 interview with Complex. "God put something in my heart to get across and that's what I'm going to focus on, using my voice as an instrument and doing what needs to be done."[18] But other religious or spiritual elements have surfaced throughout his career. Whether it's intentional, or not, has long been up for interpretation.

As he's evolved as a man and artist, Kendrick noted in a 2024 interview with SZA that his relationship with a higher power has grown even more resonant over the years. "Ain't no bullshit. Ain't no cliché. But I literally talk to God," Kendrick said. "Like, it's to a point where I'll be starting to think I'm going crazy. But then He has to remind me, 'No, this is really me.'"

Cole has also addressed his religious affiliations. On "Change," he references a man stuck between his faith in God, and his ties to a life of sin. While he's hoping to get into heaven's doors, he's also hustling the streets to feed himself and his family. But from Cole's view, the God he serves isn't "spitcful like them white folks that control the jail," he raps on the 2016 track. "See, I believe if God is real, He'd never judge a man / Because He knows us all, and therefore He would understand."

In later works, Cole said he considered practicing Islam as a religion. On his 2021 release *The Off-Season*, he acknowledged the wisdom that he gathered from the Quran in the song "let. go. my. hand." In his frequent open and transparent nature, Cole admits in the song that he doesn't have the discipline it takes to stick with the religious practices.

The two artists have both talked about how their shared practices and flaws as God-fearing men have morphed them into the individuals they are today. Along with seeking to be better versions of themselves, they have been inspired to use their platforms as musical stars for the betterment of others, including those seeking a higher education or career in the creative arts.

Rap for Change

Beyond their inspiring messages in songs and interviews, Kendrick and Cole have put their calls for social justice, equality, and advancement to action. The two artists have invested both their time and money to uplift the communities they come from, and the people who have been firm supporters of theirs from the start of their careers.

Back in 2013, Cole superfan Cierra Bosarge-Fussell called into Hot 107.9 in Philadelphia, hoping the rap star would wish her a happy birthday.[19] Months later, the South Jersey native received a call from the Dreamville artist, who wished her a happy birthday and invited her to meet him in person. When they met, the Washington Township High School student handed him a letter detailing her life. She touched on being adopted, withstanding her parents' drug addictions and incarceration. "At the time both parents were in prison, so I asked him if he could come to my graduation since they can't," Bosarge-Fussell told Complex in 2015.[20]

Cole not only agreed, he responded directly to Bosarge-Fussell, telling her he would attend the ceremony under one condition: "only IF you get into a 4 year University," he told her. The two kept in contact over social media, with Bosarge-Fussell updating Cole on her latest grade reports. "You like my grades," she tweeted on X in February 2014. "Very much," Cole replied. "Keep going." And when Bosarge-Fussell received an acceptance letter from Rowan University, Cole stayed true to his word.[21]

To make the celebration, Cole apparently rerouted the Forest Hills Drive Tour.[22] The effort culminated in a shared moment between Bosarge and Cole, who were pictured together after the ceremony concluded. "You gotta dream like you never seen obstacles," Bosarge-Fussell captioned in a 2015 X post.[23] Cole also gifted Bosarge-Fussell a handful of books, and made a second vow. After seeing her walk across the graduation stage, he promised to help pay for her college tuition.

Seven years later, Cole showed up for Bosarge-Fussell's college graduation. He took pictures with his long-time supporter, who was once again pictured in a cap and gown with the rapper, and with another quote directly from the artist she long admired. "This is for all the fans that waited, the bitch niggas that hated, old hoes we dated, look mama, we made it," she captioned in reference to Cole's 2011 hit, "Nobody's Perfect."

The move was right in line with Cole's other efforts to empower other Black men and women. He's not only willing to help aspiring college students achieve their dreams, Cole has lent a hand to single mothers who now dream to see themselves and their children reaching the same accomplishments. Along with donations to organizations like Leaders of a Beautiful Struggle and former NFL player Colin Kaepernick's Million Dollar Pledge, Cole has spearheaded charitable programs for underprivileged residents in his hometown of Fayetteville, North Carolina, through the Dreamville Foundation.

As an effort to combat financial struggles, he bought back his childhood home at 2014 Forest Hills Drive to offer rent-free housing for single mothers with children.[24] The *2014 Forest Hills Drive* album had already turned his childhood home into a local tourist attraction, but Cole's decision to convert it into a resource hub made it a haven for local families in need. "The idea is that it's a single mother with multiple kids, and she's coming from a place where all her kids is sharing a room. She might have two, three kids, they're sharing a room," Cole said in an interview with hip-hop attorney and podcaster Reggie Osse, also known as Combat Jack. "She gets to come here rent-free. I want her kids to feel how I felt when we got to the house."

"If I'm Generous at Heart, I Don't Need Recognition"

While Kendrick has rarely acknowledged his philanthropic efforts, others haven't hesitated to sing the Compton rapper's praises. In 2015, former California State Senator Isadore Hall III took to the Senate floor to award Kendrick with the Generational Icon Award.[25] The politician lauded Kendrick for his musical ascension. "In less than 10 years as a professional artist, Mr. Lamar has gone from a local Compton young boy to become a multi-platinum, Billboard chart-topping, two-time Grammy award-winning musician," Hall declared. But it wasn't musical contributions that landed him the award. He was being commemorated for his work as a community leader and public servant.

One month later, Kendrick stopped by High Tech High School in North Bergen, NJ, for an in-class visit. After hearing that educator Dr. Brian Mooney used *To Pimp a Butterfly* as a teaching tool in his freshman English class, Kendrick decided to take a trip to the North Jersey school to connect with Mooney and his students. Mooney compared Kendrick's album to Toni Morrison's 1970 novel *The Bluest Eye.*

The book is about a young Black girl who wants to have blue eyes, and Mooney recognized the similarities between Morrison's acclaimed work and Kendrick's 2015 album. "I was listening and I was like, wow, there are just so many themes that are the same," Mooney told NPR in 2015.[26] His students began writing essays and poems revolving around the ideas of beauty, Blackness, and the power of individualism, with several students drawing connections between Morrison's excerpts and Kendrick's lyrics.

After writing a blog post about the lesson, Mooney received a message from Kendrick Lamar's manager, who asked if he could stop by the classroom.[27] "I was intrigued how somebody can—other than myself—can articulate and break down the concepts of *To Pimp A Butterfly*, almost better than I can," Kendrick said in an interview inside the school's theater.

With nearly 40 students crammed into a small classroom as they awaited his arrival, Kendrick walked in with a grin as wide as students' smiles. Rather than perform or deliver a speech, he sat and listened during a school-wide assembly as students read out their poems and essays. He then watched a dance number to a mashup of his songs, and when it was his turn to grab the mic, he began rapping "Alright" as the students recited the lyrics in excitement. "It was very exciting," then-senior Sade Ford told NPR. "And this is going to be a once-in-a-lifetime-experience."

Along with class drop-ins, Kendrick has donated large sums to the Compton Unified School District to help fund their music programs. He also donated to nonprofit organizations such as Habitat for Humanity, and gifted $200,000 to twenty Los Angeles-based charities and community initiatives in June 2024.[28]

Among the twenty charities and local institutions include the Compton G.irls Club, Peace4Kids, Sisters of Watts, the Social Justice Learning Institution, and others throughout his hometown.

"We haven't seen this type of unity on the West since we lost our brother Nipsey Hussle," Tim Hinshaw, founder of the Free Lunch Agency, told *Billboard* in 2024. "All of these organizations play a pivotal role in the development of our community and the hope is that we all continue to support them moving forward."

Despite the critiques, many hip-hop artists have directly supported academic institutions through their philanthropic efforts. Jay-Z's foundation partnered with Beyonce's BeyGOOD Foundation and Tiffany & Co. to launch an initiative called "the About Love Scholarship." The initiative intentionally targeted students at historically Black colleges for scholarships. Dr. Jack Thomas, the former President of Central State University in Dayton, Ohio stated:

> This initiative exemplifies the profound influence hip-hop artists have in advocating for education. Artists like Beyoncé and Jay-Z leverage their platforms to not only entertain but also to inspire and effect meaningful change. Their commitment to educational advancement underscores the genre's potential to empower communities and foster opportunities for the next generation.

Like some of the revered legends that came before him, Kendrick Lamar has also advocated for academic advancement. In 2024, the emcee surprised students at Compton College's graduation by appearing as their commencement speaker.[29] During a casually delivered yet heartfelt speech at his hometown's public community college, Kendrick emphasized that their earned degree held value. Draped in a cap, T-shirt, and sports jacket, he stated that "this Compton degree is just as big." He added, "Now it's all about taking these resources and taking what you learned and applying. It's as simple as that."

Both Cole and Kendrick have both become staples and philanthropists in their hometowns without needing the credit from it. The mayor of Fayetteville, North Carolina, Mitch Colvin, said that Cole is "lowkey with it." He adds that Cole has "become a global staple that represents Fayetteville in a positive way. Here, of course, we look at him like that locally, but the world has a larger appreciation for him. And when he comes home … you see the effects of his work, rather than him taking the shine for it."

The mayor of Compton, California, Emma Sharif, shared the same sentiment about Kendrick's philanthropic efforts having an impact in the city. "When he comes to visit the Compton Unified School District, he is right there with his students," Sharif said. "He always makes sure that during Christmas time he does a big toy event every year here in the city of Compton for our youth, and that's something that I really want to say. I thank him and his organization, pgLang. They've done a great job as far as giving back to our community."

While Kendrick and Cole have been heavily revered due to their unique styles and appeal sonically, their music has impacted society, education, and culture in ways that many of their peers have not. Their records have created progressive dialogue about Black history, poverty, generational trauma, college, and progression. Furthermore, they have taken philanthropic action that mirrors their musical efforts. They have each taken musical and political risk within their art that would help them grow organic fanbases who are fully invested in their messages and them as individuals. The two artists both chose this community-centered approach when entering hip-hop, while another peer of theirs would rise to their success level with far less consciousness.

7

D.R.A.K.E.

Throughout J. Cole and Kendrick Lamar's stretch of massive success and impact in the 2010s and beyond, there was always another artist who was dominating record sales, radio play, streaming, and the Billboard charts. That artist is Aubrey Graham, better known as Drake. He became arguably the biggest hitmaker that hip-hop has ever seen, consistently releasing chart-topping records that rang off in clubs and parties around the globe. His consistency, success, marketability, crossover potential, and talent began to have many people mention him amongst Cole and Kendrick. In many circles, people referred to them as the "Big 3," who were running the game for the new generation.

Author and NYU professor Kathy Iandoli said Drake provided balance in the rap game. While artists like Kendrick and Cole ascended on the merit of their lyrical abilities, she said Drake sparked the hits that would expand hip-hop's sound and global appeal. The same role was shared by hip-hop greats of the past, who blended skill with commercial appeal to broaden rap audiences. "We've had the Rakims and the Big Daddy Kanes. We had Jay-Z's and Nas's. And in that regard, I think it was Drake and Kendrick. It's been Cole, too. There's always been that balance between who is swaggy and who is lyrical."

While Drake's success was undeniable, he was rejected by many hip-hop purists. Ghostwriting allegations, accusations of cultural appropriation, formulaic music; these were all common digs at why Drake could never be mentioned amongst the hip-hop greats. The larger critique was Drake's lack of conscious messaging within his music. He largely avoided pertinent issues and controversial topics like systemic racism, politics, and police brutality within his music. Renowned conscious rappers would even point out Drake's lack of depth and cultural impact. In a 2024 interview with *The Cutting Room Floor* podcast, rapper Mos Def, now known as Yasiin Bey was asked if he felt Drake represented hip-hop. Bey rejected the notion, suggesting Drake's music was suitable for a department store-run:

> Drake is pop to me. In the sense like, if I was in Target in Houston and I heard a Drake song, it feels like a lot of his music is compatible with shopping. Or shopping with an edge, in certain instances. It's likable.[1]

Bey said Drake's messaging and commercialized style of rap does nothing for society in critically political or social climates. "What happens when this thing collapses? What happens when the columns start buckling? Are we not in some early stage of that at this present hour? Are we seeing, like, the collapse of the empire? Buying and selling — where's the message that I can use? You know, what's in it for your audience apart from, like, banging the pom-poms?"

While some artists criticized Drake, a plethora of other emcees supported and collaborated with him throughout his career. He's done songs with the likes of Jay-Z, Rick Ross, Lil Wayne, and Kanye West, who all helped solidify his presence within rap and hip-hop culture. He even collaborated with J. Cole and Kendrick Lamar on several occasions throughout his career. Despite these collaborative efforts, a shift and divide were occurring. Drake was dominating the charts, but hip-hop purists were crowning Kendrick and Cole as the future of rap. The two emcees weren't afraid to let the world know they were far above their peers every chance they had.

Vulnerability on Wax

To some, Drake's vulnerability when speaking about his insecurities and relationships with women are viewed as a contribution to social discourse. While this is nothing new for hip-hop, as artists like André 3000, Common, Eminem, Ye, and even Joe Budden during his *Mood Musik* era, addressed their romantic failings well before the industry heard of Drake, he did take it to new heights.

On early projects like *The Comeback Season*, *So Far Gone*, and *Take Care*, Drake frequently rapped (and sang) about his constant pursuit of love, the sorrow he faced amid heartbreak, infidelity on both sides of his relationships, and the feeling of being used. His approach to these topics came across as genuine, and music fans of all backgrounds gravitated toward it. This alone marked his contributions to men discussing their feelings on wax, with disregard for sounding "soft" or "simpish" in a culture filled with machismo. This content and melodic sound undoubtedly influenced other artists of his era, and younger artists who came after him, such as Rod Wave, Russ, and 6lack.

On later albums, Drake began leaning into other artists' sounds and style. He was using Caribbean and Spanish accents and production on records like "Controlla," "One Dance," and "Blem" to strike a wider audience. He even released records in a UK accent on songs like "War." On other records, he leaned into Memphis, Houston, and Atlanta accents and other regional styles on records. Many viewed this approach as cultural appropriation. They were all things that would have ended or highly hindered the careers of rappers of the past, but for one reason or another, hip-hop allowed Drake to stick around.

Simultaneously, Drake adopted a "tough" persona. On records like "Mob Ties," he mentioned his street affiliations and ability to get someone "off'd" if he wanted to. He even referenced his affiliation with respected executive and founder of Rap A Lot Records, J. Prince, who's known for having street credibility. Drake was also seen wearing apparel of the biker gang Hells Angels, and subtly shouting them out on the record "God's Plan."[2] This was an alarming sign to many, as associates and members of the group have been connected to hate crimes against Black people[3] and have been known for racial intolerance.[4] This was a hard pivot from the *Degrassi* child star, whom many were first introduced to. It was beginning to become hard for fans to see where Drake stood morally, culturally, or racially.

'It's Just Big Me'

Due to competitiveness and moments of personal conflict, Kendrick and Drake would become hip-hop rivals. After a decade of subliminal blows, the musical feud between Kendrick and Drake finally erupted on March 22, 2024.

Just months after Drake and Cole released the collaboration "First Person Shooter," where the two rappers declared their positions atop the rap game, Kendrick forged a collaboration of his own. The Compton native responded with a culture-shifting verse on Future and Metro Boomin's track "Like That" that engulfed rap fans in ways unseen since his "Control" verse a decade before. "Motherfuck the big three, nigga. It's just big me," Kendrick declared on the track.

Over the Metro Boomin-produced instrumental, Kendrick fired off lyrical assaults at Drake and Cole, claiming to be the more superior artist between the three emcees. He also took aim at Drake's recent projects, with albums like *For All the Dogs* and *Honestly, Nevermind* drawing mixed reviews. He also poked fun at Drake's admiration for Michael Jackson, who was posthumously featured on his double album, *Scorpion.* "Your best work is a light pack. Nigga, Prince outlived Mike Jack,'" Kendrick rapped. The Compton emcee also dissed Cole, a long-time friend and collaborator, who linked up with Drake on the aforementioned track and joined him on the "It's All A Blur" tour stops. "Niggas clickin' up, but cannot be legit, 40 Water, tell 'em," Kendrick said.

For the first time ever, one of the "Big 3" cut the comparisons completely at the knees, with Kendrick suggesting there wasn't a rightful linkage between the three artists. Of course, all three have been vocal about their perceived supremacy in the genre. But no one was more direct than Kendrick at the moment, and Drake and J. Cole would proceed to stand their ground.

As "Like That" shot up the Billboard charts, the first artist to respond to Kendrick was Cole. He originally released the diss "7 Minute Drill" on his 2024 album *Might Delete Later.* On the rapid-fire closer to the surprise project, Cole pointed to Kendrick's musical inactivity as a point of weakness. "He averagin' one hard verse like every thirty months or somethin'. If he wasn't dissin', then we wouldn't be discussin' him." Then, in a surprising turn, he critiqued Kendrick's discography, namely 2022's *Mr. Morale and The Big Steppers.* "Your first shit was classic, your last shit was tragic. Your second shit put niggas to sleep, but they gassed it. Your third shit was massive and that was your prime. I was trailin' right behind and I just now hit mine," Cole rapped.

Many hip-hop fans and music pundits criticized Cole's Kendrick diss. While others felt Cole's "warning shot" officially sparked what would become an all-out lyrical war, others felt his jab at Kendrick's discography was underwhelming and an unmeasured attempt to respond to his fire-hot verse on "Like That." In short time, Cole also felt it was a bad move. Less than a week after releasing the song on his surprise mixtape *Might Delete Later*, Cole pulled the song from streaming services.[5] He told the crowd at his Dreamville Festival that he regretted releasing the song, calling it the "lamest shit I did in my fuckin' life."

The "Crooked Smile" rapper said the past two days "felt terrible," and that, "It let me know how good I've been sleeping for the past 10 years." The same fans that showered him with praise with the release of "7 Minute Drill" lamented Cole's retrieval. His long-time fans, however, felt Cole was making the right move because of his long-time friendship with the West Coast artist, who he's called a "brother" in past interviews and songs.

War Ready and Battle Tested

With Cole's withdrawal, the sole focus was now on Drake and Kendrick. The two rappers threw subliminal blows at one another in past interviews and songs. "There's a reason they don't call my name. I'm not the guy. I'm not the one," Drake told radio personality Angie Martinez in 2014, when asked if disses between him and Kendrick would ever happen. "There's a reason they don't call my name."[6] The decade-old interview clip would prove to be a haunting one for Drake, who was still at the top of his game.

At the time of Kendrick's "Like That" verse, Drake was two years removed from breaking The Beatles' record for most top five hits on the Billboard Hot 100. His 2023 album *For All the Dogs* secured the rapper's 13th No. 1 album, which opened with half a billion on-demand streams in the first week. That marked the largest streaming week of 2023 for any album, and the fourth largest ever recorded at the time.[7]

Drake's musical success wasn't without its challenges. Before Drake squared off against Kendrick, he was already a battle-tested emcee who went up against rappers with equal or greater lyrical ability. His past beefs with Common, Meek Mill, and Pusha T spilled over onto wax, and became pivotal moments in Drake's career for both good and bad. During the battles, each emcee exposed chinks in Drake's armor as a man and emcee. The feuds also revealed his disregard for hip-hop legends and traditions.

Drake dissed Common on Rick Ross's "Stay Schemin" featuring French Montana after the Chicago rapper dissed him on the 2011 song "Sweet." The veteran emcee called Drake a "Sweet motherfucker," on the track. He later admitted the diss was over subliminal shots he thought Drake took at him regarding Serena Williams, who Drake dated after Common's relationship with the iconic tennis star. Drake responded to Common months later on the collaborative track, calling out Common for being a seasoned emcee attempting to slight the younger, multi-platinum artist. "It bothers me when the gods get to actin' like the boards. Guess every team doesn't come complete with niggas like ours." Common's rebuttal was a remix to Ross' "Stay Schemin" beat, but Drake's initial clapback was the most memorable between the exchanges.

The short-lived spat with Common was followed by Drake's exchange with Meek Mill. The Philly rapper accused Drake of using ghostwriter, Quentin Miller, to write his rhymes, including on their collaboration, "R.I.C.O.," from Meek's 2015 album, *Dreams Worth More Than Money*. "Stop comparing Drake to me too ... He don't write his own raps!," the rapper tweeted in July 2015. Meek even said Drake is "way out of it" when it comes to contending with Kendrick and Cole atop the rap game.

Following Meek's accusation was the release of an alleged reference track, which revealed Miller's involvement in Drake's previously released album, *If You're Reading This It's Too Late*. The alleged track featured Miller's voice over what became Drake's "10 Bands." New York City's Hot 97 radio host Funkmaster Flex played the record, forcing Miller to publicly deny the ghostwriting claims. The Atlanta songwriter clarified that he was credited for a handful of songs on *IYRTITL*, rather than contributing under complete anonymity like true ghostwriters. "I am not and never will be a 'ghostwriter' for Drake," Miller wrote on his Tumblr account. Years later, Miller revealed he didn't receive any publishing compensation for his songs with Drake, pointing to a restrictive contract with producer Tricky Stewart as the source of his troubles.[8]

Rather than deny Meek's ghostwriting claims on social media, Drake released "Charged Up," a slow burning track that acted as a warning to Meek amid the allegations. "I stay silent 'cause we're at war and I'm very patient. 6

God is watching. I just hope you're prepared to face him. I'm charged up," Drake rapped.

With no response from Meek, Drake followed up with the up-tempo diss "Back to Back" less than a week later. "This for y'all that think that I don't write enough. They just mad 'cause I got the Midas touch," Drake rapped. The Canadian rapper proceeded to take jabs at Meek's love life, as Meek was dating fellow superstar Nicki Minaj at the time. The song title references the Toronto Blue Jays' run of World Series championships in 1992 and 1993. Drake's hometown team won their second consecutive championship against the Philadelphia Phillies. The diss peaked at No. 27 on the Billboard Hot 100 and was later nominated for Best Rap Performance at the Grammy Awards in 2016.

Taking a page from Jay-Z's playbook, Drake performed the song live at Toronto's OVO Fest that summer, accompanied with fan-made memes dissing Meek. For many, the move sealed Drake's victory in the beef. Meek later responded with "Wanna Know," but he eventually removed the Drake diss from SoundCloud, thus conceding his defeat in what could have been a career-ending claim for most hip-hop artists. Drake's next high-profile bout with Pusha T proved to be another substantial obstacle in Drake's career. Only this time, "The Boy" didn't come out on top in the eyes of most rap fans. It would also display how culturally out-of-touch Drake was and had been since his emergence.

Seeing Infrared

For years, Pusha T and Lil Wayne were at odds. It started with a jab at the New Orleans rapper for wearing Bathing Ape in a 2006 *Vibe* cover. The Japanese streetwear brand, also known as Bape, was popularized by Pharrell, Pusha T, and his brother and fellow emcee Malice in the early 2000s. As the hip-hop group Clipse, Pusha and Malice threw a subliminal message in Wayne's direction, accusing him of biting their style on the 2006 song, "Mr. Me Too." "Wanna know the time? Better clock us. Niggas bite the style from the shoes to the watches," Malice rapped on the Pharrell-produced beat.

That same year, Wayne sat down with Complex for an interview, and called out Pharrell and the Clipse for insinuating he was biting their style.[9] "You talking to the best. Talk to me like you're talking to the best. I don't see no f–kin' Clipse. Come on man," Wayne said. The rapper made his disdain for Pusha even clearer after Pusha released 2012's "Exodus 23:1." On the song, the Virginia-bred emcee likely threw blows about both Wayne and Drake, pointing to their label signings and affiliations as a point of weakness. "You signed to one nigga that signed to another nigga. That's signed to three niggas, now that's bad luck," Pusha rapped. At the time, Drake was signed to Lil Wayne's Young Money imprint, a subsidiary under Cash Money Records, which operated under Universal Music Group. "Fuk pusha t and anybody that love em," Wayne tweeted on the same day as the song's release.

From that moment forward, Drake inserted himself in the Pusha beef. Despite Drake's admiration for Pusha as an aspiring emcee, all was out the window when he began targeting Wayne, who Drake considered a mentor in the rap game. The rappers exchanged subliminal shots for years before releasing entire diss records. Drake questioned Pusha's street credibility and drug-dealing past on "Two Birds, One Stone," while Push reignited the ghostwriting claims on 2016's "H.G.T.V. Freestyle." But the beef reached new heights when Pusha unleashed "Infrared" in 2018.

On the closer to his album *Daytona*, Pusha continued to question Drake's songwriting abilities, insinuating that Miller was responsible for much more of Drake's success than previously believed. "It was written like Nas, but it came from Quentin," he rapped. Push also lauded Drake's two biggest contemporaries, who he felt were collectively elevating rap at a time when the "game's fucked up." "Believe in myself and the Coles and Kendricks. Let the sock puppets play in their roles and gimmicks," he rhymed.

Drake returned with the scorching "Duppy Freestyle." The rapper revealed his own songwriting contributions for Kanye West on "Father Stretch My Hands" and "30 Hours" from his 2016 album, *The Life of Pablo*. "What do you really think of the nigga that's making your beats. I've done things for him I thought that he never would need," Drake rapped in reference to West, who was the head of G.O.O.D. Music alongside Pusha at the time. Drake continued to ignite the feud by likening an old Pusha-signed microphone he purchased as a teenager to the rapper's career. "I had a microphone of yours, but then the signature faded. I think that pretty much resembles what's happenin' lately."

After the song's release, he later posted a draft of an invoice on Instagram, requesting $100,000 from the G.O.O.D. Music team for "promotional assistance and career reviving."

Pusha's clapback with "The Story of Adidon." Over Jay-Z's "The Story of O.J." instrumental, Pusha attempted to break down the rapper's psyche, suggesting his music has been "angry" and "full of lies," given what's transpired over the years. Not about the ghostwriting accusations or past bouts with other artists, but from inside the Graham home. After Drake alluded to Pusha's engagement to Virginia Williams in "Duppy Freestyle," the rapper doubled down on his family. He mentioned his father's absence from Drake's life, and revealed his son, Adonis Graham, to millions of hip-hop fans. "You are hiding a child, let that boy come home. Dead beat motherfucker, playing border patrol," he rapped.

The song featured a photo of Drake in blackface, a style of makeup that was often worn by White actors in the nineteenth and early twentieth century that conveyed negative and degrading caricatures of Black people in the entertainment industry. Drake explained the jarring image was from a 2007 project he did about young Black actors being typecast in the modern day, but no explanation could have eased the minds of fans or tempered the shocking moment.[10]

The image and news of Drake's son was a shocking revelation in the rap community, and helped solidify Drake's defeat in a hotly contested battle between him and Pusha. "The Story of Adidon" became the most famed diss record in the 2010s and changed other rappers' strategies when it came to rap beef. Instead of simply out-rapping or insulting another artist in lyrical battle, artists were now focused on exposing their dirty laundry and using social media to widen the blast radius.

A year after their back-and-forth, Drake admitted to taking the loss on the Rap Radar podcast with journalists Elliot Wilson and Brian "B. Dot" Miller.[11] He described the bout as his "first loss in the competitive sport of rapping," and waved off any potential reconciliation between him and Pusha.[162] Drake also revealed he started making a response after the release of "The Story of Adidon," but opted not to put it out because it featured lyrics that "I don't know if in two years I want to hear myself say," he said.

Royal Rumble

After the Common, Meek, and Pusha beef, and even short-lived disputes with artists like Kanye West and Chris Brown, Drake was battle-tested in lyrical warfare. He knew what it felt like to be on either side of a battle and was determined to never have the same outing as he did back in 2018. He earned his badges in previous bouts, which made his long-awaited matchup with Kendrick that much more appealing. When Kendrick's "Like Dat" verse arrived, he appeared more willing to push personal boundaries and address whatever was needed to end victorious.

After Kendrick's fiery verse, Drake responded with "Push Ups." The record was the first in a series of "leaks" between the two artists, with "Push Ups" firmly launching the long-awaited feud on wax. The song, which featured a sample of Junior M.A.F.I.A.'s "Get Money," pointed to the Compton rapper's five-foot-six frame and financial split while signed under Top Dawg Entertainment.[12] "Pull your contract 'cause we gotta see the split. The way you doin' splits, bitch, your pants might rip," he rapped.[163]

There were initial questions surrounding the song's legitimacy. Rumors about the song being AI-generated briefly surfaced, but once it was verified, it swept the hip-hop nation. Media personalities like DJ Akademiks, who was in close contact with Drake and his inner circle, began posting daily insights into the beef. Among his first was a full breakdown of "Push Ups," noting that the diss included shots at Kendrick, Metro Boomin', Rick Ross, The Weeknd, and Drake's other unnamed adversaries.

With Drake declaring himself the "hitmaker y'all depend on," Ross was the first to respond to "Push Ups." He clapped back with "Champagne Moments," filling the mafioso-styled beat with hilarious claims that Drake's obsession with plastic surgery resulted in a nose job. He also attributed Lil Wayne's connection with Drake, who Ross referred to as "white boy" throughout the song, for his acceptance in rap.

The song drew social media buzz, especially after Drake and Ross compared their physical transformations and riches, even down to the lot size of their mansions, but fans still awaited Kendrick's second outing in the feud. Their exchange would lead to an iconic series of musical moments, jarring and sometimes hideous accusations, and created a whirlwind of fan-made think pieces.

Days after "Push Ups" landed on streaming platforms, Drake and much of the culture lamented Kendrick for his delayed response. With Drake feeling enlivened by fans' support of the first diss track, he doubled up with a second record. The moment was reminiscent of his feud with Meek Mill, which saw him circle back after "Charged Up" with "Back to Back." In a similar move, he released the follow-up "Taylor Made Freestyle." But unlike the deafening blow of "Back to Back," his second Kendrick diss was pummeled by critics and listeners because of its reliance on the AI-generated voices of 2Pac and Snoop Dogg. It also once again reinforced Drake's disregard for hip-hop legends, with 2Pac being a prominent (and deceased) figure who is heavily revered by the Black community.

From the perspective of the two West Coast legends, Drake programmed their voices to dispel doubt in Kendrick's abilities, while pushing him to muster all his efforts to fulfill his role as rap's boogeyman. Then Drake ends the track with his own vocal delivery. "Since 'Like Dat,' your tone changed. You're not as enthused. How are you not in the booth? It feel like you're kinda removed," he rapped. He also critiques Kendrick's past attempts to crossover musically with pop acts like Maroon 5 and Taylor Swift. Drake quickly removed the song from streaming platforms after Shakur's estate delivered a cease-and-desist letter, demanding the record get taken down. Snoop later maligned the track, offering an apology to Kendrick for clearing the use of his likeness. But despite the uproar, Drake still managed to add fuel to the already-heated rap beef, and Kendrick's follow up helped raise the stakes.

A Moment of Euphoria

On a faithful Tuesday afternoon, Kendrick delivered "Euphoria," and brought the rap world into a standstill. The six-minute diss, released on April 30, 2024, opens with a brief and almost inaudible soundbite. The encrypted message was revealed to be a snippet from the 1978 cult classic, *The Wiz*, which sees Richard Pryor's character admit he's been falsely masquerading as an omnipotent wizard in the fictional film. Pryor's line "Everything they say about me is true" is reversed on Kendrick's track. He then dissects Drake's character like a surgeon on the operating table, unraveling how his upbringing, romantic exploits, and career has shaped him for the worse. "The famous actor we once knew, is looking paranoid and now spiraling. You're moving just like a degenerate, every antic is feeling distasteful," Kendrick rapped.

Kendrick's lyrics overlay Teddy Pendergrass's "You're My Latest, My Greatest Inspiration," then ramps up as the beat switches from a soothing cut to a hard-hitting instrumental. Kendrick later delves into Drake's manufactured accents on songs like "Controlla" and "One Dance," his collection of iconic relics like 2Pac's ruby and diamond gold ring, and his past feud with Pusha. He then went on to compare Drake to rapper Sexy Redd, who Kendrick joked mirrored the St. Louis native's "bad bitch" tendencies. "I believe you don't like women. This real competition, you might pop ass with them."

Kendrick avoided dissing Cole throughout "Euphoria," but he acknowledged where he fit among the "Big 3" with absolute confidence. "Cole and Aubrey know I'm a selfish nigga, the crown is heavy, huh. I pray they my real friends. If not, I'm YNW Melly." Within hours of the song's release, the online music website, Genius, crashed due to high traffic. People's interest in decoding Kendrick's lyrics temporarily froze the site. Fans declared the two-week wait for Kendrick's response time was worth it, as the two rappers were finally on equal ground. What came after went on to change the trajectory of the rap battle.

A Weekend for the History Books

On "Euphoria," Kendrick hinted at the discovery of damning secrets that would soon see the light. "We ain't got to get personal. This a friendly fade, you should keep it that way. I know some shit about niggas that'll make Gunna Wunna look like a saint." And before Drake responded to Kendrick's full-length diss, he dropped the soulful Al Green flip, "6:16 in LA" on May 3, 2024.[13] The song title was a play on Drake's timestamp records, like "5 AM in Toronto," and a subtle connection to the premiere of the HBO series *Euphoria*, which Drake executive produced. June 16 is also 2Pac's birthday, a figure Kendrick has admired for his musical impact and social messaging.

On the song, Kendrick claims to have moles inside Drake's OVO team, who allegedly fed him confidential information because of their own discontent with the rap star. "Have you ever thought that OVO was workin' for me? Fake bully, I hate bullies, you must be a terrible person. Everyone in your team is whispering that you deserve it." The song was more of a mild warning than a diss, but with it releasing just three days after "Euphoria," it was unclear what was to come next or when.

After the early Friday release, Drake returned fire the same day with "Family Matters." The seven-minute track was laced with a trifecta of beat switches.[14] Drake paired his witty and vengeful lyrics with an accompanying video, which featured a purple Dodge Caravan that resembled the 1996 Chrysler Town & Country that was on the cover of Kendrick's *good kid m.A.A.d city*. In the video, a driver is shown taking the truck to a junkyard, where the vehicle is crushed.

Drake, strapped with added ammunition over the past two Kendrick disses, unloaded hideous accusations about Kendrick's relationship with his high school sweetheart, Whitney Alford. "Your baby mama captions always screamin' save me. You did her dirty all her life, you tryna make peace." One of the more serious assertions was that one of Kendrick's children was actually fathered by his manager and close friend Dave Free. Drake also alleged that Kendrick supposedly abused Alford. While none of his claims were confirmed, and were later disproven, the momentum quickly swung back to Drake's direction. That same shift would inspire Kendrick to drop an immediate response, and in less than one hour, he released, "Meet the Grahams."

Like Drake's "Family Matters," Kendrick analyzed a family of his own. This time it was the Grahams. The dark and mystifying track begins with Kendrick rapping as if he was speaking directly to Drake's son Adonis. "You're a good kid, that needs good mentorship. Let me be your mentor, since your daddy don't teach you shit." After addressing Drake's parents on the diss, Kendrick delivered one of the biggest blows in the beef. He wished death on Drake for his alleged attraction to young girls, and his loyalty to OVO members with sketchy legal troubles.

Along with the predatory accusations and other claims, Kendrick turns his attention to an unnamed eleven-year-old, who he refers to as "baby girl." As the song continues, Kendrick asserts that Drake is possibly hiding a daughter.

As on Pusha's "The Story of Adidon," the rapper attempted to shed light on a second hidden child. If true, it would have been another severe blow for Drake.

Minutes after the song dropped, Drake took to Instagram to deny having a secret child. He later dismissed the predatory accusations on the follow-up, "The Heart Part 6," and called whoever leaked inside information to Kendrick "clowns." As for the alleged daughter, Drake said it was all a ruse. He and other OVO representatives had purposefully planted the information to mislead the Compton rapper. "I am a war general seasoned in preparation. My jacket is covered in metals, honor, and decoration. You waited for this moment, overcome with the desperation. We plotted for a week and then we fed you the information," Drake rapped.

It was proven Drake and Kendrick's scathing accusations were pure suspicion, old tabloid fodder, and rumors spurred from TikTok conspiracists. None of the accusations were proven true, or stuck in the minds of rap fans, making it difficult to determine a clear winner in the exchange. That was until the release of Kendrick and DJ Mustard's timely banger, "Not Like Us."

"They Not Like Us"

A hard-hitting rap song with radio potential was missing until the release of "Not Like Us." In the same way Drake's "Back to Back" flooded the airwaves and climbed the Billboard charts, Kendrick's "Not Like Us" became the biggest song in the country. It topped the Billboard charts for thirteen weeks and spent a total of fifty-three weeks on the Hot 100, making it the longest-charting rap song in history.[15] The song played at arenas during the 2024 NBA Playoffs, and even tennis star Naomi Osaka admitted to listening to "Not Like Us" on her way to a match.[16]

With "Like That" already topping the Billboard 100, the momentum of the beef and the regional appeal of "Not Like Us," the diss song became a global phenomenon. Despite Drake's attempt to temper the momentum with "The Heart Part 6," Kendrick's "Not Like Us" continued to build momentum after he performed the song a total of five times during "The Pop Out: Ken & Friends," held at Inglewood's Kia Forum later that summer. The commercial success and impact of the song led to five nominations at the 2025 Grammy Awards, including for Record of the Year and Song of the Year.

On "The Heart Part 6," Drake appeared to bow out from the musical exchange. He implies Kendrick "burnt" the feud out with his barrage of diss songs and accusations. "You would be a worthy competitor if I was really a predator. And you weren't fuckin' lying to every blogger and editor, but. It is what it is," he rapped.

The conversation went beyond who was better than who, or who would come out victorious in a lyrical death match between the two heavyweights. The beef spiraled as the accusations flew between both parties. While none of them stuck, Atlanta-based rapper LNS said Kendrick calling Drake a pedophile likely pulled the brakes on the ongoing battle, stating:

> I don't care whose feathers get ruffled, people rallied behind Kendrick because what he was saying was so tough—calling him a pedophile. Black people don't rock with that shit. Not saying Drake is one, but nobody should like that shit. All the videos and shit, nobody fucks with that. That's one of the reasons, and it's such a strong accusation. It adds up to too much. And I think a lot of people didn't secretly like Drake from the jump, so people were like, "Yeah, Kendrick, fuck him." Drake definitely put his stamp on the culture, but the accusation hit a little differently. I have daughters, so it hit differently. And it's already rooted animosity for Drake that they may have had, music-wise. Kendrick is a better artist, hands down. Kendrick won people over. I saw Drake fans say, "Damn." It was undeniable how Kendrick was on record, piecing everything together so well. He just won a massive number of people over.

The feud took a series of surprising turns from both sides. Despite the lyrical assaults between the two artists, many felt Kendrick Lamar sealed the victory with the release of "Not Like Us," although not all were happy with what media personalities like Charlamagne tha God and others called the greatest rap battle ever witnessed. "We're calling this record the greatest diss record of all time, but we're going to have to start having the conversation about this being the greatest rap record of all time," said Raney Antoine Jr., the creator of the hip-hop and R&B degree program at Loyola University New Orleans.

On the other side of the spectrum, other artists were against Drake and Kendrick's exchange. In the weeks following, legendary drummer Questlove made an Instagram post criticizing the two artists for their public spat.[17] While fans were immersed in the diss records between the two superstars, The Roots founding member said it was a sign of a fading genre that finally met its end. "Nobody Won The War. This Wasn't about skill," Questlove wrote. "This was a wrestling match level mudslinging and takedown by any means necessary—women & children (& actual facts) be damned. Same audience wanting blood will soon put up 'rip' posts like they weren't part of the problem." Followed by the headshot statement, "Hip Hop Is Truly Dead."

Port Antonio

As lyrical blows turned to warfare, many argued Cole had the right decision in mind: to back out before things got sticky. Instead of sharpening his bars and taking aim at Kendrick, whom he's long acknowledged as a brother, he withdrew his singular diss to Kendrick Lamar on streaming platforms and waved a white flag before anything serious ensued. He received a few mentions throughout the beef, namely on "Push Ups," when Drake denied Cole's claims that "Like That" caused a rift between the two artists. Beyond his retracted diss, the North Carolina native remained low throughout much of the feud.

It wasn't until October 2024 that Cole released a new track, titled "Port Antonio," where he briefly addressed the debacle. Instead of choosing a side, Cole remained neutral, rapping that "my friends went to war, I walked away with all they blood on me." This was likely referencing the backlash he got for not engaging in the battle, and the division that he believed the conflict caused. Along with acknowledging that he wasn't afraid to enter into lyrical combat, he asserted he knew that it had the potential to get personal and didn't feel it was worth losing a friend or gaining an enemy. While he understood the competitive nature that comes with wanting to be viewed as the best emcee, he expressed how his purpose is to make music that helps his listeners get through rough times in life. Not to tear his fellow peers down.

After the smoke cleared, many fans went from being disappointed that Cole didn't compete in the lyrical matchup, to believing that his decision to go the peaceful route served him better. For all intents and purposes, it appears it has. Cole refused to pick sides against two artists who he revered for attention and to appease an audience. Furthermore, he avoided being wrapped up in what nobody in the hip-hop community saw coming—an active federal lawsuit.

If You Can't Beat 'Em ... Sue 'Em

By most accounts, hip-hop fans and casual observers acknowledged Drake's defeat in the rap battle with Kendrick. "Not Like Us" was becoming both a West Coast and cultural anthem and showed no signs of leaving the Billboard charts. The music video for the song was also amassing millions of views and gaining critical acclaim, with the internet community dissecting all of the hidden messaging and symbolism within the imagery. Amidst this success, an unpredictable turn of events occurred. Instead of Drake returning fire on an upcoming album, or even recruiting some backup, he decided to take the battle into the courtroom.

On January 15, 2025, Drake filed a federal lawsuit against Universal Music Group, his own label, centered around Kendrick Lamar's diss record "Not Like Us."[18] Ironically, both artists are affiliated with the same record label. Kendrick has released music under Interscope (a subsidiary of UMG) in partnership with his own company pgLang. He's also held publishing deals with Interscope. Drake's lawsuit, filed in the Southern District of New York, claimed that UMG defamed Drake's character by promoting and amplifying the record that insinuates that he could be a child predator.

Many instantly pointed out the hypocrisy of Drake's filing after he himself made comments in his own diss records that could be perceived as defamatory. At the time of the feud, Drake accused Kendrick of abusing his fiancée, Whitney Alford. Drake also alleged that she cheated on Kendrick with his best friend Dave Free, and that his biological son is Free's instead of his. These were all meritless claims that could have impacted Kendrick's reputation or warranted a lawsuit filing of his own.

The lawsuit also prompted conversations about freedom of speech in hip-hop. Rap battling has always been a crucial part of the culture. Throughout time, artists have tested their lyrical prowess by seeing who could creatively break down their opponent, which often included insults. Many believed the lawsuit could set a precedent where artists would have to censor their lyrics when engaging in this artistic expression. Someone engaging in a rap battle, and then weaponizing the responses in legal form, was jarring for many hip-hop lovers.

Drake's move against UMG mirrored the colonization mindset that Kendrick referenced throughout the battle. Drake's actions resembled those of an outsider entering into an existing and thriving culture, then trying to shift it to best fit his own needs with total disregard for the negative implications. The lawsuit further proved that Drake was not only an outsider culturally, but was more than willing to sacrifice the integrity of the artform in his favor. This would only further fuel Kendrick's momentum. Instead of moving on from the conflict, he doubled-down on his stance.

Amplifying the Resistance

February 2025 would be a historic month for both Kendrick Lamar and hip-hop fans. Even months after its release, "Not Like Us" was still the focal point of Drake's federal lawsuit, and its impact continued to grow at rapid pace. In an unexpected sweep, the song not only became the first diss record to win a Grammy, the song and music video secured five Grammys in one night.[19] This included the coveted Song of the Year award. During his acceptance speech, Kendrick emphasized the power of the genre, "There's nothing more important than rap music. We are the culture." He also delivered a message to the younger artists, asking them to "Respect the artform and it'll get you where you need to go." He was a living testimony to that claim.

A week after the annual award show, Kendrick was scheduled to perform at the 2025 Super Bowl's Halftime Show. This was a monumental moment for hip-hop. Kendrick was the first rap artist to headline the Super Bowl Halftime Show by himself. Furthermore, having a conscious rapper perform at the most-viewed sporting event in the world was pivotal for the culture. It signaled a cultural shift and was a monumental win for hip-hop. As the Philadelphia Eagles and Kansas City Chiefs played, many viewers felt anticipation that superseded the outcome of the matchup. They wanted to know if Kendrick would still perform the controversial song during his halftime performance, disregarding the pending lawsuits. The viewership of the halftime performance surpassed that of the actual game.

During his performance, Kendrick displayed an extreme level of breath control and technical skill by rapping the entire show with no backtrack or hype man. The halftime show featured the legendary actor Samuel L. Jackson, dressed in red, white, and blue, while narrating the show as "Uncle Sam." The actor's monologue in between records showcased how society (or America) wants to simply be entertained by Kendrick's music, applauding when he performed his more commercial records with SZA, but trying to convince him not to get too edgy by performing records like "Not Like Us."

Kendrick not only performed the controversial record, but also poked fun at Drake's litigious act beforehand, saying "I want to play their favorite song … but you know they love to sue." He shook the stadium by performing "Not Like Us" in full. While he omitted the word "pedophile" from the performance, the crowd loudly filled in the gap.[20] Kendrick's halftime performance went on to become the most viewed Super Bowl halftime show to date, passing Michael Jackson's previous record.[21] For many, this marked hip-hop lyricists returning as the face and true representation of the genre.

Hip-Hop Ain't Pop

Drake's lack of lyrical substance and refusal to speak on social issues in his music was becoming more apparent, and hip-hop fans, critics, and media pundits were criticizing him for it. Former HipHopDX editor and hip-hop journalist Justin Hunte said Drake's lack of conscious records is an insult to hip-hop, and the pioneers who established its foundation:

> It's terrible. It essentially trivializes the culture, and he has a large enough voice to make an impact. If you look at the pantheon of global, titanic artists you have a "Heal the World." His closest was "God's Plan," but the song has nothing to do with the video. He's throwing jabs at XXX Tentacion, and he's shouting out the Hell's Angels. That's not the same energy, and hip-hop has represented marginalized communities—like, the history of Black music. Not even just hip-hop—jazz did the same thing. Gospel. Rock and roll. This is stuff we do as part of this community, and when you exclude that, then it's just another song. It's a pop experience, and I think his legacy really takes a beating without him doing that. Like even down to a bar or two.

While the rap feud between Drake and Kendrick Lamar was entertaining, it represented a much larger shift in the culture. It amplified a growing divide between hip-hop fans who love the substance and progressive messaging from artists like Kendrick, and those who just want catchy songs to dance and vibe to that Drake had been delivering to the world for over a decade. The wedge between those who love hip-hop for its profound and complex content, and those who simply engage with it occasionally was becoming more and more pronounced.

Rap battles at their core are defamatory. Two emcees go to lyrical war with hopes of making listeners view the other party as inferior. Battling has been at the forefront of hip-hop since Busy Bee and Kool Moe Dee's legendary bout in 1981. It's embedded within the culture. This core component of hip-hop stems from a common practice in Black culture called "The Dozens." This practice has a variety of different names for it. Whether it's "roasting," "bussing," or "joning," cracking jokes about one another is fair play in Black culture. It's a rite of passage between friends and family to form a firmer bond.

Between Kendrick and Drake, it became a war between popular and easily accessible music, and the kind of deep, enriching songs that reflect the Black experience in America. The answer is simple: there's room for both. As much as hip-hop needs artists like Kendrick and Cole, who use their voices to enrich the soul and expand the mind of listeners, hip-hop also needs a summer-time anthem, a nightclub hit, and other shades of vulnerability. Drake continued to provide that, even after suffering a historic defeat by the hands of Kendrick.

Despite his shortcomings as a conscious artist, Drake has released radio-friendly jams and memorable hits that will span the test of time. He's matched, and even exceeded, the commercial success of rap's biggest figures, and has run laps around his contemporaries because of his endless list of hit songs and projects. It's all needed for hip-hop to thrive, and to continue making pathways for other artists and subgenres to shine, though hip-hop needs much more to sustain itself.

When comparing him to other greats, Drake's lack of conscious messaging and disregard for the unspoken rules within hip-hop culture make it difficult to place his name next to emcees like Jay-Z, Ice Cube, Nas, 2Pac, and even Cole and Kendrick. These artists have proven that conscious records can be hits, that hits can be inherently conscious, and that both *should* be done for hip-hop to be at its peak.

8

The Survival of Intellectual Rap

As hip-hop continues to expand globally, so will the sound, culture, and its pool of contributors. Rap can be heard from the barrios in Brazil to villages in sub-Saharan Africa and sparsely populated towns in Eastern Europe. Murals of figures like 2Pac, Biggie Smalls, Big L and Jam Master Jay adorn their walls. Graffiti artists and break dancers perform on their street corners and cultural hubs. Over time, these little-known hip-hop communities have blossomed into international fixtures of their own, and the world has taken notice. Break dancing was even named an Olympic sport at the 2024 Paris Games, making it the first hip-hop element to achieve such a feat.

While hip-hop has become one of the world's grandest genres, there's been less regulation when it comes to quality and messaging. The Chicago Drill movement during the mid-2010s amplified and reflected gang violence and inner-city division. Fans of the genre witnessed the imprisonment and killing of fast-rising rappers, and other casualties linked to the music and lifestyle drill music embodied. Like Chicago's subsection of gangsta rap, both psychedelic trap and emo rap during the late 2010s also impacted the lives of artists and fans. It's partly responsible for birthing a generation of drug addicts at the height of America's opioid epidemic. Artists like Lil Pump, Mozzy, Lil Xan, and others acknowledged their dependence and abuse of Percocet, Xanax, OxyContin, MDMA (ecstasy), and other drugs. While they broke free of their addictions, rappers like Lil Peep and Mac Miller ultimately succumbed to their vices, with both men dying of drug overdoses.

Their deaths woke up the hip-hop community, with many fans and artists later acknowledging the dangers of drug-fueled messaging. Others continued to promote violence and drug use as a means for advancement, which indirectly led listeners to follow their footsteps. It's easy to blame rap stars and fans during the era for such a trend, but songs revolving around these topics existed well before the 2010s.

Acts such as Three 6 Mafia promoted drug use heavily in the 1990s. In the 1980s, songs like Melle Mel's "White Lines (Don't Do It)" and the KRS-One-led posse cut "Self-Destruction" provided balance. It opened people's eyes to the dark, never-ending effects of gun violence, drug addiction, and gang warfare, while illustrating ways to avoid the trappings of the underworld and make more calculated decisions. Aside from a few watershed moments in hip-hop, those kinds of records haven't garnered the same mainstream attention as they did between the 1980s and early 2000s.

Hip-hop purists and music executives have taken notice. Labels have pushed newly signed artists to lean into fast food music, or songs that draw instant virality or success, but leave listeners with little substance to absorb. Whether the artist or the fans themselves are negatively impacted by the music isn't their concern. These executives and label heads are doing what they have always done. Reap the financial benefits of the destruction and sit back as the larger hip-hop community attempts to repair itself.

As long as the money is flowing, labels will continue to push artists to make these records. They are quick, catchy, and require little attention to the lyrics. Throughout the 2010s and 2020s, drug-riddled songs over high-frequency trap beats became conventional. Rather than songs rejecting drug abuse, misogyny, or violence, labels pushed for ones filled with this messaging, as long as they landed atop streaming playlists, circulated on radio stations, and blew up on social media.

To shore up their bets, executives signed social media creators and reality TV stars to their imprints. Despite their marginal talent, they believed their large followings could translate to rap stardom. The combination led to a simpler and more formulaic mainstream sound, and fewer records drawing widespread discourse or societal change. There was a general dumbing-down of musical substance and messaging, which all threatened the survival of intellectual rap.

Dumbing Down the Audience

Conscious rap has reserved a place in hip-hop culture because of the forefathers who laid down the foundation. Artists like Kendrick Lamar and J. Cole have carried the mantle in the mainstream with pride, and new emcees who have pushed musical boundaries and addressed modern social issues have as well. While the intellectual nature of conscious rap still remains, the pressures artists face to conform or dumb down their music for "safe" or digestible consumption still prevails. For every conscious rapper who breaks into the mainstream, there are dozens of rappers being thrusted into popular culture by record labels with leading singles absent of conscious messaging, intellectualism, or redeeming qualities. Rapper and entrepreneur Chill Moody stated:

> It's the ebbs and flows of the music industry. Conscious rap is always happening underground. It's always happening in the weird space between mainstream and underground. These people are popping, but not everybody knows it yet.

Conscious rap largely remains a subgenre that must be actively sought out by hip-hop fans. While some fans stumble onto the music they regularly consume, there is a specific type of listener who is more prone to seek out conscious rap songs. It's the same kind of consumer who seeks out books about history, watches YouTube videos about conspiracy theories, or analyzes films with complex storylines and plots. The desire to both actively and critically engage with this form of media is often caused by one's desire to use media as a source for information, instead of solely for amusement or escapism. It helps them better understand society, different cultures, and the larger world they exist in. It can reflect their lived reality or allow them to experience the lived experience of others.

In the 1970s, a cultural theorist and scholar named Stuart Hall developed a theory called "encoding and decoding."[1] The concept is relatively simple. The producer of a message (in this case, a conscious rapper) develops messages based on their own experiences, viewpoints, and culture. This process is called encoding. The receiver of the message (the listener) then perceives and attempts to understand the message based on their own lived experiences, culture, and understanding of the world. This process is called decoding.

In a pivotal moment in history, where education in America is being devalued, and critical thought about race, systemic issues, and progression is being negatively stigmatized as too "woke" by elected officials, what will this impact have on the next generation of music listeners? Will future generations still crave the complex rhyme schemes and plots of a Kendrick record? Will they still desire the heartfelt, vulnerable, and transparent picture painted by an emcee like Cole? Will the audience continue to empathize with the pain of others enough to hear two or three verses that tell their story? Will they still have the attention spans to even listen to a track that's more than two minutes long? These are all valid questions considering the direction of rap today, and how the genre is consumed by the masses in the era of streaming.

The Birth of the Streaming Model

In the mid-1990s, music labels were raking in cash by the millions. The manufacturing of CDs was king, and one CD factory in Shelby, North Carolina, was the lifeline of the music industry. Labels took on marginal expenses, like royalties, packaging, and promotional costs, while receiving the bulk of album sale profits. "Capitalism was leaking money, and people figured out a way to enrich themselves with culture," rapper Rhymefest said in the 2024 documentary *How Music Got Free*. "We talk about what went wrong. What 'went wrong for who' is the question. Is it the artist or the industry?"[2]

With the rise of music-sharing sites like Napster and LimeWire in the early 2000s, the formula slowly descended. A growing community of music fans wanted to bypass the cost of music and began uploading MP3 files for easy access and storage. Like the Warez scene during the 1980s, which saw underground piracy groups obtain and share video games, TV shows, movies, and other digital media for free through online communities, the music industry took a similar path. While physical pirates sold CDs or cassettes at local flea markets or street corners, online sharing technology forced music labels to shift their operations.

With broadband internet and the formation of the MP3 audio format, file sharing became much simpler. What would have taken hours was now down to minutes, and the transmission of free music was in high circulation as online communities expanded. The online movement flipped the industry on its head. Hip-hop album leaks grew more frequent, forcing artists to re-record or rework their releases completely. For his fifth album, Nas had to re-record and split it into two parts, which became … *I Am* and *Nastradamus*. The threat of album leaks made artists paranoid of in-studio and outside interference. Even with the Recording Industry Association of America suing peer-to-peer sites like Napster, online piracy groups continued to rise. It became the second wave of the Warez scene and later evolved into the streaming model music fans experience today.

Napster expanded from thousands of users to upwards of 50 million users by the early 2000s.[3] Napster and other copycat sites vastly impacted artist sales and label profits. As a result, labels had fewer promotional resources and less agility when it came to supporting seasoned emcees or building newly signed acts. They were forced to become their own A&Rs and build their own marketing street teams. It pushed artists to steer their own careers from the driver's seat. And as the internet became an even bigger access point, the independent rap scene rose to new heights.

In 1998, Chuck D and Flavor Flav released free Public Enemy songs online, making them the first major recording artists to use internet releases to combat their own label, Def Jam.[4] While they didn't make money from the move, their intention was to prove that artists could use the internet to their advantage by overstepping the barriers set by record labels and execs. "Technology is leveling the playing field," Chuck D said in a 1998 interview with *The New York Times*. "No longer can executives, accountants and lawyers dictate the flow."

Weeks after receiving lawsuit threats by Def Jam, Public Enemy offered fans free downloads of unheard remixed hits like "Bring the Noise 2000." While Public Enemy's proclamation didn't fully come to form, as streaming platforms like Spotify and Apple Music would offer artists revenue splits as low as $0.003 per play or stream, Chuck D prophesized ways signed acts and independent artists could leverage the internet to build their audience, develop partnership deals, and generate wealth without having to rely on the formulaic structure set out by the music industry. In 1998, Chuck D wrote a statement on the Public Enemy website, stating:

> It seems like the weasels have stepped into the fire. The execs, lawyers and accountants who lately have made most of the money in the music biz are now running scared from the technology that evens out the creative field and makes artists harder to pimp. Let 'em all die … I'm glad to be a contributor to the bomb …[5]

In the 2010s, artists like Kendrick, Cole, Nipsey Hussle, Joey Bada$$, and others applied direct-to-consumer strategies to build cache, widen their audiences, and encourage major labels to invest in their music. Other artists opted to remain independent, so they could make, sell, and distribute the kind of music they wanted without any barriers, especially those revolving around social issues. It also lowered the barrier for entry, with less talented artists garnering buzz in spaces where more accredited rappers resided. Labels attached themselves to artists and social media stars with viral hit songs. They tried to morph them into hip-hop artists until failure throughout the 2010s and 2020s. While the moves may have spawned momentary interest, it eventually oversaturated the industry with "rappers" who weren't contributing to the genre for the better. Former HipHopDX editor and hip-hop journalist Justin Hunte stated:

> We're in a brand-heavy and brand-focused environment. I believe we're in the, "I fuck with you era," where [people] fuck with you more than they're critical of the stuff you're doing. Or, perhaps we're in a, "I really like your music, and maybe I'm not necessarily into this genre all like that" era. It's a whole lot of things like that, too. It doesn't really matter how good or bad you are.

It was becoming increasingly evident that both labels and streaming platforms were exploiting artists. Independence was becoming the most logical route for entertainers to retain ownership of their music, maximize their earning potential, and maintain their artistic expression and freedom of speech.

Independence or Death

Record labels and executives have largely gone unscathed in their promotion of music with destructive messaging and their silencing of progressive acts. While artists with music glorifying dangerous and destructive behaviors such as murder, drug use, and sexual violence against women are often criticized, the labels amplifying and profiting from their music have been largely unaffected. Companies continue to line their pockets from music that glorifies Black death and crime, and by exploiting uneducated or inexperienced Black youth with predatory recording contracts and unfair streaming practices.

Prolific emcees with powerful messages are shelved and overlooked by labels, while lesser talent is encouraged to push negative stereotypes about Black people for profit. While hip-hop is a Black American genre, its fate and legacy have largely been dictated by people from outside of the culture. Capitalistic greed has been just as impactful as the art itself.

Conscious rap has been able to impact music and society through profound and riveting messaging, but it has hit a major fork in the road. Hip-hop music and culture have become overly commercialized, and are now being treated like the profitable commodities they are. While Kendrick and Cole have been able to push the boundaries as mainstream artists, it's possible their messaging has been limited because of their affiliations with large corporations and record companies. Would they have pushed their pens and messaging further if they fully controlled their music and artistry? Questions of authenticity and the navigation of commercial success have arisen for Cole, Kendrick, and other conscious artists. Would they have put out more songs that challenged the system more directly if they had no attachments to corporate entities?

There is a growing movement of artists who are choosing to remain independent, despite their growing popularity and increased offers from big-name record companies. One influential rapper who's been a fixture in the new wave of indie artists is Chicago emcee Chance the Rapper. At the height of his career, Chance refused to sign a traditional recording contract and was aggressively vocal about this decision. He expressed his disdain for the music industry system by jokingly mocking major record labels at live shows, addressing the predatory nature of labels, and emphasizing why artists should have full control over art publicly.[6] In a 2017 interview with Yahoo Global News, he stated:

> I think there's a lot of attention on me not signing a record deal. But I also don't believe in publishing deals or most of the traditional upper management style of music being distributed. I think whoever makes [the music] should have a say in when they release it, what they release, how much it costs.[7]

Other notable rappers like LaRussell, Russ, Tech N9ne, and Larry June have also flaunted their independence with pride, seemingly making, releasing, and promoting their music at will. They have built large organic fanbases who follow their tours, purchase their merchandise, and choose to buy physical CDs and vinyls from them directly, despite having full access to their digital catalogs.

There is no true freedom of speech when a creative is attached to a billion-dollar corporation. That freedom diminishes when the group making the art doesn't own and control the company. An artist is likely limited in subject matter and content that's deemed "acceptable." If Black artists don't begin claiming ownership of their art, the future of conscious rap could be dead. "As ownership grows more conscious rap pops up," Moody said. "When we start controlling the messages, it will help the music be seen in different ways."

The Exploitation of Black Art

The exploitation of Black art has been a glaring issue throughout music history. At the turn of the twentieth century, Black musicians were at the heart of genres like ragtime and the blues. Many even helmed all-black orchestras, but due to overly priced studio equipment and discrimination, Black musicians were often forced to play in the background. They were unable to record their own music, and they sold songs to White-owned phonograph companies for little money, fame, or recognition. Many even re-recorded and released these records with a White vocalist, without crediting the original songwriters.

These songs, then-known as "race records," reflected their lived experiences.[8] Many became hit records, but a large portion of the artists responsible for their success were erased from music history.

There were few exceptions. Singer George W. Johnson, known for popular ragtime songs like "The Laughing Song," is credited as the first Black person ever recorded, in 1890. Vaudevillians like George Walker and Bert Williams were among the first performers to cross racial lines. The duo performed alongside White musicians and actors in Broadway venues. Their songs "Good Morning, Carrie" and others were recorded at a time when Black musicians were barred from studios or priced out of purchasing studio equipment, which empowered White musicians to reap the benefits of their musical talents.

It wasn't until 1920 that Black composer Perry Bradford convinced Okeh Records to record a Black artist. The New York-based label had a division of foreign records in languages like Yiddish and Norwegian, but no other songs were targeted outside of those immigrant communities. Bradford eventually encouraged the label to give blues singer Mamie Smith a chance, and she delivered. Smith's 1920 hit "Crazy Blues," sung from the mind of a woman enraged by mistreatment, sold 75,000 copies in its first month of release. The song marked the world's first major blues record, and established the artform as a lasting memento of American music. The song also inspired other record labels to produce race records to garner the Black audiences they had once excluded from recording music.

Race records became a sought-after commodity for White record labels. It was easier to exploit and underpay Black artists than White ones. Since many of their songs were unpublished, labels purchased recording rights, and even the recordings themselves. Black artists were given pseudonyms, or their names were left out entirely, to ensure they didn't receive compensation for the success of the releases. And with Black artists largely excluded from organizations like the American Society of Composers, Artists, and Performers (ASCAP), they recorded without contracts and or paid royalties. These predatory actions led to serious financial issues. Artists like Bessie Smith, known as the "Empress of the Blues," generated Columbia Records millions in revenue, but she never received royalties for her music.

Throughout the mid-1920s, traveling scouts brought recording equipment to the American South, where they offered local musicians the opportunity to record their music. They profited from one-time, local recordings, without revealing the names of the artists, or crediting them for the music they crafted. While the recordings of artists like Bessie Smith, Ethel Waters, Louis Armstrong, and others have transcended time, other contributors have been scrubbed from music history. These unnamed and uncredited recordings serve as a reminder of how Black music and creatives were taken advantage of during a time of discrimination and exploitation.

It's crucial for the history of early Black American music to be preserved and taught to the next generation. Obtaining knowledge of this dark past can and should be internalized by today's artists and listeners to prevent it from repeating itself. Music fans and artists should actively support and advocate for museums, academic programs, and historians who teach and advance the conversations about Black music and its legacy of exploitation globally. In many ways, the past issues these genres endured have surfaced in hip-hop.

The Colonization of Rap

Born from the experiences of marginalized talents, hip-hop was a vehicle for Black Americans to better understand and reflect the world around them. The years of formation by Black artists in the 1970s built what became the house of hip-hop, and for a time, only true contributors of the culture were allowed entry. When it became a larger commodity, others were granted keys in the 1980s and 1990s. Many sought invitations into the house, while others peeked through side doors and cracked windows for entry. There were also cultural assailants, who attempted to bulldoze their way through hip-hop's doors. Others disguised themselves as true ambassadors of hip-hop, only to later reveal their impure intentions.

In time, questions about their intention, or intrusion, became harder to decipher. These same cultural invaders have infiltrated other musical genres established by Black musicians, especially blues, R&B, and rock and roll. As of late, hip-hop has become the grounds for non-contributors to camouflage themselves as champions of the culture, only to disregard its founding principles for their own success. It's the colonization of rap—or the appropriation of certain hip-hip elements or aesthetics for monetary gain—and it's been an issue for decades.

The colonization of rap has had many names, iterations, and phases. Like the real effects of colonialism within human history, which disproportionately affected Black communities throughout time, the raw materials of hip-hop have been extracted for the benefit of others. One example is Robert Van Winkle, better known as Vanilla Ice, who was on a meteoric rise with his massive 1990 hit, "Ice Ice Baby." After the release of his debut album *To the Extreme*, which became the fastest selling hip-hop album of all time, Ice was established as rap's first White solo star. He toured with MC Hammer, starred in the feature film *Cool as Ice*, and had a board game in his likeness. The fame proved too overwhelming for Ice, who later fell into drug addiction before regaining his footing years later. While he opened pathways for other White rappers to emerge, his journey largely served as a cautionary tale for non-Black rappers.

Growing up between Dallas and Miami, Ice had firm roots in hip-hop. He fronted a breakdancing troupe, battle rapped at parties, and opened up for the likes of MC Hammer, N.W.A., Public Enemy, and The D.O.C. before launching his own rap career. It wasn't until he signed with SBK that things went off the rails. The label encouraged him to adopt a mainstream look, more reflective of ones helmed by the likes of MC Hammer, and embrace a background that exaggerated and plainly fabricated his upbringing. His bio under SBK claimed he attended the same Miami high school as 2 Live Crew leader Luther "Uncle Luke" Campbell, that his mother was a music teacher at a Florida university, and that he was a national championship-winning motocross athlete for Team Honda—none of which was true.

The lies were uncovered by reporters at the *Miami Herald* and *Dallas Morning News*, and Ice was forced to come out publicly to address them. Many believed the bio was made to hide an affluent upbringing, or to falsify his street credibility. However, Ice contends that he grew up in impoverished neighborhoods in Dallas and Miami, was stabbed five times, and that the other altered details were to protect him and his family from the public eye. "I was trying to protect my privacy," Ice *told The Los Angeles Times* in a 1990 interview. "I didn't want people to find out who I was. I twisted a couple of things in the bio so people couldn't look me up. I was a bad kid growing up, always in trouble. My background is worse than I've said."[9]

His fabricated backstory, paired with his less-than-stellar rap skills, drew criticism from fans and fellow hip-hop acts. Among them was 3rd Bass, a group consisting of MC Serch, DJ Richie Rich, and Pete Nice, who compared Ice to Elvis Presley. They felt the King of Rock and Roll was a figure who was beloved for adopting a sound and style pioneered by Black musicians, without crediting them for their influence.

While the rise of Vanilla Ice is widely considered a low point in the golden era of rap, his momentary reign broadened rap audiences and opened doors for other non-Black hip-hop stars, who expressed genuine interest in springing the culture forward. The Beastie Boys established firm ground in the 1980s, and years after Vanilla Ice's rise and drastic fall, acts like Eminem emerged. They became permanent residents in the pantheons of hip-hop, who were revered for their work and influence.

Eminem went on to become one of the highest-selling rappers of all-time, while simultaneously elevating the careers of Curtis "50 Cent" Jackson, Detroit supergroup D12, the rap collective Slaughterhouse, and other musical acts. Eminem was also embraced for acknowledging his privilege in the culture within songs like "White America," where he raps "if I was Black I would've sold half. I ain't have to graduate from Lincoln High School to know that." However, others weren't so well intentioned. There have been several artists, record executives, and label heads who have had other motives, mostly those focused on generating dollars rather than uplifting or changing hip-hop for the better.

Throughout decades, hip-hop has seen artists use hip-hop music and a "rap aesthetic" to rise to prominence, and then completely alter their sound and image to appease a different audience. In the 1990s, a Michigan artist named Kid Rock released multiple hip-hop projects, including a multi-platinum album called *Devil Without a Cause* in 1998. By the early 2000s, Kid Rock was performing on stages with a confederate flag flying in the background, singing country and rock music.[10] He was also reportedly using the n-word in an interview with *Billboard* in 2024.[11] And after a video surfaced of country singer Morgan Wallen using the racial slur himself, Rock hosted Wallen's first show amid the controversy.[12]

Yelawolf, a rapper discovered by Eminem, also raised the confederate flag at his shows.[13] When faced with backlash from the Black community, he defended this decision publicly before changing his stance. Post Malone rose to prominence through a song called "White Iverson" rocking a grill and braided hair. A few years later, Post switched to country music and voiced his opposition to hip-hop, stating, 'If you're looking to think about life, don't listen to hip-hop.'[14] Many of these acts use hip-hop's popularity and edginess to spark their career, and later show disregard and disdain for the culture and people who got them there. Being a "rapper" was merely a costume.

To avoid this occurrence, cultural gatekeeping in hip-hop is mandatory. This could consist of boycotting artists who are appropriating the sound of Black artists and musicians without paying homage and crediting them appropriately. Also, banishing record executives or cultural figures who leech off the fruits of the culture, without supporting the artists or hip-hop figures who push it forward could also be a protective measure. Setting this precedent can keep hip-hop's sound and culture intact, while protecting the legacy of the genre's originators and fending off culture vultures.

Culture Vultures

The term was coined by fellow Roc-A-Fella Records CEO Damon "Dame" Dash, who took aim at long-time music executives like Lyor Cohen, formerly of Def Jam and 300 Entertainment. In 2017's *Culture Vultures: Conversations with Damon Dash*, writer Kenyatta Griggs and Dash defined the term. They said a culture vulture isn't based on race or skin color. It's centered on a person's "state of mind" or "honor code," with Griggs and Dash writing:

A culture vulture can be Black or White. It's the people who exploit other cultures and make money from them when they can't make money off of their own culture, not giving back, and robbing people like robbing a child because he doesn't know any better.

Dash and Griggs pointed to Cohen and other record executives like Steve Stoute, Alan Grunblatt, Joie Manda, and Todd Moscowitz. These were all figures who they felt exploited a life and culture they didn't live or respect, and were willing to lie, cheat, and steal from their artists to get ahead. The two authors also noted how they profited from rappers' beef, refusing to de-escalate certain disputes if it meant stopping the money from rolling in, no matter how far things could go. In the book, they pinpoint these figures as some of the culprits responsible for the decline of conscious rap in the mainstream and the promotion of the genre's most damning qualities. However, executives with this mindset have been lurking throughout hip-hop since its inception.

The culture vultures Dash and Griggs described are the same figures Chuck D and A Tribe Called Quest called out in the 1990s. On "Check the Rhime," Q-Tip rapped "Industry Rule No. 4080, record company people are shady." And after years calling out executives for their predatory business practices, including at his own label, Chuck D filed a $100 million class action lawsuit against Universal Music Group in 2011.[15] He and Andrew Titus of Black Sheep, Rick James's estate, and other artists alleged there were millions of miscalculated royalties for digital downloads owed to them. The filing suggests MP3 and ringtone downloads were improperly classified as sales instead of licenses, leaving artists with only 15 percent of collected income rather than the 50 percent they claimed were due.

In 2015, UMG settled the lawsuit.[16] The company had to pay $11.5 million in supplemental royalties for past digital downloads, and increase future download royalties by 10 percent to specific artists submitting claims. It was a significant win for hip-hop amid the pivot from physical to online digital distribution, but disputes between record execs and hip-hop stars didn't end there. The same issues persisted after 2015's legal victory. Artists like Lil Wayne and Megan Thee Stallion publicly clashed with their labels for blocking the release of new music. Stars like Big Sean, Kanye West, De La Soul, and others sought ownership of their masters, or original song recordings, to dictate how their music would be used and monetized.[17] Others fought for creative control, pushing back against their labels' expectations in exchange for their own musical vision.

Throughout the 2020s, the demand for viral or Spotify playlist-friendly hits was a top priority for record labels, but not all artists were willing to forfeit their artistic vision, sound, or brand to spark short-term interest. Despite the shift toward drill, emo, and psychedelic rap, artists like Cole and Kendrick remained true to their musicality. They remained firm in their creative pursuits and spearheaded conscious rap at the highest level in music. "They have found a delicate balance of undeniable focus and care for the craft, while simultaneously making hits year after year," said artist and Loyola University New Orleans professor Raney Antoine Jr.

Other artists didn't have the same fervor. Many fell victim to the same trappings of old. Certain industry demands and societal pressures stripped them of their authenticity and artistic voices. They collaborated with specific rappers or stirred up social media beefs, solely for clicks and views. Attention became the new capital.

Past artists would have scoffed at the lengths rappers go to for fame or virality. The reasons they conform, or resort to social media antics, are the same reasons past artists adopted popular aesthetics or sounds foreign to their own. It was for financial gain and widespread acceptance. Anything in opposition made their climb to stardom that much steeper, but even with social media opening doors for certain personalities to break through, the era of cancel culture made the move much more challenging.

Denouncing Cancel Culture

As hip-hop becomes more valuable to corporate entities, a layer of new expectations is being placed on artists. In past decades, emcees were able to function as rebels within the larger scope of the music industry, but to reach a high level of mainstream success, they are expected to "play the game." In the age of social media, the fear of being "cancelled" is now a perceived reality for music acts of today. This fear is likely to hinder how far artists are willing to push the boundaries when it comes to addressing societal issues, local and international politics, and their own controversial ideologies.

A public figure being cancelled typically consists of them being stripped of financial opportunities such as endorsements, live performances, and brand collaborations due to them making inappropriate or offensive statements in the eyes of the general public, or a group with significant influence.

Ironically, artists glorifying murder, gang activity, or drug dealing rarely face cancellation by corporate affiliates. A brand may decide not to attach themselves to a certain kind of artist to begin with, but once they have bought in it's rarely considered a deal-breaker. There are few, if any, cases of artists losing their clothing or endorsement deals due to lyrics about wanting to kill an enemy. Instead, companies are able to dictate what positions, statements, or behaviors are deemed accepted for artists. This inherently hinders an artist's creative process, in a similar way a nontenured professor would be limited in their research potential.

It's important for fans to denounce the concept and notion of cancel culture when it pertains to hip-hop. At its core, hip-hop is a genre filled with a range of perspectives, ideologies, and viewpoints that are integral in solving or shedding light on societal issues. It's rooted in the very fabric of hip-hop. While corporations will always act to protect their bottom line, rap fans and musicians need to take the same liberties to protect their freedom of speech and combat cancel culture.

The Power of Lyrical Substance

Without lyrical substance, social issues would have gone unchecked, revolutions would have been squandered, and the state of music (and the world) would look vastly different. Hip-hop artists have urged listeners to fight against their oppressors, to embrace their individualism, and abandon any destructive paths stopping them from attaining self-fulfillment.

These messages have been woven into songs by rap's most celebrated poets, whose sizzling punchlines and memorable verses have been permanently inscribed in the minds of music fans. From 2Pac's "Keep Ya Head Up" to Talib Kweli's "Get By" and Joey Bada$$'s "Land of the Free," they all conveyed different messages. 2Pac's 1993 classic serves as a reminder to stay strong in the face of adversity and takes a stand for women's reproductive rights nearly thirty years before the overturning of Roe v. Wade in 2022, when the U.S. Supreme Court ruling eliminated women's constitutional right to an abortion. Kweli's "Get By" reflects on the overcoming of life's challenges, particularly when money is tight and opportunities are limited. "Land of the Free" placed a mirror in the face of America, with Joey Bada$$ noting just how destructive the country had become under President Donald Trump.

That's the power of quality lyrics, and among the sharpest wordsmiths in rap history are Cole and Kendrick. They have proven their ability to spark cultural movements, shine light on the wrongdoings of power-hungry oppressors, and present ways for Black America to push forward. The result has been a more evolved hip-hop. Even when lyricism became a secondary focus in the 2010s, they remained two of the few mainstream hitmakers placing songwriting at the forefront. There were fewer artists taking the same artistic leaps, and hip-hop culture ultimately suffered.

The gap between the Coles and the Kendricks, and the rest of rap's headliners, grew exponentially wider. The drop-off in lyrical substance had lessened the impact and longevity of many hit records and albums. They didn't stick to the bones quite as much as they used to, and that falls on the artists themselves, as well as the labels and fans consuming their music. It's their responsibility to inject songs with messages that promote self-empowerment, echo the thoughts and feelings of those in underserved communities, and inform listeners on the lessons they have learned. The mayor of Fayetteville Mitch Colvin said Cole and Kendrick's push to social consciousness and reformation is "beautiful," and it harks back to the pioneers before them – namely KRS-One and Public Enemy. Colvin stated:

> I think that's what makes them different, right? That there [are] the things that are best for you and your career, and then there [are] the best things for society, because they have an incredible bully pulpit, right? The words that they say can instantly go out to millions of people. I think them using that to push a message of social consciousness or change or reform is huge, and that's commendable for both of them to do that.

That's not to say Cole and Kendrick are the only two emcees pushing penmanship in modern rap. Artists like Wale, Joey Bada$$, Rapsody, Vic Mensa, Vince Staples, Doechii, Tyler, The Creator, and others have generated hits with their lyrical abilities at center. Though, younger emcees and audiences have favored artists with simpler rhyme schemes, flows, and less redeeming messages. It coincides with the emergence of mumble rap, where lyrics are delivered in a slow, unintelligible manner. It encourages fans to be hyperfocused on artists' production and image, rather than the actual content of their music.

By the mid-2010s, lyricism was almost looked at as a handicap. Artists prioritized accessibility over substance, and mainstream audiences were calling for it. It's a phenomenon that's emerged with the oversaturation of music on streaming platforms. The challenges these algorithm-driven platforms present are steep for many artists, particularly those who make thought-provoking music.

Along with Kendrick's ability to camouflage conscious records, Cole has struck similar chords. Through most of his career, his music has been deemed more easily digestible. Cole has released music more frequently, and he's leaned into new musical trends far more often than Kendrick. Justin Hunte said Cole takes less artistic risks between the two emcees, but that's also why Cole's music is more appealing to casual or non-traditional hip-hop fans. Hunte stated:

> Cole has a more palatable approach when he puts out music. I also think Cole connects with people easier. Between Kendrick's voice changes, flow switches, and third person stories, he forces you to pay attention. Cole as an artist is more direct, and I think that's what Cole fans really love about him. He doesn't take long to get to the point, and that's a powerful thing.

Despite their different approaches to music, neither Cole nor Kendrick cheat fans out of lyrical substance. Cole's lyrics on "Love Yourz" strengthened the minds of his listeners. Records like "amari" and "Grown Simba" motivated his fans to broaden their horizons, assuring them that one day they could reach the peak of their powers. Kendrick did the same on songs like "DNA," "Alright," and "Complexion (A Zulu Love)." The songs reassured listeners that their ancestry is linked to kings and queens of past centuries, and that they can overcome any barriers in their way.

Without lyrical substance or reason, there's no longevity or societal change. Artists who placed the same emphasis on lyricism and conscious messaging have withstood the test of time. No matter how long it's been since Public Enemy's "Fight the Power," The Roots' "You Got Me," Lauryn Hill's "Doo Wop (That Thing)," and other conscious records, they always have a place in music history because of the messages they bear. From the time of their release until now (and so on), these songs and their memorable lyrics will continue to touch the souls of hip-hop fans. The lessons imbued in each line will serve as a call for action, self-empowerment, and internal reflection for generations of listeners to come. And future artists need to take note.

Don't Rap Without Reason

Without lyrical substance and conscious messaging, all the work of hip-hop's pioneers would be undone. Music, community, activism, and artistic expression are the sources of hip-hop's power, and it's the reason why the genre is a global phenomenon. 2Pac's "Changes" directly addressed police brutality amid rising tensions between Black Americans and law enforcement. Lil Wayne's "Georgia Bush" highlighted the devastation of Hurricane Katrina in his hometown of New Orleans. Wayne criticized then-President George W. Bush and his decision to send American troops to Iraq instead of deploying them to provide aid to Louisiana. While Wayne is an artist who is not often known for speaking up on social issues through his music, this record's impact could be felt worldwide.

> *Fuck it he just let him kill all of our troops*
> *Look at the bullshit we been through*
> *Had the niggas sittin on top they roofs*
> *Hurricane Katrina, we shoulda called it Hurricane (Georgia) Bush*

These songs brought added awareness to issues impacting Black Americans and other underserved communities, including those on foreign soil. Lupe Fiasco's "Words I Never Said" addressed the Israeli-Palestinian conflict, long before the Hamas-led attack into Israeli territory on October 7, 2023, that sparked global debate and protest. He also criticized former President Barack Obama, who he felt was complacent in the Middle Eastern conflict because of his silence concerning the two parties. On the day of Obama's second presidential inauguration, Fiasco was booted off stage by security during an unofficial inaugural ball in Washington DC after performing "Words I Never Said" for thirty minutes.[18] The party organizer denied Fiasco was removed for his political views, but the timing of the incident drew opposing views.

While fans have been mixed on Fiasco's pro-Palestinian views, and his critiques of US foreign policy, it's undeniably impacted his career. After sparring with fans on social media over the freestyle "NERD," with some claiming he spewed antisemitic rhetoric, Lupe announced the cancellation of three forthcoming albums and threatened retirement in December 2016.[19] He soon un-retired with the release of 2017's *Drogas Light*, but his stake in mainstream rap never reached the same height as it did before 2011's *Lasers*.

The risks taken by Fiasco and earlier musical revolutionaries like KRS-One, Dead Prez, and Immortal Technique inspired international emcees to take on similar racial and political matters. Global stars like M.I.A., who was born in London to Sri Lankan Tamil parents, criticized the government of Sri Lanka for the ongoing civil war with the Liberation Tigers of Tamil Eelam (LTTE).[20] The militant organization attempted to establish a separate Tamil state due to discrimination by the largely Sinhalese-dominated government. Through a series of artful vignettes, the music video for M.I.A.'s "Born Free" reflected the hostility, tension, and violence happening in her ancestral grounds.

Other international artists used hip-hop to expose the discriminatory and inhumane conditions impacting their native countries. On 2019's "This Is Iraq," Iraqi-New Zealand rapper I-NZ condemned the political corruption and foreign intervention plaguing the Middle Eastern country. Dominican-Spanish rapper Arianna Puello's "Asi es la negra," which translates to "That's what the Black woman is like," addressed the racist attitudes towards her and other Black migrants in Spain. Racionals MC's, considered the most influential hip-hop group in Brazilian history, criticized the country's prisons and deeply flawed justice system on songs like "Diário de um Detento." This trend needs to continue for the survival of conscious rap.

Trial by Lyrics

No matter the consequences faced, American and international artists have boldly inserted conscious messaging in their music. Not all succeeded in reversing discrimination action or harmful political policy, but their musical protests paid dividends much later. The same goes for artists who have pushed more harmful rhetoric. Not only did it further glamorize violence and drug use, in many cases, their irresponsible lyrics have placed them in legal turmoil.

In a 2022 study by Andrea Dennis, co-author of the 2019 book, *Rap on Trial: Race, Lyrics and Guilt in America*, she found nearly 500 criminal trial cases that date back to the late 1980s, where rap lyrics were successfully used as evidence.[21] One such case involved Atlanta rappers Young Thug, Gunna, and other affiliates connected to the Young Slime Life imprint. In 2023, the state of Georgia prosecuted Thug, born Jeffrey Williams, and the YSL collective for racketeering. The crime is defined by the act of operating an illegal business entity, often involving bribery, fraud, drug or human trafficking, and extortion to make a profit.

Fulton County District Attorney Fani Willis announced she would pursue legal action against the alleged YSL gang using the Racketeer Influenced and Corrupt Organizations Act (RICO) statute.[22] Willis claimed the Young Thug-led group was responsible for several shootings and homicides in the Atlanta area over a decade and had ties with the national Bloods gang. Following months of contentious court filings and debates about the admissibility of song lyrics, Fulton County Superior Court Judge Ural Glanville ruled that seventeen specific sets of lines from Young Thug and other YSL artists' music could be used in the case.[23] Defense lawyers tried to suppress the use of their lyrics, arguing the practice violated the First Amendment right of free speech, and would wrongfully prejudice the jury.

After more than 500 days of litigation, it became the longest-running criminal trial in Georgia history. While the state secured nineteen convictions in total through plea deals and other verdicts, the case ended with no murder convictions.[24] Thug agreed to a plea deal of his own on October 31, 2024. The deal required him to serve fifteen years on probation, perform quarterly anti-violence lectures, have no contact with gang members or victims, and he was barred from the metro Atlanta area for ten years. During sentencing, Superior Court Judge Paige Whitaker encouraged Thug to use his music to encourage more positive messaging and action, rather than violence and crime. Whitaker stated:

> If you choose to continue to rap, you need to try to use your influence to let kids know that is not the way to go. There are ways out of poverty besides

hooking up with the powerful guy at the end of the street selling drugs ...
I want you to be more of the solution and less of the problem.

The high-profile case was among the biggest in hip-hop history, but it wasn't
the first to include artists' rap lyrics as evidence. In 1992, lyrics from Mac Dre's
"Punk Police" were used to convict the Bay Area legend, who was sentenced
to five years in prison. And when artists like Snoop Dogg and Boosie Badazz
faced first-degree murder trials, prosecutors used lyrics from Snoop's "Murder
Was the Case" and Boosie's "187" to link the two artists to homicides. Both
received not-guilty verdicts.

Debates about the use of song lyrics in legal trials have always been
contentious. Many believe lyrics should be used in a case if directly linked or
relevant to a crime. Others believe it violates free speech, thus making it a flawed
and unfair prosecutive tool. The lines blurred with the emergence of the drill
movement, which saw artists diss opposing emcees or gang members who were
killed, or allude to taking part in robberies or deadly crimes on record. Rap fans
and law professionals continue to be split on the matter, but what's undeniable is
the importance of the written word, and the responsibilities held by high-profile
artists. Rap lyrics can fuel positive change in society or be weaponized for its
destruction. It's up to artists to step up their penmanship, and for consumers to
embrace higher-quality music for intellectual rap to survive.

Despite some popular opinions, the testimonials of artists with crime-filled
pasts are still valuable for the genre and culture. Hearing tales from people who
escaped deadly circumstances to chase their dreams and become successful
often serves as a source of inspiration for listeners. Furthermore, the artists
who express the full scope of their past without omitting the pain, loss of loved
ones, incarceration, and PTSD can also deter someone from thinking about
entering that lifestyle.

However, rappers with past (or present) street affiliations should strongly
reconsider openly attaching themselves through songs and visuals. With RICO
cases on the rise, and hip-hop artists often being targeted by state and federal
agencies, rappers attaching themselves to any organizations that are deemed
"criminal" or labeled "gangs" is risky to their careers, livelihood, and freedom.
Even if the artist is not engaging in any illegal behaviors, the public association

alone can cause artists to be the focus of an investigation. Due to the current state of the legal system, artists must be strategic when addressing their pasts.

Responsibility of the Consumer

While record labels and artists play a significant role in the future of rap music, the genre's consumers also hold a crucial responsibility. Given the amount of media that users are force-fed daily through algorithms, the ability to accept or reject content is still available. Many listeners have become comfortable listening to messaging for entertainment that completely contradicts their actual belief system. Amplifying the music that spreads awareness to real-world problems is key, though.

It's crucial for music fans to actively support and advocate for artists who speak to social issues that they deem important. The praise for those artists should match or surpass the public disdain expressed for artists with messaging that they oppose. Support could mean sharing their music on social media, attending concerts, or purchasing their merch. Music executive Richie Abbott said the key to a musical shift is in the hands of the fans themselves:

> I've said for a long time, the music industry and record execs don't run the music business, the fans do, always have and always will. Music that makes you think may not be for those who just want to feel, but artists like Kendrick have successfully proven to do both and that's a beautiful thing. We need more artists like him, and they are coming.

Both record labels and fans often gravitate to musical trends. In the early 2000s, when "snap" dance records like "Laffy Taffy" and "Lean Wit It, Rock Wit It" picked up steam out of Atlanta and climbed the charts, labels flooded the market with other dance records from new and older acts. When Chicago rapper Chief Keef's record "I Don't Like" rose to prominence in 2012, labels flocked to sign other Chicago rappers who were making music that fit the "drill" sound and aesthetic. This same reality can exist again for music with deeper, progressive, and thought-provoking substance. All that's needed is a collective push from fans, artists, and the labels themselves.

Elements Needed for Survival

The year 2023 marked fifty years in rap, yet the culture was facing one of its most abysmal commercial droughts in recent memory.[25] Even with rappers Killer Mike, Larry June, and Gunna dropping during the first half of the year, hip-hop didn't secure a No. 1 spot on the Billboard 200 albums chart or Hot 100 for six months. It marked the longest stretch without a No. 1 rap album since 1993. It wasn't until Lil Uzi Vert's *Pink Tape* that rap's dry spell ended, but the project did little to represent or build up to the significance of year fifty. There were award show tributes and televised dedications to celebrate the historic mark, but for a moment, hip-hop was stuck in suspension. As fans looked back on the genre's pioneers and pivotal milestones, they began to question what rap had become and where it was headed. The genre was in need of a facelift, and artists like Cole and Kendrick stepped up to the operation table.

Cole's 2024 project *Might Delete Later* was a quality release that further teased his long-awaited album, *The Fall Off*. Kendrick continued his musical tear with the release of *GNX*, a welcomed ode to his West Coast roots that set the stage for rising talents like AzChike and others throughout the album. Their projects and the genre-shifting debacle between Cole, Kendrick, and Drake set hip-hop ablaze. Amid the smoke, rap's competitive fire returned to the main stage in ways unseen since Kendrick's "Control" verse. Rappers like Joey Bada$$, Ray Vaughn, Daylyt, and others exchanged fiery verses over which coast reigned supreme. Joyner Lucas and Skepta also drew lyrical arms, releasing a series of diss records to decide whether the US or UK had superior talent.

The musical disses reminded purists of the days when rappers battled on street corners, and shook hands as a sign of mutual respect. It also placed lyricism at the forefront. No longer were social media exchanges or viral memes suitable for rap beef. They laid their grievances on wax, and didn't resort to violence when tensions ran hot. It also pushed artists to drop more music of substance, rather than the same continuous cycle of baseless releases fans were accustomed to. It seemed like more established artists were addressing societal issues, and that long-time hip-hop fans were finally having their wishes granted. They endured the decline of trap music, the devastation of the drill and psychedelic rap movements, and the low lights of the mumble rap era for the long-awaited resurgence of intellectual rap.

It's a movement many hope fully returns to mainstream rap. For its protection, it takes more than a small collection of artists to exemplify what's made rap such an integral part of music. It requires record labels, streaming services, and fans to support conscious rap. Artists like Cole and Kendrick are certainly doing their part as artists and torchbearers, but it's up to the other parties to hold up their weight. By championing conscious rap, it's honoring the legends who first formed hip-hop, and pressed it forward as a brand, culture, and sound. This also ensures Cole and Kendrick aren't the last megastars to carry on the hip-hop tradition. It's time for all others to embrace the power of conscious rap, and encourage future contributors to continue the legacy. Conscious rap lives.

Acknowledgments

We first and foremost have to thank hip-hop. Music from the genre motivated, uplifted, educated, and inspired us throughout our journeys. Rap has gotten us through the rough times, and provided us a soundtrack throughout the good times. We want to acknowledge our Bloomsbury editor Michael Tan for believing in the vision of this book from the very beginning. We also want to acknowledge all of the scholars, artists, producers, journalists, and authors who agreed to be interviewed for the book. Their insight and perspectives were crucial in crafting this narrative.

Dr. Jeremy C. McCool Personal Acknowledgments

I want to thank my mother for always supporting my passion for hip-hop throughout my journey. I also want to acknowledge programs in Chicago such as After School Matters and The Happiness Club for giving me an opportunity to expose myself to other kids who were just as passionate about the arts as me in the city, giving me a safe and productive outlet. I want to thank the city of Chicago and Mississippi for exposing me to homegrown music influences such as Juke, House, Gospel, and Blues at a young age. I also want to thank the hip-hop artists who impacted my life personally, such as 2Pac, Jay-Z, Scarface, OutKast, and Common.

I also have to thank my mentor Dr. Jack Thomas, who encouraged me to enter academia. I thank Taylor for her constant support and encouragement. I want to thank all of my past, present, and future students. I learn just as much from you as you do from me. Lastly, I want to thank you for purchasing and reading this book. I hope it informed and/or reinforced the impact of hip-hop in society.

Earl Hopkins Personal Acknowledgments

I have to thank my parents, Mr. Earl and Vivian Hopkins. Without your guidance and reassurance, I wouldn't have life, direction, or purpose. You are my foundation. I also have to thank my siblings Lelia, TaMara, Vicci, and Dejuan. In your own unique way, you each pushed me to be a better me. You kept me grounded when my thoughts ran wild, and gave me confidence when tasks appeared too large. I love you all.

I have to thank the city of Columbus, Ohio. It's a criminally underrated Midwest city booming with creative talent. While artists like Nas, 2Pac, and Jay-Z made me fall in love with hip-hop, it was the rap shows at Newport Music Hall and Woodlands Tavern between 2014–17 that inspired me to become a music writer. I still think about the artists and sounds that came from that era.

I also want to thank my mentors Justice Hill and Allison Hunter. Whenever I was at a professional or personal crossroads, you offered time, opportunity, and wisdom at pivotal moments in my life and career. Thank you forever. And to Ashley, the love of my life, I thank you for your patience and unwavering support. I couldn't have done this without you.

Lastly, we want to thank *you* for reading *Raps of Resistance*. By purchasing and reading this book, it's proof that meaningful art still has a place in this increasingly frayed world. We hope the book sparked or reinvigorated your love of conscious rap. We hope it gave you a deeper appreciation for the hip-hop icons, freedom fighters, and musical activists of the past, present, and future. We hope this gives you a clearer view of the power of Blackness in all its forms. And we hope this book inspired you to make your own positive mark on society, whatever or however it may be.

Notes

Chapter 1

1 Noreen Nasir, "In the Beginning, There Was the Bronx," AP News, 2023. https://proje
cts.apnews.com/features/2023/hip-hop-50th-history/in-the-beginning-there-was-the-
bronx.html.

2 John Leland, "THE SPIN INTERVIEW: DJ Kool Herc," *SPIN*, 2023. https://www.spin.
com/2023/08/the-spin-interview-dj-kool-herc/.

3 Questlove, and Ben Greenman, *Hip-Hop is History* (AUWA, 2024). https://questlove.
com/hip-hop-is-history/.

4 "500 Greatest Songs of All Time (2004)," *Rolling Stone*, 2003. https://www.rollingstone.
com/music/music-lists/500-greatest-songs-of-all-time-151127/grandmaster-flash-
and-the-furious-five-the-message-56194/.

5 djvlad, "Melle Mel Explains Why 'The Message' Was the Single Most Important
Song in Hip Hop History (Part 4)," YouTube, 2021. https://www.youtube.com/
watch?v=9QBDNsbBHSE.

6 Alec Wilkinson, "New York Is Killing Me," *The New Yorker*, 2010. https://www.newyor
ker.com/magazine/2010/08/09/new-york-is-killing-me.

7 Dorian Lynskey, "The Forgotten 'Godfathers' of Hip-hop," *BBC News*, 2023. https://
www.bbc.com/culture/article/20230807-the-last-poets-and-watts-prophets-the-radi
cal-poets-overshadowed-by-hip-hop.

8 Dart Adams, "How Stop the Violence Movement's 'Self Destruction' Became One of
Rap's Most Important Releases," *Okayplayer*, 2019. https://www.okayplayer.com/origin
als/the-making-krs-one-stop-the-violence-movements-self-destruction-single-89.html.

9 Michel Marriott, "One Is Killed and 12 Are Injured as L.I. Rap Concert Turns Violent,"
The New York Times, 1988. https://www.nytimes.com/1988/09/12/nyregion/one-is-kil
led-and-12-are-injured-as-li-rap-concert-turns-violent.html.

10 Michel Marriott, "9 Charged, 4 with Murder, in Robbery Spree at L.I. Rap Concert,"
The New York Times, 1988. https://www.nytimes.com/1988/09/19/nyregion/9-char
ged-4-with-murder-in-robbery-spree-at-li-rap-concert.html.

11 Greg McKevitt, "'It's Time to Retaliate in Song'—Why NWA's Provocative 80s Rap
Became an Anthem," *BBC News*, 2024. https://www.bbc.com/culture/article/20240
802-the-nwa-protest-anthem-that-foreshadowed-riots-in-the-us.

12 "Race & Policing—'to Protect and to Serve'—L.A.P.D. Culture," *PBS*. https://www. pbs.org/wgbh/pages/frontline/shows/lapd/race/protectserve.html. Accessed August 14, 2025.

13 Paul Meara, "J. Cole Celebrates Nas Lyrics & 'I Gave You Power' in Speech," *HipHopDX*, 2014. https://hiphopdx.com/news/id.27225/title.j-cole-celebrates-nas-lyr ics-i-gave-you-power-in-speech.

Chapter 2

1 "The Complete List of Platinum Hip-Hop Albums by Year," *DJBooth*, 2015. https://djbooth.net/features/2015-10-20-platinum-hip-hop-albums-year-breakd own/#:~:text=To%20extend%20that%20even%20further,%2D1997%29%20there%20w ere%2012.

2 The Roots, "Ice-T Says He Based 6 N' the Morning on Schoolly D's PSK (What Does It Mean)?", YouTube, 2023. https://www.youtube.com/watch?v=syFagoTn77c.

3 Chuck Philips, "Anti-Rap Crusader Under Fire," *Los Angeles Times*, 1996. https://www. latimes.com/local/la-fi-tupacdelores20march2096-story.html.

4 Naima Cochrane, "Music Sermon: The Groundbreaking Sprite and St. Ides Hip-Hop Campaigns," *VIBE*, 2018. https://www.vibe.com/features/editorial/music-sermon-spr ite-st-ides-hip-hop-625444/.

5 "Rap Artist Tupac Shakur Shot in Robbery," *The New York Times*, 1994. https://www. nytimes.com/1994/11/30/nyregion/rap-artist-tupac-shakur-shot-in-robbery.html.

6 Brian Haack, " 'The Miseducation of Lauryn Hill': For the Record," *GRAMMY Awards*, 2018. https://www.grammy.com/news/miseducation-lauryn-hill-record.

7 Sean Michaels, "Ice T Tells Soulja Boy: You Killed Hip-Hop," *The Guardian*, 2008. https://www.theguardian.com/music/2008/jun/19/news.culture1#:~:text=%22Sou lja%20Boy%2C%20I%20know%20you,of%20the%20gangsta%2Drap%20era.

8 djvlad, "Khujo Goodie: Andre 3000 Was the First Artist to Say 'Trappin" on a Song (Part 2)," YouTube, 2020. https://www.youtube.com/watch?v=DIxQ-zAHr18.

9 The Angie Martinez Show, "T.I. Claims He Created Trap Music," YouTube, 2017. https://www.youtube.com/watch?v=4Zc1RWcQcfY.

Chapter 3

1 Andres Tardio, "Jay Z Gives J. Cole His Original Roc-A-Fella Chain," HipHopDX, 2013. https://hiphopdx.com/news/jay-z-gives-j-cole-his-original-roc-a-fella-chain/.

2 Francesca Gariano, "All About J. Cole's Parents, James and Kay Cole," PEOPLE, 2024. https://people.com/all-about-j-cole-parents-8622187.

3 Frannie Kelley, "J. Cole on Competition and Writing Honest Songs," NPR, 2013. https://www.npr.org/sections/microphonecheck/2013/06/23/194594097/j-cole-on- competition-and-writing-honest-songs.

4 Galindo Thomas, "J. Cole Shares List of Hip-Hop Artists Who Inspired Him," *American Songwriter*, 2023. https://americansongwriter.com/j-cole-sha res-list-of-hip-hop-artists-who-inspired-him/.

5 "J. Cole Says His Early Music Was Him 'Literally Just Sounding Like Eminem & Nas,'" DJBooth, 2016. https://djbooth.net/features/2016-06-07-j-cole-eminem-nas/.

6 Nardwuar Serviette, "Nardwuar vs. J. Cole (2021)," YouTube, 2021. https://www.yout ube.com/watch?v=GxVXEd_G_60.

7 On Air with Ryan Seacrest, "J. Cole Confesses His First Rapper Name | Interview | On Air with Ryan Seacrest," YouTube, 2013. https://www.youtube.com/watch?v=rKv0 ZMlwjhU.

8 "J. Cole Gives Us a Tour of 2014 Forest Hills Drive in Fayetteville, N.C.," Complex News, YouTube, 2014. https://www.youtube.com/watch?v=QR-Nw5LV BgI&t=220s.

9 Bryan Armen Graham, "J. Cole on His Hoop Dreams, And Why the World Won't Allow LeBron to Be as Great as MJ," SI, 2013. https://www.si.com/extra-mustard/2013/06/12/ j-cole-on-his-hoop-dreams-and-why-the-world-wont-allow-lebron-to-be-as-great-as-mj.

10 Nathalie Weiner, "The Oral History of J. Cole's Basketball Career," Bleacher Report, 2017. https://bleacherreport.com/articles/2704529-the-oral-history-of-j-coles-basketball-career.

11 "From Rock Stars to Rappers, St. John's Hosts a Who's Who of Musicians on Campus," St. John's University, 2019. https://www.stjohns.edu/news-media/news/2019-10-29/ rock-stars-rappers-st-johns-hosts-whos-who-musicians-campus.

12 David Shapiro, "J. Cole's Tales Out of School," *Interview Magazine*, 2013. https://www. interviewmagazine.com/music/j-cole-harvard.

13 Michael Futch, "'I Lived It:' Fayetteville State Has History in Civil Rights Movement," *The Fayetteville Observer*, 2020. https://www.fayobserver.com/story/news/local/murchi son-road/2020/02/22/lsquoi-lived-itrsquo-fayetteville-state-has-history-in-civil-rig hts-movement/41821221/.

14 "Fayetteville's Black Community Calls for Change in Police Culture in Wake of Tyre Nichols' Death," ABC11,, January 27, 2023. https://abc11.com/post/police-cult ure-tyre-nichols-brutality-fayetteville/12742566/.

15 Power 106 Los Angeles, "J. Cole Speaks on His Alicia Keys Crush," YouTube, 2013. https://www.youtube.com/watch?v=ud5FMX1a3jo.

16 "Rapper J. Cole Talks Graduating Magna Cum Laude," *The Wall Street Journal*, 2013. https://www.wsj.com/video/rapper-j-cole-talks-graduating-magna-cum-laude/B1FD0 DF5-F6EE-4F69-8C28-476300B9410F.

17 Sophie Caraan, "J. Cole's 'The Come Up' Mixtape Is Now on Streaming Services," Hypebeast, 2024. https://hypebeast.com/2024/11/j-cole-the-come-up-mixt ape-vol-1-now-on-streaming-services.

18 Danielle Harling, "J. Cole Says 'Lights Please' Secured His Meeting with Jay-Z, Refers to the Song as a 'J. Cole Classic,'" HipHopDX, 2012. https://hipho pdx.com/news/j-cole-says-lights-please-secured-his-meeting-with-jay-z-ref ers-to-the-song-as-a-j-cole-classic/.

19 Ajacobs, "J. Cole, Tiye Phoenix, Statik Selektah, HipHopDX Win at Underground Music Awards," HipHopDX, 2010. https://hiphopdx.com/news/j-cole-tiye-phoenix-sta tik-selektah-hiphopdx-win-at-underground-music-awards/.

20 Petar Kujundzic, "MTV's Hottest Breakthrough MCS,—J. Cole," Hypebeast, 2010. https://hypebeast.com/2018/7/mtvs-hottest-breakthrough-mcs-j-cole.

21 ionehiphopwiredstaff, "BET Releases List of Nominees for 2010 Hip-Hop Awards," Hip-Hop Wired, 2010. https://hiphopwired.com/56131/bet-releases-list-of-nomin ees-for-2010-hip-hop-awards-22222/.

22 Xxlstaff, "Meet the 2010 XXL Freshman Class (XXL April 2010 Issue)," *XXL Mag*, 2010. https://www.xxlmag.com/2010-xxl-freshman-class/.

23 Eddie Washington, "J. Cole Scores His First #1 Hit on Billboard Hot 100," *The Black Wall Street Times*, 2024. https://theblackwallsttimes.com/2023/10/18/j-cole-sco res-his-first-1-hit-on-billboard-hot-100/.

24 William Goodman, "J. Cole Explains Personal Story behind 'Born Sinner' Track 'Let Nas Down,'" Fuse, 2013. https://web.archive.org/web/20130619201119/https://www. fuse.tv/videos/2013/06/j-cole-let-nas-down.

25 Brittany Lewis, "J. Cole Talks About His 'Splinter Cell' Collaboration & His Favorite Childhood Video Game," Global Grind, 2013. https://globalgrind.com/3853 047/j-cole-splinter-cell-collaboration-favorite-childhood-video-game-interview-photos/.

26 Rose Lilah, "J. Cole Explains 'Miss America' Single, Album May Be Delayed," HotNewHipHop, 2022. https://www.hotnewhiphop.com/7769-j-cole-explains-miss-america-single-album-may-be-delayed-news.

27 Tyrone Smith and Jeremy C. McCool, "The Silencing of Intellectuals in Music. Study Finds Racial Bias in How People Perceive Hip-Hop about Police Brutality," *Diverse Issues in Higher Education*, 2022. https://www.diverseeducation.com/opinion/arti cle/15288842/the-silencing-of-intellectuals-in-music-study-finds-racial-bias-in-how-people-perceive-hiphop-about-police-brutality.

28 Earn Your Leisure, "Common 30 Yrs of Evolution: Artists Investing in Their Bodies, Early Kanye, & Streaming Hurting Music," YouTube, 2024. https://www.youtube.com/watch?v=3JDmGyZUUbU.

Chapter 4

1 hawaiiangroove, "Kendrick Lamar Gets Passed Down Torch HiiiPower Live Music Box Los Angeles, CA 8/19/11," YouTube, 2011. http://1.https//www.youtube.com/watch?v=KYjyVjI2-z0&t=343s.

2 SZA, and Kaitlyn Greenidge, "Kendrick Lamar's Inner Drive," *Harper's Bazaar*, 2024. https://www.harpersbazaar.com/culture/art-books-music/a62568151/kendr ick-lamar-sza-interview-2024/.

3 Josh Eells, "The Trials of Kendrick Lamar," *Rolling Stone*, 2015. https://www.rollingst one.com/music/music-news/the-trials-of-kendrick-lamar-33057/2/.

4 NardwuarServiette, "Nardwuar vs. Kendrick Lamar," YouTube, 2012. https://www.yout ube.com/watch?v=6s5vlQdQp4s.

5 Jessica Hopper, "Kendrick Lamar: Not Your Average Everyday Rap Savior," SPIN, 2012. https://www.spin.com/2012/10/kendrick-lamar-not-your-average-every

day-rap-savior/#:~:text=%E2%80%9CCompton%20was%20just%20as%20ro
ugh,tree%20and%20for%20my%20birthday.%E2%80%9D.

6 Andrew Noz, "Black Hippy: A View from the Center," The FADER, 2012. https://www.
thefader.com/2012/02/20/black-hippy-a-view-from-the-center/.

7 Kendrick Lamar, *Youngest Head Nigga in Charge (Hub City Threat: Minor of the Year)*
(Konkrete Jungle Muzik, 2003). https://genius.com/albums/Kendrick-lamar/Young
est-head-nigga-in-charge-hub-city-threat-minor-of-the-year.

8 Mosi Reeves, "Mixtape Primer: Reviewing Kendrick Lamar's Pre-Fame Output,"
Rolling Stone, 2017. https://www.rollingstone.com/music/music-album-reviews/mixt
ape-primer-reviewing-kendrick-lamars-pre-fame-output-126139/.

9 Matt Diehl, "Top Dawg's Kendrick Lamar & Schoolboy?Q Cover Story: Enter the
House of Pain," *Billboard*, 2014. https://www.billboard.com/pro/top-dawg-entertainm
ent-cover-story-kendrick-lamar-schoolboy-q-anthony-tiffith/.

10 Datwon Thomas, "Kendrick Lamar and Anthony 'Top Dawg' Tiffith on How
They Built Hip-Hop's Greatest Indie Label," *Billboard*, 2017. https://www.billbo
ard.com/music/features/kendrick-lamar-anthony-tiffith-interview-billbo
ard-cover-story-2017-7964649/.

11 Danielle Harling, "Kendrick Lamar Speaks on Previously Being Signed to Def Jam,"
HipHopDX, 2012. https://hiphopdx.com/news/kendrick-lamar-speaks-on-previou
sly-being-signed-to-def-jam/.

12 Top Dawg Entertainment, "Kendrick Lamar—Interview / A Little Appalled
(Freestyle)," YouTube, 2009. https://www.youtube.com/watch?v=56GO5PkBrMI.

13 The Howard Stern Show, "Kendrick Lamar Hung Up on Dr. Dre When the Rap Mogul
First Called Him (2017)," YouTube, 2019. https://www.youtube.com/watch?v=0-
YF3cszc3c.

14 Melanie Davis, "'Designed in Destiny': The Pivotal Childhood Moment That Inspired
Kendrick Lamar's Musical Career," American Songwriter, 2025. https://americanson
gwriter.com/designed-in-destiny-the-pivotal-childhood-moment-that-inspired-kendr
ick-lamars-musical-career/.

15 NardwuarServiette, "Nardwuar vs. J. Cole."

16 The Come Up Show, "Kendrick Lamar Talks J.Cole, His Father, Hiiipower," YouTube,
2011. https://www.youtube.com/watch?v=lWTcT3fdgAc.

17 Jordan Darville, "J. Cole on Collab Album with Kendrick Lamar: 'We Put It to Bed
Years Ago,'" The FADER, 2023. https://www.thefader.com/2023/11/03/j-cole-col
lab-album-kendrick-lamar.

18 Home Grown Media Group, "Kendrick Lamar Defines HiiiPower & Having a Vision
of 2pac," YouTube, 2011. https://www.youtube.com/watch?v=KCGS25RXaDE.

19 Erika Ramirez, "Kendrick Lamar Talks 'Section.80,' New Album and Upcoming
Videos," *Billboard*, 2011. https://www.billboard.com/music/music-news/kendr
ick-lamar-talks-section80-new-album-and-upcoming-videos-467608/.

20 Marisa Mendez, "Kendrick Lamar's 'Good Kid, m.A.A.d City' Hits New Chart
Milestone After 12th Anniversary," HipHopDX, 2024. https://hiphopdx.com/news/
kendrick-lamar-good-kid-m-a-a-d-city-chart-milestone-12th-anniversary/.

21 Jonah Weiner, "Drake: High Times at the Yolo Estate," *Rolling Stone*, 2014. https://www.
rollingstone.com/music/music-news/drake-high-times-at-the-yolo-estate-72518/.

22 Andreas Hale, "'To Pimp a Butterfly': Kendrick Lamar Shares History," GRAMMY Awards, 2017. https://www.grammy.com/news/aoty-to-pimp-a-butterfly-oral-history.

23 Recording Academy / GRAMMYs, "Kendrick Lamar Wins Best Rap Album for 'To Pimp a Butterfly' in 2016 | GRAMMY Rewind," YouTube, 2024. https://www.youtube.com/watch?v=zLONqF1-icI.

24 Nick Williams, "Producer Sounwave on Kendrick Lamar's Historic No. 1 Album 'To Pimp a Butterfly,'" *Billboard*, 2020. https://www.billboard.com/music/music-news/sounwave-kendrick-lamar-to-pimp-a-butterfly-interview-9334666/.

25 Kendrick Lamar, "The Making of Kendrick Lamar's To Pimp a Butterfly," GRAMMY Awards, 2016. https://www.grammy.com/news/the-making-of-kendrick-lamars-to-pimp-a-butterfuly.

26 Ryan White, "'Damn': Kendrick Lamar Reveals New Album Artwork and Tracklist," *i-D*, 2017. https://i-d.co/article/damn-kendrick-lamar-reveals-new-album-artwork-and-tracklist/.

27 Nerisha Penrose, "4 Wildest Fan Theories About Kendrick Lamar's 'Damn.' Album," *Billboard*, 2017. https://www.billboard.com/music/rb-hip-hop/kendrick-lamar-damn-conspiracy-theories-8061639/.

28 Moriba Cummings, "Kendrick Lamar Bests Drake to Earn the Highest First Week Sales of 2017, So Far," BET, 2017. https://www.bet.com/article/yazw9u/kendrick-bests-drake-for-highest-opening-sales-of-2017.

29 Gregory Krieg, "It's Official: Clinton Swamps Trump in Popular Vote," CNN, 2016. https://www.cnn.com/2016/12/21/politics/donald-trump-hillary-clinton-popular-vote-final-count/index.html.

30 "Obama Undone: In First Year, Trump Unravels Predecessor's Signature Achievements," ABC News, 2018. https://abcnews.go.com/Politics/obama-undone-year-trump-unravels-predecessors-signature-achievements/story?id=52234311.

Chapter 5

1 Liz Fields, "The Story Behind Nina Simone's Protest Song, 'Mississippi Goddam,'" PBS, 2021. https://www.pbs.org/wnet/americanmasters/the-story-behind-nina-simones-protest-song-mississippi-goddam/16651/.

2 Jim Salter, "Timeline of Events in Ferguson, Missouri, After a Police Officer Fatally Shot Michael Brown," AP News, 2024. https://apnews.com/article/michael-brown-timeline-ferguson-410824a723f91caeddce01e13860ce30.

3 Ray Sanches, "Choke Hold by Cop Killed NY Man, Medical Examiner Says," CNN, 2014. https://www.cnn.com/2014/08/01/justice/new-york-choke-hold-death/index.html.

4 Ben Sisario, "J. Cole Releases an Impassioned Song About Michael Brown, 'Be Free,'" *The New York Times*, 2014. https://www.nytimes.com/2014/08/16/arts/music/j-coles-be-free-spreads-around-the-world-in-hours.html.

5 Bethonie Butler, "Rapper J. Cole Responds to Michael Brown Slaying with a Song, 'Be Free,'" *The Washington Post*, 2014. https://www.washingtonpost.com/news/

arts-and-entertainment/wp/2014/08/15/rapper-j-cole-responds-to-michael-brown-slaying-with-a-song-be-free/.

6 Brandon Jenkins, "Interview: J. Cole Talks About His Visit to Ferguson and Shares His Thoughts on the Michael Brown Shooting," Complex, 2014. https://www.complex.com/music/a/brandon-jenkins/interview-j-cole-michael-brown-ferguson.

7 "Music Stars React to Michael Brown Shooting, Ferguson Crisis," BET. https://www.bet.com/photo-gallery/ljp2l2/music-stars-react-to-michael-brown-shooting-ferguson-crisis/5bn9j3.

8 Mapping Police Violence, Website, https://mappingpoliceviolence.org/.

9 Gavin Edwards, "Billboard Cover: Kendrick Lamar on Ferguson, Leaving Iggy Azalea Alone and Why 'We're in the Last Days,'" *Billboard*, 2015. https://www.billboard.com/music/music-news/kendrick-lamar-billboard-cover-story-on-new-album-iggy-azalea-police-violence-the-rapture-6436268/.

10 Kimberly Foster, "Azealia Banks Calls Out Kendrick Lamar's 'Dumb' Ferguson Comments," The Culture, 2015. https://theculture.forharriet.com/2015/01/azealia-banks-calls-out-kendrick-lamars.html#google_vignette.

11 "How George Floyd Died, and What Happened Next," *The New York Times*, 2022. https://www.nytimes.com/article/george-floyd.html.

12 Bryan Rolli, "Childish Gambino's 'This Is America' And Kendrick Lamar's 'Alright' See Massive Spotify Gains Amid George Floyd Protests," Forbes, 2020. https://www.forbes.com/sites/bryanrolli/2020/06/03/childish-gambino-kendrick-lamar-spotify-george-floyd-protests/.

13 K. C. Orcutt, "See the SWAT Team Footage That Inspired J. Cole's Track 'Neighbors,'" BET, April 16, 2017. https://www.bet.com/article/qufhmm/see-the-swat-team-footage-that-inspired-j-cole.

14 Danielle Ransom, "J. Cole Explains How 'New Jim Crow' Inspired His '4 Your Eyez Only' Tour," BET, 2020. https://www.bet.com/article/fung4w/j-cole-explains-how-new-jim-crow-inspired-him-musically.

15 MONTREALITY, "J. Cole x Ryan Coogler—Full Interview," YouTube, 2016. https://www.youtube.com/watch?v=i2hozWdwSK0.

16 Rose A. Rudd, Puja Seth, Felicita Davis, and Lawrence Sholl, "Increases in Drug and Opioid- Involved Overdose Deaths—United States, 2010–2015," Centers for Disease Control and Prevention, 2016. https://www.cdc.gov/mmwr/volumes/65/wr/mm6550511e1.htm.

17 "Fentanyl," National Institutes of Health. https://nida.nih.gov/research-topics/fentanyl.

18 Evan Minsker, "J. Cole Releasing New Album This Week," Pitchfork, 2018. https://pitchfork.com/news/j-cole-releasing-new-album-this-week/.

19 Michael Jackman, "J. Cole's New Album Cover Is Designed by a Detroit-Based Artist," *Detroit Metro Times*, 2018. https://www.metrotimes.com/music/j-coles-new-album-cover-is-designed-by-a-detroit-based-artist-12866442.

20 "'Chain Gang' by Sam Cooke," National Museum of African American History & Culture. https://www.searchablemuseum.com/chain-gang-by-sam-cooke/.

21 Jgray, "Kendrick Lamar Says No to Voting," VIBE, 2012. https://www.vibe.com/music/music-news/kendrick-lamar-says-no-voting-108874/.

22 Megan Armstrong, "From the Stage to the Stump: 7 Rappers with Political Side Hustles," *Billboard*, 2011. https://www.billboard.com/music/music-news/rappers-run-political-office-8543143/.

23 "Kanye West Election: How Many Votes Did He Get?" BBC News, 2020. https://www.bbc.com/news/election-us-2020-54849605.

24 Mass Appeal, "Kendrick Lamar Explains 'To Pimp a Butterfly' Album Artwork," YouTube, 2015. https://www.youtube.com/watch?v=VN2IteZRHvc.

25 The Independent, "Footage from 2016 Shows Obama Predicting Winner of Kendrick vs Drake Feud," YouTube, May 6, 2024. https://www.youtube.com/watch?v=f888 9Ucg2hc.

26 Adelle Platon, "Kendrick Lamar Opens Up About Meeting President Obama: 'No Matter How High-Ranking You Get, You're Human,'" *Billboard*, February 4, 2016. https://www.billboard.com/music/features/kendrick-lamar-meeting-presid ent-obama-6866105/.

27 Kellie Meyer, "What Has Trump Accomplished During the First Month of His Second Term?" *NewsNation*, February 20, 2025. https://www.newsnationnow.com/politics/trump-first-month-second-term-recap/.

28 José Olivares, "US Citizen Wrongfully Arrested by Border Patrol in Arizona Held for Nearly 10 Days," *The Guardian*, April 21, 2025. https://www.theguardian.com/us-news/2025/apr/20/us-citizen-jose-hermosillo-border-patrol.

29 Andrea Castillo, "'It Is Time for You to Leave': DHS Mistakenly Sends Notices to U.S. Citizens," *Los Angeles Times*, April 23, 2025. https://www.latimes.com/politics/story/2025-04-23/homeland-security-immigration-termination-notices-deportation.

30 Anna Helhoski, "Federal Job Cuts by the Numbers: Will Layoffs Affect the Economy?" CBS42, March 29, 2025. https://www.cbs42.com/news/national/fede ral-job-cuts-by-the-numbers-will-layoffs-affect-the-economy/.

31 J. Cole, "cLOUDs," Inevitable Audio Series: Jermaine Cole & Ibrahim Hamad, February 20, 2017. https://www.inevitable.live/algorithm/clouds.

32 "Shooting at the Trump Rally in Butler, PA—July 13, 2024," C-SPAN, July 13, 2024. https://www.c-span.org/liveEvent/?Trump-Rally-Shooting.

33 Joseph Gedeon, "Joe Biden Warns 'Oligarchy Is Taking Shape in America' in Farewell Address," *The Guardian*, January 15, 2025. https://www.theguardian.com/us-news/2025/jan/15/joe-biden-farewell-address-trump-oligarchy-america.

34 Brian Hiatt, "Kendrick Lamar: The Best Rapper Alive on Bono, Mandela, Stardom and More," *Rolling Stone*, August 9, 2017. https://www.rollingstone.com/music/music-featu res/kendrick-lamar-the-rolling-stone-interview-199817/.

35 J. Cole, "J. Cole x Angie Martinez Interview at Salaam's House," YouTube, May 16, 2018. https://www.youtube.com/watch?v=gsKjJRSmYio.

36 Kamleshun Ramphul and Stephanie G. Mejias, "Is 'Snapchat Dysmorphia' A Real Issue?" *PubMed Central*, March 3, 2018. https://pmc.ncbi.nlm.nih.gov/articles/PMC5933578/.

37 Andy Bustard, "Kendrick Lamar Theory Offers Meaning Behind Oklama Nickname," HipHopDX, May 11, 2022.

38 Sunil Iyengar, "Federal Data on Reading for Pleasure: All Signs Show a Slump," *National Endowment for the Arts*, October 3, 2024. https://www.arts.gov/stories/blog/2024/federal-data-reading-pleasure-all-signs-show-slump

Chapter 6

1 "First of Its Kind." Loyola University New Orleans. Accessed August 18, 2025. https://www.loyno.edu/academics/colleges/college-music-media/hip-hop-rb.

2 "Who Is Melissa Heholt, J. Cole's Wife?" *People*, August 8, 2023. https://people.com/who-is-melissa-heholt-j-cole-wife-7502700.Aleyna Rentz, "Acclaimed Rapper Lupe Fiasco Joins Peabody as Visiting Professor," The Hub, January 7, 2025. https://hub.jhu.edu/2025/01/07/lupe-fiasco-joins-peabody-faculty/.

3 "Distinguished Visiting Lecturer." Center for Engaged Research and Collaborative Learning (CERCL) | Rice University.

4 "9th Wonder." The Kennedy Center. Accessed August 18, 2025. https://www.kennedy-center.org/artists/n/na-nn/9th-wonder/.

5 Rashad Grove, "Stic.Man of Dead Prez on Legacy, Wellness in Hip Hop, and Partnering with eBay & Kirpa House for Hip Hop 50." BET, August 23, 2023. https://www.bet.com/article/tuei8r/stic-man-documenting-hip-hop-50-wellness-is-the-future-of-the-culture.

6 Julian Kimble, "We Major: Rappers Who Went to College and What They Studied." Complex, February 10, 2014. https://www.complex.com/pop-culture/a/julian-kimble/rappers-who-went-to-college.

7 Maddie Ellis, "'A Different World' Is Now Streaming on Netflix. 11 Facts to Know About the Beloved Sitcom." TODAY.com, February 21, 2025. https://www.today.com/popculture/tv/a-different-world-streaming-rcna192841.

8 "Earnings and Education in the First Quarter of 2004." U.S. Bureau of Labor Statistics, April 20, 2004. https://www.bls.gov/opub/ted/2004/apr/wk3/art02.htm#:~:text=April%2020%2C%202004,had%20median%20earnings%20of%20$1%2C149 .

9 "Holding a Four-Year College Degree Brings Blacks Close to Economic Parity with Whites." *The Journal of Blacks in Higher Education*, 2005. https://www.jbhe.com/news_views/47_four-year_collegedegrees.html.

10 djvlad, "J Cole on Having Advantage in Rap by Going to College, Posting Raps on Message Boards (Flashback)." YouTube, April 9, 2024. https://www.youtube.com/watch?v=f5Y26KI-VvM.

11 "Loans for Undergraduate Students and Debt for Bachelor's Degree Recipients." National Center for Education Statistics, May 2023. https://nces.ed.gov/programs/coe/indicator/cub.

12 Danielle Harling, "Nas to Pursue His High School Diploma." HipHopDX, March 16, 2010. https://hiphopdx.com/news/nas-to-pursue-his-high-school-diploma/.

13 Brittny Meija, "Kendrick Lamar, the Pride of Compton, Receives Key to the City Today." *Los Angeles Times*, February 13, 2016. https://www.latimes.com/local/lanow/la-me-ln-kendrick-lamar-compton-key-to-the-city-20160213-story.html.

14 UCLA, "Photos from 2022, but the Lesson Stays the Same—UCLA Is Where You Level Uup 🐻✌️." X, February 26, 2025. https://x.com/UCLA/status/1894843770212098301.

15 Danielle Harling, "Kendrick Lamar Says 'The Autobiography of Malcolm X' Changed Him." HipHopDX, October 13, 2014. https://hiphopdx.com/news/kendrick-lamar-says-the-autobiography-of-malcolm-x-changed-him/.

16 Sam Kestenbaum, "Explained: Rapper Kendrick Lamar's Hebrew Israelite Connection." Forward, April 24, 2017. https://forward.com/news/369749/explained-rapper-kendrick-lamars-hebrew-israelite-connection/.

17 Reggie Ugwu, "The Radical Christianity of Kendrick Lamar." BuzzFeed, February 3, 2015. https://www.buzzfeed.com/reggieugwu/the-radical-christianity-of-kendrick-lamar.

18 Mark Elibert, "Kendrick Lamar Says He 'Literally Talks to God' While Reflecting on His 'Spiritual Practices.'" Complex, October 22, 2024. https://www.complex.com/music/a/markelibert/kendrick-lamar-can-hear-god.

19 Elias Leight, "J. Cole Followed Through on a 2013 Promise to Attend Fan's High School Graduation." The FADER, June 25, 2015. https://www.thefader.com/2015/06/25/j-cole-highschool-graduation.

20 Tamara Dhia, "J. Cole Keeps 2 Year Promise to Attend Fan's Graduation." Complex, June 26, 2015. https://www.complex.com/music/a/cmplxtamaradhia/j-cole-keeps-2-year-promise-to-attend-fan-graduation.

21 sim. "@JColeNC You like My Grades?" X, February 14, 2014. https://x.com/princess_simba/status/434373139167186944..

22 Ibrahim H., "@princess_simba i'm Happy It All Worked out for You. Had to Route the Tour around Your Graduation Lol. You Deserved It Now Keeping It Going." X, June 24, 2015. https://x.com/KingOfQueenz/status/613737765839204352.

23 sim, "'You Gotta Dream like You Never Seen Obstacles' #DreamsDoComeTrue @JColeNC." X, June 24, 2015. https://x.com/princess_simba/status/613739466407211008.

24 Darian Lusk, "J. Cole Will Let Single Mothers Stay in His Childhood Home for Free." CBS News, January 28, 2015. https://www.cbsnews.com/news/j-cole-will-let-single-mothers-stay-in-his-childhood-home-forfree/#:~:text=In%20a%20recent%20interview%20with,live%20there%2C%22%20Cole%20stated.

25 Eric Diep, "Kendrick Lamar Receives Generational Icon Award from California State Senate." BET, May 12, 2015.

26 Sami Yenigun, "A Visit from Kendrick Lamar—Best Day of School Ever?" NPR, June 13, 2015. https://www.npr.org/sections/ed/2015/06/13/413966099/a-visit-from-kendrick-lamar-best-day-of-school-ever.

27 Brian Mooney, "Why I Dropped Everything and Started Teaching Kendrick Lamar's New Album." Brian Mooney, Ph.D., April 27, 2015. https://bemoons.wordpress.com/2015/03/27/why-i-dropped-everything-and-started-teaching-kendrick-lamars-new-album/.

28 Carl Lamarre, "Kendrick Lamar, pgLang and Free Lunch Donate $200,000 to L.A. Charities and Community Initiatives." *Billboard*, June 28, 2024. https://www.billboard.com/music/rb-hip-hop/kendrick-lamar-pop-out-donation-charities-los-angeles-1235720142/#:~:text=Mustard&text=%E2%80%9CWe%20haven%27t%20seen%20this,irls%20Club.

29 Gil Kaufman, "Kendrick Lamar Makes Surprise Speech at 2024 Compton College Graduation: 'There's No Place Like This One Right Here.'" *Billboard*, June 10, 2024. https://www.billboard.com/music/music-news/kendrick-lamar-surprise-speech-2024-compton-college-graduation-1235705540/.

Chapter 7

1 Rashad Grove, "Yasiin Bey Says Drake's Music Is 'Pop' Not Hip-Hop," BET, 2024. https://www.bet.com/article/jjq8q0/yasiin-bey-says-drakes-music-is-pop-not-hip-hop.

2 Connor Garel, "Toronto Police Chief Shames Drake for Hells Angels Hoodie," VICE, 2018. https://www.vice.com/en/article/toronto-police-chief-shames-drake-for-hells-angels-hoodie/.

3 Vanessa Arredondo, "Hells Angels Club Members, Supporters Indicted in 'Vicious' Hate Crime Attack in San Diego," *USA Today*, 2023. https://www.usatoday.com/story/news/nation/2023/09/26/hells-angels-attack-three-black-men-in-hate-crime-in-san-diego-california/70966586007/.

4 Anand N. Bosmia, James F. Quinn, Todd B. Peterson, Christoph J. Griessenauer, and R. Shane Tubbs, "Outlaw Motorcycle Gangs: Aspects of the One-Percenter Culture for Emergency Department Personnel to Consider," *Western Journal of Emergency Medicine* 15, no. 4 (2014): 523–8. https://doi.org/10.5811/westjem.2014.2.17919.

5 Steven J. Horowitz, "J. Cole Removes Kendrick Lamar Diss '7 Minute Drill' from Streaming Services," *Variety*, 2024. https://variety.com/2024/music/news/j-cole-7-minute-drill-removed-streaming-kendrick-lamar-diss-1235969657/.

6 HOT 97, "Drake's First Radio Exclusive with Angie Martinez," YouTube, 2014. https://www.youtube.com/watch?v=MRYFeqG4ncU.

7 Xander Zellner, "All 23 Songs from Drake's 'For All the Dogs' Hit Top Half of Hot 100," *Billboard*, 2023. https://www.billboard.com/music/chart-beat/drake-for-all-the-dogs-all-songs-hot-100-top-half-1235443806/.

8 Barnaby Lane, "Drake's Former Songwriter Claims He Never Got Paid for Writing Tracks for the Rapper's Hit Mixtape 'If You're Reading This It's Too Late,'" *Business Insider*, 2023. https://www.businessinsider.com/drake-songwriter-quentin-miller-never-got-paid-songs-2023-1#:~:text=Miller%20is%20credited%20as%20a%20writer%20on%20four%20songs.&text=Speaking%20with%20VladTV%20on%20Wednesday,Tricky%20Stewart%20at%20the%20time.

9 Toshitaka Kondo, "Interview: Lil Wayne's 2006 Cover Story Uncut," Complex, 2012. https://www.complex.com/music/a/toshitaka-kondo/interview-lil-wayne-2006-cover-story-uncut.

10 Joe Coscarelli, "Drake Addresses Blackface Photo Used for Pusha-T Cover Art," *The New York Times*, 2018. https://www.nytimes.com/2018/05/31/arts/music/drake-blackface-photo-pusha-t.html.

11 Drake, "Rap Radar: Drake," YouTube, 2019. https://www.youtube.com/watch?v=mmsasEoupO4.

12 Steven J. Horowitz, "Drake Officially Releases Kendrick Lamar Diss 'Push Ups' to Streaming Platforms," *Variety*, 2024. https://variety.com/2024/music/news/drake-push-ups-kendrick-lamar-official-release-1235976597/.

13 Paul A. Thompson, "Kendrick Lamar: '6:16 in LA,'" Pitchfork, 2024. https://pitchfork.com/reviews/tracks/kendrick-lamar-616-in-la/.

14 Jennifer Zhan, "Let's Just Hope Drake and Kendrick's Kids Aren't Listening," Vulture, 2024. https://www.vulture.com/article/drake-kendrick-lamar-new-disses-family-matters-meet-the-grahams.html.

15 Sophie Caraan, "Kendrick Lamar's 'Not Like Us' Becomes Longest-Charting Rap Song on Billboard Hot 100," Hypebeast, 2025. https://hypebeast.com/2025/5/kendrick-lamar-not-like-us-longest-charting-rap-song-billboard-hot-100-record.

16 Michael Saponara, "Naomi Osaka Reveals Whether She's Team Kendrick Lamar or Team Drake," *Billboard*, May 9, 2024. https://www.billboard.com/music/rb-hip-hop/naomi-osaka-team-kendrick-lamar-drake-feud-1235678683/.

17 Rodney Carmichael, "In an Industry of Conformity, Questlove Remains a Hip-Hop Iconoclast," NPR, 2024. https://www.npr.org/2024/06/25/g-s1-5948/questlove-interview-hip-hop-is-history#:~:text=In%20a%20late%2Dnight%20Instagram,lens%2C%20or%20a%20publicity%20nightmare.

18 Marina Watts, Elizabeth Rosner, and Jeff Nelson, "Drake Sues His Own Record Label for Alleged Defamation over Kendrick Lamar's Diss Track 'Not Like Us,'" *People*, 2025. https://people.com/drake-sues-own-record-label-for-alleged-defamation-over-kendrick-lamar-diss-track-not-like-us-8775091.

19 Douglas Markowitz, "Kendrick Lamar Sweeps the 2025 GRAMMYs with Song of the Year Win," GRAMMY Awards, 2025. https://www.grammy.com/news/kendrick-lamar-not-like-us-wins-song-of-the-year-2025-grammys.

20 Sean Mandell, "Kendrick Lamar Performed Drake Diss Track 'Not Like Us' at Super Bowl 2025 Halftime Show—with One Big Change," *New York Post*, 2025. https://nypost.com/2025/02/09/entertainment/kendrick-lamar-performs-drake-diss-track-not-like-us-at-super-bowl-2025-halftime-show-with-one-big-change/.

21 Heran Mamo, "Kendrick Lamar's 2025 Super Bowl Halftime Show Is Now the Most-Watched of All Time," *Billboard*, 2025. https://www.billboard.com/music/rb-hip-hop/kendrick-lamar-2025-super-bowl-halftime-show-most-watched-all-time-1235899552/.

Chapter 8

1 Simon During, "Encoding, Decoding," *The Cultural Studies Reader* (Routledge, 2007), 89–103. https://homepage.villanova.edu/silvia.nagyzekmi/cultural/hall_Encoding-Decoding.pdf.

2 Alex Stapleton, *How Music Got Free* (Paramount, 2024). https://www.paramountplus.com/shows/how-music-got-free/.

3 Tom Lamont, "Napster: The Day the Music Was Set Free," *The Guardian*, 2013. https://www.theguardian.com/music/2013/feb/24/napster-music-free-file-sharing.

4 Matt Richtel, "Public Enemy Fights the Music Industry with Online Releases," *The New York Times*, 1998. https://archive.nytimes.com/www.nytimes.com/library/tech/98/12/cyber/articles/04enemy.html.

5 Chuck D wrote a statement on the Public Enemy website.

6 Andrew Flanagan, "Chance the Rapper Cheekily Roasts the Major Labels Onstage," NPR, 2017. https://www.npr.org/sections/therecord/2017/04/27/525869410/chance-the-rapper-cheekily-roasts-the-major-labels-onstage.

7 Melody Hahm, "How Chance the Rapper Got Big Without a Record Deal," Yahoo! Finance, 2017. https://finance.yahoo.com/news/chance-the-rapper-grammys-rec ord-deal-independent-artist-unsigned-213355505.html.

8 Erin Blakemore, "How 'Race Records' Turned Black Music into Big Business," History. com, 2018. https://www.history.com/articles/race-records-bessie-smith-big-bill-broo nzy-music-business.

9 Dennis Hunt, "Vanilla Ice's Official Bio Is Melting in Media Heat: Pop Music: The Hot-Selling Rap Star, Who Appears in Anaheim on Dec. 29, Admits He Made Up Some of the Colorful Details About His Background," *Los Angeles Times*, 1990. https://www.lati mes.com/archives/la-xpm-1990-12-05-ca-5589-story.html.

10 "A Timeline of Kid Rock's Controversies," *Billboard*, 2021. https://www.billboard.com/ music/music-news/kid-rock-controversies-timeline-9585206/.

11 Gil Kaufman, "Kid Rock Reportedly Waves Gun During Interview, Uses Racial Slurs: 'Write the Most Horrific Article About Me,' " *Billboard*, 2024. https://www.billbo ard.com/music/music-news/kid-rock-racial-slurs-waves-gun-rolling-stone-interview-1235687600/.

12 Heran Mamo, "Morgan Wallen Performs for First Time Since Racial Slur at Kid Rock's Nashville Bar, Gains Airplay," *Billboard*, 2021. https://www.billboard.com/music/coun try/morgan-wallen-performs-kid-rock-bar-nashville-racial-slur-video-9575704/.

13 Mark Lelinwalla, "Yelawolf Defends Confederate Flag," BET, 2015. https://www.bet. com/article/rhqxky/yelawolf-defends-confederate-flag.

14 Ben Dandridge-Lemco, "Post Malone: 'If You're Looking to Think About Life, Don't Listen to Hip-Hop,'" The FADER, 2017. https://www.thefader.com/2017/11/20/post-malone-polish-interview-dont-listen-to-hip-hop.

15 Eriq Gardner, "Public Enemy's Chuck D Files $100M Lawsuit Against Universal Music Group," *Billboard*, 2011. https://www.billboard.com/music/music-news/public-ene mys-chuck-d-files-100m-lawsuit-against-universal-music-group-465294/.

16 Mike Heuer, "Settlement with Musicians Will Cost UMG $11.5 Million," Courthouse News Service, 2015. https://www.courthousenews.com/settlement-with-musici ans-will-cost-umg-11-5-million/#:~:text=Settlement%20With%20Musicians%20W ill%20Cost%20UMG%20$11.5%20Million%20%7C%20Courthouse%20News%20 Service.

17 Preezy Brown, "De La Soul Finally Owns the Rights to Their Masters," VIBE.com, 2021. https://www.vibe.com/music/music-news/de-la-soul-owns-rights-masters-rec ordings-1234625360/.

18 Eyder Peralta, "Rapper Lupe Fiasco Booted Off Inaugural Party Stage After Criticizing Obama," NPR, 2013. https://www.npr.org/sections/thetwo-way/2013/01/21/169902 969/rapper-lupe-fiasco-booted-off-inaugural-party-stage-after-criticizing-obama.

19 "Lupe Fiasco Retires Again, Launching a New Career as a Guy Retiring from Being a Rapper," VICE, 2016. https://www.vice.com/en/article/lupe-fiasco-may-have-finally-retired-from-rap-for-good-this-time/.

20 Preeti Bhattacharji, "Liberation Tigers of Tamil Eelam (Aka Tamil Tigers) (Sri Lanka, Separatists)," Council on Foreign Relations, 2009. https://www.cfr.org/backgrounder/ liberation-tigers-tamil-eelam-aka-tamil-tigers-sri-lanka-separatists#:~:text=Introduct ion,the%20use%20of%20child%20soldiers.

21 Andrea L. Dennis, "Schoolhouse Rap," *Popular Music* 41, no. Special Issue 4 (2022). https://doi.org/https://doi.org/10.1017/S0261143022000599.

22 Erik Ortiz, "Young Thug Released After Changing Plea to Guilty in Georgia's Longest-Running Criminal Trial," NBC News, 2024. https://www.nbcnews.com/news/us-news/young-thug-changes-plea-guilty-georgias-longest-running-criminal-trial-rcna177873.

23 Joe Coscarelli, "Young Thug Lyrics Will Be Allowed as Evidence in YSL Rico Trial," *The New York Times*, 2023. https://www.nytimes.com/2023/11/09/arts/music/young-thug-lyrics-ysl-rico-trial.html.

24 Jozsef Papp and Shaddi Abusaid, "Atlanta's YSL Racketeering Trial Is Over; 'Everybody Lost,' Experts Say," The Atlanta Journal-Constitution, 2025. https://www.ajc.com/news/2025/06/the-ysl-case-has-finally-ended-and-absolutely-everybody-lost-experts-say/#:~:text=Despite%20going%20after%20what%20prosecutors,ones%20in%20the%20YSL%20case.

25 Kyle Denis, "Five Reasons Why 2023 Has Yet to Yield a No. 1 Hip-Hop Album or Single," *Billboard*, 2023. https://www.billboard.com/music/rb-hip-hop/hip-hop-no-number-one-albums-singles-charts-reasons-why-1235350404/.

Bibliography

"9th Wonder." The Kennedy Center. Accessed August 18, 2025. https://www.kennedy-cen ter.org/artists/n/na-nn/9th-wonder/.

Adams, Dart. "How Stop the Violence Movement's 'Self Destruction' Became One of Rap's Most Important Releases." Okayplayer, January 15, 2019. https://www.okayplayer.com/ originals/the-making-krs-one-stop-the-violence-movements-self-destruction-sin gle-89.html.

Ajacobs. "J. Cole, Tiye Phoenix, Statik Selektah, HipHopDX Win at Underground Music Awards." HipHopDX, August 24, 2010. https://hiphopdx.com/news/j-cole-tiye-phoe nix-statik-selektah-hiphopdx-win-at-underground-music-awards/.

Aleaziz, Hamed. "Biden Finally Got Border Numbers Down. Will He See the Political Benefits?" The New York Times, July 16, 2024. https://www.nytimes.com/2024/07/16/ us/politics/biden-border-immigration.html.

Apple, Amari. "Candace Owens Calls Gangsta Rap 'A Creation of Federal Authorities.'" Rolling Out, September 23, 2024. https://rollingout.com/2024/09/23/candace-owens-gangsta-rap-creation/.

Armstrong, Megan. "From the Stage to the Stump: 7 Rappers with Political Side Hustles." Billboard, November 11, 2011. https://www.billboard.com/music/music-news/rapp ers-run-political-office-8543143/.

Arredondo, Vanessa. "Hells Angels Club Members, Supporters Indicted in 'Vicious' Hate Crime Attack in San Diego." USA Today, September 26, 2023. https://www.usato day.com/story/news/nation/2023/09/26/hells-angels-attack-three-black-men-in-hat e-crime-in-san-diego-california/70966586007/.

"A Timeline of Kid Rock's Controversies." Billboard, June 10, 2021. https://www.billboard. com/music/music-news/kid-rock-controversies-timeline-9585206/.

Bhattacharji, Preeti. "Liberation Tigers of Tamil Eelam (Aka Tamil Tigers) (Sri Lanka, Separatists)." Council on Foreign Relations, May 20, 2009. https://www.cfr.org/ backgrounder/liberation-tigers-tamil-eelam-aka-tamil-tigers-sri-lanka-separati sts#:~:text=Introduction,the%20use%20of%20child%20soldiers.

Blakemore, Erin. "How 'Race Records' Turned Black Music into Big Business." History.com, August 7, 2018. https://www.history.com/articles/race-records-bes sie-smith-big-bill-broonzy-music-business.

Bosmia, Anand N., James F. Quinn, Todd B. Peterson, Christoph J. Griessenauer, and R. Shane Tubbs. "Outlaw Motorcycle Gangs: Aspects of the One-Percenter Culture for Emergency Department Personnel to Consider." Western Journal of Emergency Medicine 15, no. 4 (July 7, 2014): 523–8. https://doi.org/10.5811/westjem.2014.2.17919.

Brown, Preezy. "De La Soul Finally Owns the Rights to Their Masters." VIBE.com, August 10, 2021. https://www.vibe.com/music/music-news/de-la-soul-owns-rights-masters-recordings-1234625360/.

Bustard, Andy. "Kendrick Lamar Theory Offers Meaning Behind Oklama Nickname." HipHopDX, May 11, 2022. https://hiphopdx.com/news/kendrick-lamar-oklama-meaning-explained/.

Butler, Bethonie. "Rapper J. Cole Responds to Michael Brown Slaying with a Song, 'Be Free.'" *The Washington Post*, August 15, 2014. https://www.washingtonpost.com/news/arts-and-entertainment/wp/2014/08/15/rapper-j-cole-responds-to-michael-brown-slaying-with-a-song-be-free/.

Caraan, Sophie. "J. Cole's 'The Come Up' Mixtape Is Now on Streaming Services." Hypebeast, November 19, 2024. https://hypebeast.com/2024/11/j-cole-the-come-up-mixtape-vol-1-now-on-streaming-services.

Caraan, Sophie. "Kendrick Lamar's 'Not Like Us' Becomes Longest-Charting Rap Song on Billboard Hot 100." Hypebeast, May 21, 2025. https://hypebeast.com/2025/5/kendrick-lamar-not-like-us-longest-charting-rap-song-billboard-hot-100-record.

Carmichael, Rodney. "In an Industry of Conformity, Questlove Remains a Hip-Hop Iconoclast." NPR, June 25, 2024. https://www.npr.org/2024/06/25/g-s1-5948/questlove-interview-hip-hop-is-history#:~:text=In%20a%20late%2Dnight%20Instagram,lens%2C%20or%20a%20publicity%20nightmare.

Castillo, Andrea. "'It Is Time for You to Leave': DHS Mistakenly Sends Notices to U.S. Citizens." *Los Angeles Times*, April 23, 2025. https://www.latimes.com/politics/story/2025-04-23/homeland-security-immigration-termination-notices-deportation.

Cochrane, Naima. "Music Sermon: The Groundbreaking Sprite and St. Ides Hip-Hop Campaigns." VIBE.com, December 9, 2018. https://www.vibe.com/features/editorial/music-sermon-sprite-st-ides-hip-hop-625444/.

Cole, J. "cLOUDs." Inevitable Audio Series: Jermaine Cole & Ibrahim Hamad, February 20, 2017. https://www.inevitable.live/algorithm/clouds.

Cole, J. "J. Cole x Angie Martinez Interview at Salaam's House." YouTube, May 16, 2018. https://www.youtube.com/watch?v=gsKjJRSmYio.

Complex News. "J. Cole Gives Us a Tour of 2014 Forest Hills Drive in Fayetteville, N.C." YouTube, November 24, 2014. https://www.youtube.com/watch?v=QR-Nw5LVBgI&t=220s.

Coscarelli, Joe. "Drake Addresses Blackface Photo Used for Pusha-T Cover Art." *The New York Times*, May 31, 2018. https://www.nytimes.com/2018/05/31/arts/music/drake-blackface-photo-pusha-t.html.

Coscarelli, Joe. "Young Thug Lyrics Will Be Allowed as Evidence in YSL Rico Trial." *The New York Times*, November 9, 2023. https://www.nytimes.com/2023/11/09/arts/music/young-thug-lyrics-ysl-rico-trial.html.

Cummings, Moriba. "Kendrick Lamar Bests Drake to Earn the Highest First Week Sales of 2017, So Far." BET, April 23, 2017. https://www.bet.com/article/yazw9u/kendrick-bests-drake-for-highest-opening-sales-of-2017.

Dandridge-Lemco, Ben. "Post Malone: 'If You're Looking to Think About Life, Don't Listen to Hip-Hop.'" The FADER, November 20, 2017. https://www.thefader.com/2017/11/20/post-malone-polish-interview-dont-listen-to-hip-hop.

Darville, Jordan. "J. Cole on Collab Album with Kendrick Lamar: 'We Put It to Bed Years Ago.'" The FADER, November 3, 2023. https://www.thefader.com/2023/11/03/j-cole-collab-album-kendrick-lamar.

Davis, Melanie. "'Designed in Destiny': The Pivotal Childhood Moment That Inspired Kendrick Lamar's Musical Career." American Songwriter, February 7, 2025. https://americansongwriter.com/designed-in-destiny-the-pivotal-childhood-moment-that-inspired-kendrick-lamars-musical-career/.f

Denis, Kyle. "Five Reasons Why 2023 Has Yet to Yield a No. 1 Hip-Hop Album or Single." *Billboard*, June 12, 2023. https://www.billboard.com/music/rb-hip-hop/hip-hop-no-number-one-albums-singles-charts-reasons-why-1235350404/.

Dennis, Andrea L. "Schoolhouse Rap." *Popular Music* 41, no. 4, Special Issue (n.d.). https://doi.org/https://doi.org/10.1017/S0261143022000599.

Dhia, Tamara. "J. Cole Keeps 2 Year Promise to Attend Fan's Graduation." Complex, June 26, 2015. https://www.complex.com/music/a/cmplxtamaradhia/j-cole-keeps-2-year-promise-to-attend-fan-graduation.

Diehl, Matt. "Top Dawg's Kendrick Lamar & Schoolboy? Q Cover Story: Enter the House of Pain." *Billboard*, February 28, 2014. https://www.billboard.com/pro/top-dawg-entertainment-cover-story-kendrick-lamar-schoolboy-q-anthony-tiffith/.

Diep, Eric. "Kendrick Lamar Receives Generational Icon Award from California State Senate." BET, May 12, 2015. https://www.bet.com/article/y4wb1u/kendrick-lamar-receives-generational-icon-award.

"Distinguished Visiting Lecturer." Center for Engaged Research and Collaborative Learning (CERCL) | Rice University. Accessed August 18, 2025. https://cercl.rice.edu/distinguished-visiting-lecturer.

DJBooth. "J. Cole Says His Early Music Was Him 'Literally Just Sounding Like Eminem & Nas.'" DJBooth, June 7, 2016. https://djbooth.net/features/2016-06-07-j-cole-eminem-nas/.

djvlad. "J Cole on Having Advantage in Rap by Going to College, Posting Raps on Message Boards (Flashback)." YouTube, April 9, 2024. https://www.youtube.com/watch?v=f5Y26KI-VvM.

djvlad. "Khujo Goodie: Andre 3000 Was the First Artist to Say 'Trappin'' on a Song (Part 2)." YouTube, March 19, 2020. https://www.youtube.com/watch?v=DIxQ-zAHr18.

djvlad. "Melle Mel Explains Why 'The Message'' was the Single Most Important Song in Hip Hop History (Part 4)." YouTube, March 29, 2021. https://youtu.be/WxXQfkCFYCA?feature=shared&t=1010.

Drake. "Rap Radar: Drake." YouTube, December 25, 2019. https://www.youtube.com/watch?v=mmsasEoupO4.

During, Simon. "Encoding, Decoding." Essay. In *The Cultural Studies Reader*, 89–103. Abingdon: Routledge, n.d. https://homepage.villanova.edu/silvia.nagyzekmi/cultural/hall_Encoding-Decoding.pdf.

"Earnings and Education in the First Quarter of 2004." U.S. Bureau of Labor Statistics, April 20, 2004. https://www.bls.gov/opub/ted/2004/apr/wk3/art02.htm#:~:text=April%2020%2C%202004,had%20median%20earnings%20of%20$1%2C149.

Earn Your Leisure. "Common 30yrs of Evolution: Artists Investing in Their Bodies, Early Kanye, & Streaming Hurting Music." YouTube, December 19, 2024. https://www.yout ube.com/watch?v=3JDmGyZUUbU.

Edwards, Gavin. "Billboard Cover: Kendrick Lamar on Ferguson, Leaving Iggy Azalea Alone and Why 'We're in the Last Days.'" *Billboard*, January 9, 2015. https://www. billboard.com/music/music-news/kendrick-lamar-billboard-cover-story-on-new-albu m-iggy-azalea-police-violence-the-rapture-6436268/.

Eells, Josh. "The Trials of Kendrick Lamar." *Rolling Stone*, June 22, 2015. https://www.rolli ngstone.com/music/music-news/the-trials-of-kendrick-lamar-33057/2/.

Elibert, Mark. "Kendrick Lamar Says He 'Literally Talks to God' While Reflecting on His 'Spiritual Practices.'" Complex, October 22, 2024. https://www.complex.com/music/a/ markelibert/kendrick-lamar-can-hear-god.

Ellis, Maddie. "'A Different World' Is Now Streaming on Netflix. 11 Facts to Know About the Beloved Sitcom." TODAY.com, February 21, 2025. https://www.today.com/popcult ure/tv/a-different-world-streaming-rcna192841.

"Fayetteville's Black Community Calls for Change in Police Culture in Wake of Tyre Nichols' Death." ABC11, January 27, 2023. https://abc11.com/post/police-culture-tyre- nichols-brutality-fayetteville/12742566/.

"Fentanyl." National Institutes of Health. Accessed August 15, 2025. https://nida.nih.gov/ research-topics/fentanyl.

"First of Its Kind." Loyola University New Orleans. Accessed August 18, 2025. https:// www.loyno.edu/academics/colleges/college-music-media/hip-hop-rb.

Fields, Liz. "The Story behind Nina Simone's Protest Song, 'Mississippi Goddam.'" PBS, January 14, 2021. https://www.pbs.org/wnet/americanmasters/the-story-behind-nina- simones-protest-song-mississippi-goddam/16651/.

Flanagan, Andrew. "Chance The Rapper Cheekily Roasts the Major Labels Onstage." NPR, April 27, 2017. https://www.npr.org/sections/therecord/2017/04/27/525869410/cha nce-the-rapper-cheekily-roasts-the-major-labels-onstage.

Foster, Kimberly. "Azealia Banks Calls Out Kendrick Lamar's 'Dumb' Ferguson Comments." The Culture, 2015. https://theculture.forharriet.com/2015/01/azea lia-banks-calls-out-kendrick-lamars.html#google_vignette.

"From Rock Stars to Rappers, St. John's Hosts a Who's Who of Musicians on Campus." St. John's University, October 29, 2019. https://www.stjohns.edu/news-media/ news/2019-10-29/rock-stars-rappers-st-johns-hosts-whos-who-musicians-campus.

Futch, Michael. "'I Lived It:' Fayetteville State Has History in Civil Rights Movement." *The Fayetteville Observer*, February 22, 2020. https://www.fayobserver.com/story/news/ local/murchison-road/2020/02/22/lsquoi-lived-itrsquo-fayetteville-state-has-hist ory-in-civil-rights-movement/41821221/.

Galindo, Thomas. "J. Cole Shares List of Hip-Hop Artists Who Inspired Him." American Songwriter, August 1, 2023. https://americansongwriter.com/j-cole-sha res-list-of-hip-hop-artists-who-inspired-him/.

Gardner, Eriq. "Public Enemy's Chuck D Files $100M Lawsuit Against Universal Music Group." *Billboard*, November 4, 2011. https://www.billboard.com/ music/music-news/public-enemys-chuck-d-files-100m-lawsuit-against-univer sal-music-group-465294/.

Garel, Connor. "Toronto Police Chief Shames Drake for Hells Angels Hoodie." VICE, September 4, 2018. https://www.vice.com/en/article/toronto-police-chief-shames-drake-for-hells-angels-hoodie/.

Gariano, Francesca. "All About J. Cole's Parents, James and Kay Cole." People.com, April 6, 2024. https://people.com/all-about-j-cole-parents-8622187.

Gedeon, Joseph. "Joe Biden Warns 'Oligarchy Is Taking Shape in America' in Farewell Address." *The Guardian*, January 15, 2025. https://www.theguardian.com/us-news/2025/jan/15/joe-biden-farewell-address-trump-oligarchy-america.

Goodman, William. "J. Cole Explains Personal Story behind 'Born Sinner' Track 'Let Nas Down.'" Fuse, June 7, 2013. https://web.archive.org/web/20130619201119/https://www.fuse.tv/videos/2013/06/j-cole-let-nas-down.

Graham, Bryan Armen. "J. Cole on His Hoop Dreams, And Why the World Won't Allow LeBron to Be as Great as MJ." SI, June 12, 2013. https://www.si.com/extra-mustard/2013/06/12/j-cole-on-his-hoop-dreams-and-why-the-world-wont-allow-lebron-to-be-as-great-as-mj.

Grove, Rashad. "Stic.Man of Dead Prez on Legacy, Wellness in Hip Hop, and Partnering with eBay & Kirpa House for Hip Hop 50." BET, August 23, 2023. https://www.bet.com/article/tuei8r/stic-man-documenting-hip-hop-50-wellness-is-the-future-of-the-culture.

Grove, Rashad. "Yasiin Bey Says Drake's Music Is 'Pop' Not Hip-Hop." BET, January 16, 2024. https://www.bet.com/article/jjq8q0/yasiin-bey-says-drakes-music-is-pop-not-hip-hop.

H., Ibrahim. "@princess_simba i'm Happy It All Worked out for You. Had to Route the Tour around Your Graduation Lol. You Deserved It Now Keeping It Going." X, June 24, 2015. https://x.com/KingOfQueenz/status/613737765839204352.

Haack, Brian. "'The Miseducation of Lauryn Hill': For the Record." GRAMMY Awards, March 15, 2018. https://www.grammy.com/news/miseducation-lauryn-hill-record.

Hahm, Melody. "How Chance the Rapper Got Big Without a Record Deal." Yahoo! Finance, February 27, 2017. https://finance.yahoo.com/news/chance-the-rapper-grammys-record-deal-independent-artist-unsigned-213355505.html.

Hale, Andreas. "'To Pimp a Butterfly': Kendrick Lamar Shares History." GRAMMY Awards, May 15, 2017. https://www.grammy.com/news/aoty-to-pimp-a-butterfly-oral-history.

Hamilton, Xavier. "Political Commentator Ben Shapiro Catches Heat for Saying Rap Isn't Music." Complex, September 16, 2019. https://www.complex.com/music/a/fnr-tigg/political-commentator-ben-shapiro-saying-rap-isnt-music.

Harling, Danielle. "J. Cole Says 'Lights Please' Secured His Meeting with Jay-Z, Refers to the Song as a 'J. Cole Classic.'" HipHopDX, January 26, 2012. https://hiphopdx.com/news/j-cole-says-lights-please-secured-his-meeting-with-jay-z-refers-to-the-song-as-a-j-cole-classic/.

Harling, Danielle. "Kendrick Lamar Says 'The Autobiography of Malcolm X' Changed Him." HipHopDX, October 13, 2014. https://hiphopdx.com/news/kendrick-lamar-says-the-autobiography-of-malcolm-x-changed-him/.

Harling, Danielle. "Kendrick Lamar Speaks on Previously Being Signed to Def Jam." HipHopDX, May 22, 2012. https://hiphopdx.com/news/kendrick-lamar-speaks-on-previously-being-signed-to-def-jam/.

Harling, Danielle. "Nas To Pursue His High School Diploma." HipHopDX, March 16, 2010. https://hiphopdx.com/news/nas-to-pursue-his-high-school-diploma/.

hawaiiangroove. "Kendrick Lamar Gets Passed Down Torch HiiiPower Live Music Box Los Angeles, CA 8/19/11." YouTube, August 22, 2011. https://www.youtube.com/watch?v=KYjyVjI2-z0&t=343s.

Helhoski, Anna. "Federal Job Cuts by the Numbers: Will Layoffs Affect the Economy?" CBS42, March 29, 2025. https://www.cbs42.com/news/national/federal-job-cuts-by-the-numbers-will-layoffs-affect-the-economy/.

Heuer, Mike. "Settlement with Musicians Will Cost UMG $11.5 Million." Courthouse News Service, April 17, 2015. https://www.courthousenews.com/settlement-with-musicians-will-cost-umg-11-5-million/#:~:text=Settlement%20With%20Musicians%20Will%20Cost%20UMG%20$11.5%20Million%20%7C%20Courthouse%20News%20Service.

Hiatt, Brian. "Kendrick Lamar: The Best Rapper Alive on Bono, Mandela, Stardom and More." *Rolling Stone*, August 9, 2017. https://www.rollingstone.com/music/music-features/kendrick-lamar-the-rolling-stone-interview-199817/.

"Holding a Four-Year College Degree Brings Blacks Close to Economic Parity with Whites." *The Journal of Blacks in Higher Education*, 2005. https://www.jbhe.com/news_views/47_four-year_collegedegrees.html.

Home Grown Media Group. "Kendrick Lamar Defines HiiiPower & Having a Vision of 2pac." YouTube, July 13, 2011. https://www.youtube.com/watch?v=KCGS25RXaDE.

Hopper, Jessica. "Kendrick Lamar: Not Your Average Everyday Rap Savior." SPIN, October 9, 2012. https://www.spin.com/2012/10/kendrick-lamar-not-your-average-everyday-rap-savior/#:~:text=%E2%80%9CCompton%20was%20just%20as%20rough,tree%20and%20for%20my%20birthday.%E2%80%9D

Horowitz, Steven J. "Drake Officially Releases Kendrick Lamar Diss 'Push Ups' to Streaming Platforms." Variety, April 19, 2024. https://variety.com/2024/music/news/drake-push-ups-kendrick-lamar-official-release-1235976597/.

Horowitz, Steven J. "J. Cole Removes Kendrick Lamar Diss '7 Minute Drill' from Streaming Services." Variety, April 12, 2024. https://variety.com/2024/music/news/j-cole-7-minute-drill-removed-streaming-kendrick-lamar-diss-1235969657/.

HOT 97. "Drake's First Radio Exclusive with Angie Martinez." YouTube, February 13, 2014. https://www.youtube.com/watch?v=MRYFeqG4ncU.

"How George Floyd Died, and What Happened Next." *The New York Times*, July 29, 2022. https://www.nytimes.com/article/george-floyd.html.

How Music Got Free. Paramount+, 2024. https://www.paramountplus.com/shows/how-music-got-free/.

Hunt, Dennis. "Vanilla Ice's Official Bio Is Melting in Media Heat: Pop Music: The Hot-Selling Rap Star, Who Appears in Anaheim on Dec. 29, Admits He Made Up Some of the Colorful Details About His Background." *Los Angeles Times*, December 5, 1990. https://www.latimes.com/archives/la-xpm-1990-12-05-ca-5589-story.html.

ionehiphopwiredstaff. "BET Releases List of Nominees for 2010 Hip-Hop Awards." Hip-Hop Wired, September 8, 2010. https://hiphopwired.com/56131/bet-releases-list-of-nominees-for-2010-hip-hop-awards-22222/.

Iyengar, Sunil. "Federal Data on Reading for Pleasure: All Signs Show a Slump." National Endowment for the Arts, October 3, 2024. https://www.arts.gov/stories/blog/2024/fede ral-data-reading-pleasure-all-signs-show-slump.

Jackman, Michael. "J. Cole's New Album Cover Is Designed by a Detroit-Based Artist." *Detroit Metro Times*, June 11, 2018. https://www.metrotimes.com/ music/j-coles-new-album-cover-is-designed-by-a-detroit-based-artist-12866442.

Jenkins, Brandon. "Interview: J. Cole Talks About His Visit to Ferguson and Shares His Thoughts on the Michael Brown Shooting." Complex, August 19, 2014. https:// www.complex.com/music/a/brandon-jenkins/interview-j-cole-michael-brown- ferguson.

Jgray. "Kendrick Lamar Says No to Voting." VIBE.com, August 27, 2012. https://www.vibe. com/music/music-news/kendrick-lamar-says-no-voting-108874/.

"Kanye West Election: How Many Votes Did He Get?" BBC News, November 6, 2020. https://www.bbc.com/news/election-us-2020-54849605.

Kaufman, Gil. "Kendrick Lamar Makes Surprise Speech at 2024 Compton College Graduation: 'There's No Place Like This One Right Here.'" *Billboard*, June 10, 2024. https://www.billboard.com/music/music-news/kendrick-lamar-surprise-speech-2024- compton-college-graduation-1235705540/.

Kaufman, Gil. "Kid Rock Reportedly Waves Gun During Interview, Uses Racial Slurs: 'Write the Most Horrific Article About Me.'" *Billboard*, May 20, 2024. https:// www.billboard.com/music/music-news/kid-rock-racial-slurs-waves-gun-rolling-stone- interview-1235687600/.

Kelley, Frannie, and Ali Shaheed Muhammad. "J. Cole on Competition and Writing Honest Songs." NPR, June 23, 2013. https://www.npr.org/sections/microphonech eck/2013/06/23/194594097/j-cole-on-competition-and-writing-honest-songs.

Kestenbaum, Sam. "Explained: Rapper Kendrick Lamar's Hebrew Israelite Connection." Forward, April 24, 2017. https://forward.com/news/369749/explained-rapper-kendr ick lamars hebrew-israelite-connection/.

Kimble, Julian. "We Major: Rappers Who Went to College and What They Studied." Complex, February 10, 2014. https://www.complex.com/pop-culture/a/julian-kimble/ rappers-who-went-to-college.

Kondo, Toshitaka. "Interview: Lil Wayne's 2006 Cover Story Uncut." Complex, January 4, 2012. https://www.complex.com/music/a/toshitaka-kondo/interview-lil-wayne-200 6-cover-story-uncut.

Krieg, Gregory. "It's Official: Clinton Swamps Trump in Popular Vote." CNN, December 22, 2016. https://www.cnn.com/2016/12/21/politics/donald-trump-hillary-clinton- popular-vote-final-count/index.html.

Kujundzic, Petar. "MTV's Hottest Breakthrough MCS—J. Cole." Hypebeast, July 1, 2010. https://hypebeast.com/2018/7/mtvs-hottest-breakthrough-mcs-j-cole.

Lamar, Kendrick. "The Making of Kendrick Lamar's *To Pimp a Butterfly*." GRAMMY Awards, April 12, 2016. https://www.grammy.com/news/the-making-of-kendrick-lam ars-to-pimp-a-butterfuly.

Lamar, Kendrick. *Youngest Head Nigga in Charge (Hub City Threat: Minor of the Year)*. Konkrete Jungle Muzik, 2003. https://genius.com/albums/Kendrick-lamar/Young est-head-nigga-in-charge-hub-city-threat-minor-of-the-year.

Lamarre, Carl. "Kendrick Lamar, pgLang and Free Lunch Donate $200,000 to L.A. Charities and Community Initiatives." *Billboard*, June 28, 2024. https://www.billbo ard.com/music/rb-hip-hop/kendrick-lamar-pop-out-donation-charities-los-angeles- 1235720142/#:~:text=Mustard&text=%E2%80%9CWe%20haven%27t%20seen%20t his,irls%20Club.

Lamont, Tom. "Napster: The Day the Music Was Set Free." *The Guardian*, February 23, 2013. https://www.theguardian.com/music/2013/feb/24/napster-music-free-file- sharing.

Lane, Barnaby. "Drake's Former Songwriter Claims He Never Got Paid for Writing Tracks for the Rapper's Hit Mixtape 'If You're Reading This It's Too Late.'" Business Insider, January 6, 2023. https://www.businessinsider.com/drake-songwriter-quentin-mil ler-never-got-paid-songs-2023-1#:~:text=Miller%20is%20credited%20as%20a%20wri ter%20on%20four%20songs.&text=Speaking%20with%20VladTV%20on%20Wednes day,Tricky%20Stewart%20at%20the%20time.

Leight, Elias. "J. Cole Followed Through on a 2013 Promise to Attend Fan's High School Graduation." The FADER, June 25, 2015. https://www.thefader.com/2015/06/25/j-cole- highschool-graduation.

Leland, John. "The Spin Interview: DJ Kool Herc." SPIN, August 1, 2023. https://www. spin.com/2023/08/the-spin-interview-dj-kool-herc/.

Lelinwalla, Mark. "Yelawolf Defends Confederate Flag." BET, August 26, 2015. https:// www.bet.com/article/rhqxky/yelawolf-defends-confederate-flag.

Lewis, Brittany. "J. Cole Talks About His 'Splinter Cell' Collaboration & His Favorite Childhood Video Game." Global Grind, August 23, 2013. https://globalgrind.com/3853 047/j-cole-splinter-cell-collaboration-favorite-childhood-video-game-interview- photos/.

Lilah, Rose. "J. Cole Explains 'Miss America' Single, Album May Be Delayed." HotNewHipHop, September 26, 2022. https://www.hotnewhiphop.com/7769-j-cole- explains-miss-america-single-album-may-be-delayed-news.

"Loans for Undergraduate Students and Debt for Bachelor's Degree Recipients." National Center for Education Statistics, May 2023. https://nces.ed.gov/programs/coe/indica tor/cub.

"Lupe Fiasco Retires Again, Launching a New Career as a Guy Retiring from Being a Rapper." VICE, December 13, 2016. https://www.vice.com/en/article/lupe-fia sco-may-have-finally-retired-from-rap-for-good-this-time/.

Lusk, Darian. "J. Cole Will Let Single Mothers Stay in His Childhood Home for Free." CBS News, January 28, 2015. https://www.cbsnews.com/news/j-cole-will-let-single- mothers-stay-in-his-childhood-home-for-free/#:~:text=In%20a%20recent%20interv iew%20with,live%20there%2C%22%20Cole%20stated.

Lynskey, Dorian. "The Forgotten 'Godfathers' of Hip-Hop." BBC News, August 7, 2023. https://www.bbc.com/culture/article/20230807-the-last-poets-and-watts-prophets-the- radical-poets-overshadowed-by-hip-hop.

Malone, Vocab. "Spirituality in Modern Hip Hop: The Theology of Kendrick Lamar and Chance the Rapper." Christian Research Institute, February 11, 2019. https:// www.equip.org/articles/spirituality-in-modern-hip-hop-the-theology-of-kendr ick-lamar-and-chance-the-rapper/.

Mamo, Heran. "Kendrick Lamar's 2025 Super Bowl Halftime Show Is Now the Most-Watched of All Time." *Billboard*, February 11, 2025. https://www.billboard.com/music/rb-hip-hop/kendrick-lamar-2025-super-bowl-halftime-show-most-watched-all-time-1235899552/.

Mamo, Heran. "Morgan Wallen Performs for First Time Since Racial Slur at Kid Rock's Nashville Bar, Gains Airplay." *Billboard*, May 5, 2021. https://www.billboard.com/music/country/morgan-wallen-performs-kid-rock-bar-nashville-racial-slur-video-9575704/.

Mandell, Sean. "Kendrick Lamar Performed Drake Diss Track 'Not Like Us' at Super Bowl 2025 Halftime Show—with One Big Change." *New York Post*, February 9, 2025. https://nypost.com/2025/02/09/entertainment/kendrick-lamar-performs-drake-diss-track-not-like-us-at-super-bowl-2025-halftime-show-with-one-big-change/.

Mapping Police Violence. Accessed August 15, 2025. https://mappingpoliceviolence.org/.

Markowitz, Douglas. "Kendrick Lamar Sweeps the 2025 GRAMMYs with Song of the Year Win." GRAMMY Awards, February 3, 2025. https://www.grammy.com/news/kendrick-lamar-not-like-us-wins-song-of-the-year-2025-grammys.

Marriott, Michel. "9 Charged, 4 with Murder, in Robbery Spree at L.I. Rap Concert." *The New York Times*, September 19, 1988. https://www.nytimes.com/1988/09/19/nyregion/9-charged-4-with-murder-in-robbery-spree-at-li-rap-concert.html.

Marriott, Michel. "One Is Killed and 12 Are Injured as L.I. Rap Concert Turns Violent." *The New York Times*, September 12, 1988. https://www.nytimes.com/1988/09/12/nyregion/one-is-killed-and-12-are-injured-as-li-rap-concert-turns-violent.html.

Mass Appeal. "Kendrick Lamar Explains 'To Pimp a Butterfly' Album Artwork." YouTube, April 28, 2015. https://www.youtube.com/watch?v=VN2IteZRHvc.

McKevitt, Greg. "'It's Time to Retaliate in Song'—Why NWA's Provocative 80s Rap Became an Anthem." BBC News, August 5, 2024. https://www.bbc.com/culture/article/20240802-the-nwa-protest-anthem-that-foreshadowed-riots-in-the-us.

Meara, Paul. "J. Cole Celebrates NAS Lyrics & 'I Gave You Power' in Speech." HipHopDX, January 25, 2014. https://hiphopdx.com/news/j-cole-celebrates-nas-lyrics-i-gave-you-power-in-speech/.

Mejia, Brittny. "Kendrick Lamar, the Pride of Compton, Receives Key to the City Today." *Los Angeles Times*, February 13, 2016. https://www.latimes.com/local/lanow/la-me-ln-kendrick-lamar-compton-key-to-the-city-20160213-story.html.

Mendez, Marisa. "Kendrick Lamar's 'Good Kid, m.A.A.d City' Hits New Chart Milestone After 12th Anniversary." HipHopDX, October 31, 2024. https://hiphopdx.com/news/kendrick-lamar-good-kid-m-a-a-d-city-chart-milestone-12th-anniversary/.

Meyer, Kellie. "What Has Trump Accomplished During the First Month of His Second Term?" NewsNation, February 20, 2025. https://www.newsnationnow.com/politics/trump-first-month-second-term-recap/.

Michaels, Sean. "Ice T Tells Soulja Boy: You Killed Hip-Hop." *The Guardian*, June 19, 2008. https://www.theguardian.com/music/2008/jun/19/news.culture1#:~:text=%22Soulja%20Boy%2C%20I%20know%20you,of%20the%20gangsta%2Drap%20era.

Minsker, Evan. "J. Cole Releasing New Album This Week." Pitchfork, April 16, 2018. https://pitchfork.com/news/j-cole-releasing-new-album-this-week/.

MONTREALITY. "J. Cole x Ryan Coogler—Full Interview." YouTube, January 22, 2016. https://www.youtube.com/watch?v=i2hozWdwSK0.

Mooney, Brian. "Why I Dropped Everything and Started Teaching Kendrick Lamar's New Album." Ph.D., April 27, 2015. https://bemoons.wordpress.com/2015/03/27/why-i-dropped-everything-and-started-teaching-kendrick-lamars-new-album/.

"Music Stars React to Michael Brown Shooting, Ferguson Crisis." BET. Accessed August 15, 2025. https://www.bet.com/photo-gallery/ljp2l2/music-stars-react-to-michael-brown-shooting-ferguson-crisis/5bn9j3.

NardwuarServiette. "Nardwuar vs. J. Cole (2021)." YouTube, December 25, 2021. https://www.youtube.com/watch?v=GxVXEd_G_60.

NardwuarServiette. "Nardwuar vs. Kendrick Lamar." YouTube, March 23, 2012. https://www.youtube.com/watch?v=6s5vlQdQp4s.

Nasir, Noreen. "In the Beginning, There Was the Bronx." August 9, 2023. https://projects.apnews.com/features/2023/hip-hop-50th-history/in-the-beginning-there-was-the-bronx.html.

NMAAHC. "'Chain Gang' by Sam Cooke." National Museum of African American History & Culture. Accessed August 15, 2025. https://www.searchablemuseum.com/chain-gang-by-sam-cooke/.

Noz, Andrew. "Black Hippy: A View from the Center." The FADER, February 20, 2012. https://www.thefader.com/2012/02/20/black-hippy-a-view-from-the-center/.

"Obama Undone: In First Year, Trump Unravels Predecessor's Signature Achievements." ABC News, January 17, 2018. https://abcnews.go.com/Politics/obama-undone-year-trump-unravels-predecessors-signature-achievements/story?id=52234311.

Olivares, José. "US Citizen Wrongfully Arrested by Border Patrol in Arizona Held for Nearly 10 Days." The Guardian, April 21, 2025. https://www.theguardian.com/us-news/2025/apr/20/us-citizen-jose-hermosillo-border-patrol.

On Air with Ryan Seacrest. "J. Cole Confesses His First Rapper Name | Interview | On Air with Ryan Seacrest." YouTube, October 25, 2013. https://www.youtube.com/watch?v=rKv0ZMlwjhU.

Orcutt, KC. "See the SWAT Team Footage That Inspired J. Cole's Track 'Neighbors.'" BET, April 16, 2017. https://www.bet.com/article/qufhmm/see-the-swat-team-footage-that-inspired-j-cole.

Ortiz, Erik. "Young Thug Released After Changing Plea to Guilty in Georgia's Longest-Running Criminal Trial." NBC News, October 31, 2024. https://www.nbcnews.com/news/us-news/young-thug-changes-plea-guilty-georgias-longest-running-criminal-trial-rcna177873.

Papp, Jozsef, and Shaddi Abusaid. "Atlanta's YSL Racketeering Trial Is over; 'Everybody Lost,' Experts Say." The Atlanta Journal-Constitution, June 9, 2025. https://www.ajc.com/news/2025/06/the-ysl-case-has-finally-ended-and-absolutely-everybody-lost-experts-say/#:~:text=Despite%20going%20after%20what%20prosecutors,ones%20in%20the%20YSL%20case.

Pawa, Vandana. "Who Is J. Cole's Wife? All About Melissa Heholt." People, August 8, 2023. https://people.com/who-is-melissa-heholt-j-cole-wife-7502700.

Penrose, Nerisha. "4 Wildest Fan Theories About Kendrick Lamar's 'Damn.' Album." Billboard, December 5, 2017. https://www.billboard.com/music/rb-hip-hop/kendrick-lamar-damn-conspiracy-theories-8061639/.

Peralta, Eyder. "Rapper Lupe Fiasco Booted Off Inaugural Party Stage After Criticizing Obama." NPR, January 21, 2013. https://www.npr.org/sections/thetwo-way/2013/01/21/169902969/rapper-lupe-fiasco-booted-off-inaugural-party-stage-after-criticizing-obama.

Philips, Chuck. "Anti-Rap Crusader Under Fire." *Los Angeles Times*, March 20, 1996. https://www.latimes.com/local/la-fi-tupacdelores20march2096-story.html.

Platon, Adelle. "Kendrick Lamar Opens Up About Meeting President Obama: 'No Matter How High-Ranking You Get, You're Human.'" *Billboard*, February 4, 2016. https://www.billboard.com/music/features/kendrick-lamar-meeting-president-obama-6866105/.

Power 106 Los Angeles. "J. Cole Speaks on His Alicia Keys Crush." YouTube, July 13, 2013. https://www.youtube.com/watch?v=ud5FMX1a3jo.

Questlove, and Ben Greenman. *Hip Hop is History*. New York: AUWA, 2024.

"Race & Policing—'to Protect and to Serve'—L.A.P.D. Culture." PBS. Accessed August 14, 2025. https://www.pbs.org/wgbh/pages/frontline/shows/lapd/race/protectserve.html.

Ramirez, Erika. "Kendrick Lamar Talks 'Section.80,' New Album and Upcoming Videos." *Billboard*, September 9, 2011. https://www.billboard.com/music/music-news/kendrick-lamar-talks-section80-new-album-and-upcoming-videos-467608/.

Ramphul, Kamleshun, and Stephanie G. Mejias. "Is 'Snapchat Dysmorphia' A Real Issue?" PubMed Central, March 3, 2018. https://pmc.ncbi.nlm.nih.gov/articles/PMC5933578/.

Ransom, Danielle. "J. Cole Explains How 'New Jim Crow' Inspired His '4 Your Eyez Only' Tour." BET, January 21, 2020. https://www.bet.com/article/fung4w/j-cole-explains-how-new-jim-crow-inspired-him-musically.

"Rap Artist Tupac Shakur Shot in Robbery." *The New York Times*, November 30, 1994. https://www.nytimes.com/1994/11/30/nyregion/rap-artist-tupac-shakur-shot-in-robbery.html.

Recording Academy / GRAMMYs. "Kendrick Lamar—Seeing Dr. Dre and Tupac as a Kid | GRAMMYs." YouTube, October 8, 2013. https://www.youtube.com/watch?v=KdUhlV_Si2E.

Recording Academy / GRAMMYs. "Kendrick Lamar Wins Best Rap Album For 'To Pimp a Butterfly' in 2016 | GRAMMY Rewind." YouTube, August 23, 2024. https://www.youtube.com/watch?v=zLONqF1-icI.

Reeves, Mosi. "Mixtape Primer: Reviewing Kendrick Lamar's Pre-Fame Output." *Rolling Stone*, July 14, 2017. https://www.rollingstone.com/music/music-album-reviews/mixtape-primer-reviewing-kendrick-lamars-pre-fame-output-126139/.

Rentz, Aleyna. "Acclaimed Rapper Lupe Fiasco Joins Peabody as Visiting Professor." The Hub, January 7, 2025. https://hub.jhu.edu/2025/01/07/lupe-fiasco-joins-peabody-faculty/.

Richtel, Matt. "Public Enemy Fights the Music Industry with Online Releases." *The New York Times*, December 4, 1998. https://archive.nytimes.com/www.nytimes.com/library/tech/98/12/cyber/articles/04enemy.html.

Rolli, Bryan. "Childish Gambino's 'This Is America' and Kendrick Lamar's 'Alright' See Massive Spotify Gains amid George Floyd Protests." Forbes, June 3, 2020. https://www.forbes.com/sites/bryanrolli/2020/06/03/childish-gambino-kendrick-lamar-spotify-george-floyd-protests/.

Rolling Stone. "500 Greatest Songs of All Time." December 11, 2003. https://www.rolli ngstone.com/music/music-lists/500-greatest-songs-of-all-time-151127/grandmas ter-flash-and-the-furious-five-the-message-56194/.

Rudd, Rose A., Puja Seth, Felicita Davis, and Lawrence Sholl. "Increases in Drug and Opioid-Involved Overdose Deaths—United States, 2010–2015." Centers for Disease Control and Prevention, December 30, 2016. https://www.cdc.gov/mmwr/volumes/65/ wr/mm655051e1.htm.

Salter, Jim. "Timeline of Events in Ferguson, Missouri, after a Police Officer Fatally Shot Michael Brown." AP News, August 9, 2024. https://apnews.com/article/mich ael-brown-timeline-ferguson-410824a723f91caeddce01e13860ce30.

Sanchez, Ray. "Choke Hold by Cop Killed NY Man, Medical Examiner Says." CNN, August 2, 2014. https://www.cnn.com/2014/08/01/justice/new-york-choke-hold-death/ index.html.

Saponara, Michael. "Naomi Osaka Reveals Whether She's Team Kendrick Lamar or Team Drake." *Billboard*, May 9, 2024. https://www.billboard.com/music/rb-hip-hop/ naomi-osaka-team-kendrick-lamar-drake-feud-1235678683/.

Shapiro, David. "J. Cole's Tales Out of School." *Interview Magazine*, February 4, 2013. https://www.interviewmagazine.com/music/j-cole-harvard.

"Shooting at the Trump Rally in Butler, PA—July 13, 2024." C-SPAN, July 13, 2024. https:// www.c-span.org/liveEvent/?Trump-Rally-Shooting.

sim. "@JColeNC You like My Grades?" X, February 14, 2014. https://x.com/princess_si mba/status/434373139167186944.

sim. "'You Gotta Dream like You Never Seen Obstacles' #DreamsDoComeTrue @ JColeNC." X, June 24, 2015. https://x.com/princess_simba/status/61373946640 7211008.

Sisario, Ben. "J. Cole Releases an Impassioned Song about Michael Brown, 'Be Free.'" *The New York Times*, August 14, 2014. https://www.nytimes.com/2014/08/16/arts/ music/j-coles-be-free-spreads-around-the-world-in-hours.html.

Smith, Tyrone, and Jeremy C. McCool. "The Silencing of Intellectuals in Music. Study Finds Racial Bias in How People Perceive Hip-Hop about Police Brutality." *Diverse Issues in Higher Education*, February 22, 2022. https://www.diverseeducation.com/ opinion/article/15288842/the-silencing-of-intellectuals-in-music-study-finds-rac ial-bias-in-how-people-perceive-hiphop-about-police-brutality.

Soulr. "Kendrick Lamar: The Come Up | Part 1." YouTube, August 4, 2020. https://www. youtube.com/watch?v=1R8fk870ipc&t=12s.

SZA, and Kaitlyn Greenidge. "Kendrick Lamar's Inner Drive." *Harper's Bazaar*, October 21, 2024. https://www.harpersbazaar.com/culture/art-books-music/a62568151/kendr ick-lamar-sza-interview-2024/.

Tardio, Andres. "Jay Z Gives J. Cole His Original Roc-A-Fella Chain." HipHopDX, January 29, 2014. https://hiphopdx.com/news/jay-z-gives-j-cole-his-origi nal-roc-a-fella-chain/.

The Angie Martinez Show. "T.I. Claims He Created Trap Music." YouTube, April 11, 2017. https://www.youtube.com/watch?v=4Zc1RWcQcfY.

The Come Up Show. "Kendrick Lamar Talks J. Cole, His Father, Hiiipower." YouTube, July 1, 2011. https://www.youtube.com/watch?v=lWTcT3fdgAc.

"The Complete List of Platinum Hip-Hop Albums by Year." DJBooth, October 20, 2015. https://djbooth.net/features/2015-10-20-platinum-hip-hop-albums-year-breakd own/#:~:text=To%20extend%20that%20even%20further,%2D1997%29%20there%20w ere%20129.

The Howard Stern Show. "Kendrick Lamar Hung Up on Dr. Dre When the Rap Mogul First Called Him (2017)." YouTube, October 13, 2019. https://www.youtube.com/ watch?v=0-YF3cszc3c.

The Independent. "Footage from 2016 Shows Obama Predicting Winner of Kendrick vs Drake Feud." YouTube, May 6, 2024. https://www.youtube.com/watch?v=f888 9Ucg2hc.

The Roots. "Ice-T Says He Based 6 N' The Morning on Schoolly D's PSK (What Does It Mean)?" YouTube, August 9, 2023. https://www.youtube.com/watch?v=syFagoTn77c.

The Wall Street Journal. "Rapper J. Cole Discusses Graduating Magna Cum Laude." YouTube, August 14, 2013. https://www.youtube.com/watch?v=IZ2dlLToxoI&t=159s.

Thomas, Datwon. "Kendrick Lamar and Anthony 'Top Dawg' Tiffith on How They Built Hip-Hop's Greatest Indie Label." *Billboard*, September 14, 2017. https://www. billboard.com/music/features/kendrick-lamar-anthony-tiffith-interview-billbo ard-cover-story-2017-7964649/.

Thompson, Paul A. "Kendrick Lamar: '6:16 in LA.'" Pitchfork, May 3, 2024. https://pitchf ork.com/reviews/tracks/kendrick-lamar-616-in-la/.

Top Dawg Entertainment. "Kendrick Lamar—Interview / A Little Appalled (Freestyle)." YouTube, December 18, 2009. https://www.youtube.com/watch?v=56GO5PkBrMI.

UCLA. "Photos from 2022, but the Lesson Stays the Same—UCLA Is Where You Level Up 🎥." X, February 26, 2025. https://x.com/UCLA/status/1894843770212098301.

Ugwu, Reggie. "The Radical Christianity of Kendrick Lamar." BuzzFeed, February 3, 2015. https://www.buzzfeed.com/reggieugwu/the-radical-christianity-of-kendrick-lamar.

Wall Street Journal. "Rapper J. Cole Talks Graduating Magna Cum Laude." August 20, 2013. https://www.wsj.com/video/rapper-j-cole-talks-graduating-magna-cum-laude/ B1FD0DF5-F6EE-4F69-8C28-476300B9410F.

Washington, Eddie. "J. Cole Scores His First #1 Hit on Billboard Hot 100." *The Black Wall Street Times*, September 12, 2024. https://theblackwallsttimes.com/2023/10/18/j-cole-scores-his-first-1-hit-on-billboard-hot-100/.

Watts, Marina, Elizabeth Rosner, and Jeff Nelson. "Drake Sues His Own Record Label for Alleged Defamation over Kendrick Lamar's Diss Track 'Not Like Us.'" People, January 15, 2025. https://people.com/drake-sues-own-record-label-for-alleged-defamat ion-over-kendrick-lamar-diss-track-not-like-us-8775091.

Weiner, Jonah. "Drake: High Times at the Yolo Estate." *Rolling Stone*, February 13, 2014. https://www.rollingstone.com/music/music-news/drake-high-times-at-the-yolo-est ate-72518/.

Weiner, Natalie. "The Oral History of J. Cole's Basketball Career." Bleacher Report, April 19, 2017. https://bleacherreport.com/articles/2704529-the-oral-history-of-j-coles-bas ketball-career.

White, Ryan. "'Damn': Kendrick Lamar Reveals New Album Artwork and Tracklist." *i-D*, April 11, 2017. https://i-d.co/article/damn-kendrick-lamar-reveals-new-album-artw ork-and-tracklist/.

Wilkinson, Alec. "The Unlikely Survival of the Godfather of Rap." *The New Yorker*, August 2, 2010. https://www.newyorker.com/magazine/2010/08/09/new-york-is-killing-me.

Williams, Nick. "Producer Sounwave on Kendrick Lamar's Historic No. 1 Album 'To Pimp a Butterfly.'" *Billboard*, March 16, 2020. https://www.billboard.com/music/music-news/sounwave-kendrick-lamar-to-pimp-a-butterfly-interview-9334666/.

XXL Staff. "Meet the 2010 XXL Freshman Class (XXL April 2010 Issue)." *XXL Mag*, April 1, 2010. https://www.xxlmag.com/2010-xxl-freshman-class/.

Yenigun, Sami. "A Visit from Kendrick Lamar—Best Day of School Ever?" NPR, June 13, 2015. https://www.npr.org/sections/ed/2015/06/13/413966099/a-visit-from-kendrick-lamar-best-day-of-school-ever.

Zellner, Xander. "All 23 Songs from Drake's 'For All the Dogs' Hit Top Half of Hot 100." Billboard, October 16, 2023. https://www.billboard.com/music/chart-beat/drake-for-all-the-dogs-all-songs-hot-100-top-half-1235443806/.

Zhan, Jennifer. "Let's Just Hope Drake and Kendrick's Kids Aren't Listening." Vulture, May 4, 2024. https://www.vulture.com/article/drake-kendrick-lamar-new-disses-family-matters-meet-the-grahams.html.

Index

Boosie Badazz 175
Born Sinner 60–3
Bosarge-Fussell, Cierra 130–1
Bradford, Perry 163
Brand Nubian 22
braggadocio 55
"The Breaks" 26
Brother D 5
Brown, Mike 92
Bun B 115
Bush, George W. 173

C4 73, 76
"Caged Bird" 97
cancel culture 169–70
Cam'ron 33
Cash Money Records 73, 142
Center for Disease Control (CDC) 101
Chahta Anumpa 111
"Chain Gang" 102
Chance the Rapper 16, 161
"Change" 98, 129
Chappelle's Show 36
"Charged Up" 140–1, 145
Chauvin, Derek 94
Chicago Drill 155
Childish Gambino 95
Chill Moody 29
Choctaw 111
Chuck D 159
Clipse 13
"cLOUDs" 107–8
"College Boy" 122
The College Dropout 120
The Comeback Season 137
The Come Up 55–6
"Complexion (A Zulu Love)" 172
Compton Unified School District 132
Concepcion, Mike 71
conscious rap 1
consciousness 1
    Socially conscious rap 3–8, 22, 29, 36
"Control (HOF)" 83, 138

"Controlla" 137, 146
Coogler, Ryan 100
Cooke, Sam 102
The Cosby Show 118
"Cream" 27
Crunk movement 39
Crunk music 39–40
Culture Vultures: Conversations with Damon Dash 167–8
Curry, Denzel 16
Cyhi the Prynce 79

DAMN. 76, 87–9
Dapper Dan 28
Dash, Damon 167
DatPiff 55
David Letterman 94
Davis, Miles 2
Dead Prez 11–12, 117, 174
Death Certificate 24
Death Row Records 24
decoding 157–8
De La Soul 12
Degrassi 137
Department of Government Efficiency (DOGE) 107
DJ Akademiks 144
DJ Kool Herc 2–3
DJ Quik 70
DJ Vlad 5, 40
DJ Yella 24
The D.O.C. 165
Doechii 171
The Dozens 154
Drake 79, 83–4, 90, 135–50
Dr. Dre 24, 70, 73, 78, 83
Dreamville Foundation 131
Dreamville Records 49
drug overdose deaths 101
D12 166
"Duppy Freestyle" 142–3

EarthGang 96
East Coast rap 14
East–West friction 35–6